Organising the Firm

Petri Mäntysaari

Organising the Firm

Theories of Commercial Law, Corporate Governance and Corporate Law

Springer

Prof. Dr. Petri Mäntysaari
Hanken School of Economics
Department of Accounting and Commercial Law
Handelsesplanaden 2
65100 Vaasa
Finland
petri.mantysaari@hanken.fi

ISBN 978-3-642-22196-5 e-ISBN 978-3-642-22197-2
DOI 10.1007/978-3-642-22197-2
Springer Dordrecht Heidelberg London New York

Library of Congress Control Number: 2011937439

Printed on acid-free paper

Springer is part of Springer Science+Business Media (www.springer.com)

Contents

Chapter 1
Introduction

Organisation form has an important impact on business performance.[1] Legal institutions such as laws and legal instruments help to organise the firm.[2] This makes commercial law, the law of corporate governance, and corporate law important research areas in legal science.

However, commercial law, the law of corporate governance, and corporate law all share the same problem: they lack a proper theoretical basis. This is unfortunate, because all scientific research is theory-based in social sciences. The lack of a proper theoretical foundation can raise doubts about the scientific quality of research, reduce access to leading journals and to external funding, reduce universities' internal funding, and make the area less attractive to researchers. Moreover, if the purpose of a theory is to predict objective reality, the lack of a proper theoretical basis raises questions about the relevance of existing research.

These three areas of law share this problem partly for the same reasons. (a) First, these areas are *interlinked*. Commercial law is a large branch of law that covers commercial contract law, corporate law, the regulation of corporate governance, and many other issues. Since the codification of commercial law in France and Germany, commercial contract law and corporate law have been regarded as its main areas. Large parts of corporate law regulate questions of corporate governance. (b) Second, mainstream legal research has as its starting point existing *legal norms* applied and interpreted by the court. Because of the vast number and diversity of legal norms, it is difficult to define their common characteristics in a relevant way and to formulate theories that would explain sector-specific

[1] Williamson OE, The Modern Corporation: Origins, Evolution, Attributes, J Econ Lit 19 (1981) p 1543 (on Chandler 1962).

[2] For institutions in general, see North DC, Institutions, Institutional Change and Economic Performance. Cambridge U P, Cambridge (1990) pp 3–4 (definition); Ostrom E, Crawford S, Classifying Rules. In: Ostrom E, Understanding Institutional Diversity. Princeton U P, Princeton Oxford (2005), Chapter 7, pp 190–191 (classification); Aoki M, Toward a Comparative Institutional Analysis. The MIT Press, Cambridge, Mass. (2001) pp 26–27, 186 and 197 (elements).

P. Mäntysaari, *Organising the Firm*,
DOI 10.1007/978-3-642-22197-2_1,

phenomena rather than phenomena common to all legal norms. (c) Third, it may be difficult to fill the theoretical void by using *economic theories* as a model, because economic theories are not necessarily compatible with existing norms. (d) Fourth, both corporate law and corporate governance are heavily influenced by *theories of the firm*.[3]

The problem will thus require a coordinated solution in legal science. The purpose of this book is to discuss the reasons for the absence of theories in present research, and to develop a theoretical framework for commercial law, the law of corporate governance, and corporate law. In legal science, the theoretical framework should be able to predict legal phenomena.

The key to the proposed theoretical framework is the choice of the *perspective of the firm* in commercial law and corporate governance. In this book, it will replace competing perspectives such as the perspective of the judge (legal dogmatics), the investor (shareholder primacy), or the stakeholder (the stakeholder theory). Choosing the perspective of the firm can, perhaps contrary to popular wisdom,[4] make it easier to formulate theories and develop commercial law as a science. One of the obvious benefits is that it can help to explain the behaviour of firms and many legal institutions used by firms. The choice of the perspective of the firm does not mean that managers would be given freedom to pursue whatever interests they choose or society directs (managerialism).[5]

The perspective of the firm must, of course, be defined. Once this has been accomplished, one can study the firm's generic commercial objectives and the legal tools and practices that firms use to reach them. This is the area of general commercial law. Corporate governance is a particular context in which the firm uses legal tools and practices to address particular governance-related issues in addition to the generic issues. This is the area of the law of corporate governance. Corporate law is a collection of legal norms that regulate three important contexts: corporate governance; corporate finance; and the existence of corporations.

The chapters of this book reflect the fact that theories of commercial law, corporate governance, and corporate law are connected.

Chapter 2 discusses economic theories of the firm. As the chosen perspective is that of the firm, economic theories of the firm set the scene for much of the rest of the book.

Chapters 3 and 4 provide the foundation for the study of commercial phenomena in legal science. A reader interested in corporate governance can skip these two chapters. Chapter 3 discusses existing theories of commercial law. Whereas

---

[3] For corporate law, see Bratton WW, The New Economic Theory of the Firm: Critical Perspectives from History, Stanford L Rev 41 (1989) pp 1471–1527.

[4] See, for example, Merkt H, Wirtschaftsrechtsvergleichung im Zeitalter der Globalisierung: Tendenzen, Aufgaben, Perspektiven, ZVglRWiss 103 (2004) p 266: "Am Ende: von der Wissen- zur Wirtschaft?"

[5] See, for example, Bainbridge S, Director Primacy: The Means and Ends of Corporate Governance, Northw U L Rev 97 (2003) pp 547–549.

theories of the firm are irrelevant for existing theories of commercial law, they are very important for Management-based Commercial Law (MBCL), a new theory of commercial law proposed in Chap. 4. MBCL is defined as a "functional" rather than normative area of law.[6] According to MBCL, the firm uses legal tools and practices in order to reach its objectives.

Chapters 5 and 6 discuss existing theories of corporate law and corporate governance. A new legal theory of corporate governance is proposed in Chap. 7. The starting point of the proposed theory of corporate governance is that there are legal entities and organisations. Certain issues must be addressed because of the existence of legal entities, and further questions because of the existence of organisations.

Chapters 8 and 9 develop the theory of corporate governance further. While Chap. 7 answers the question what issues must be addressed, it does not tell you how they should be addressed. According to Chaps. 8 and 9, the self-enforcement of the governance model and its ability to foster innovation are important drivers when firms choose their governance models.[7] Chapter 8 explains how the sustainability of the firm can be increased by making its governance model more self-enforcing. In Chap. 9, it is argued that the firm is not sustainable unless its governance model also fosters innovation.

A new theory of corporate law is proposed in Chap. 10. According to the proposed theory of corporate law, corporations are legal tools used by firms. Corporate law consists of three main areas: corporate governance; corporate finance; and existential issues. Self-enforcement and innovation-related issues are incorporated into the proposed theory.

[6] All theories should be functional, but there is a distinction between normative and functional areas of law in legal science.

[7] A related approach can be found in Aoki M, Toward a Comparative Institutional Analysis. The MIT Press, Cambridge, Mass. (2001) pp 2–3: "... the synchronic problem, where the goal is to understand the complexity and diversity of overall institutional arrangements across the economies as an instance of multiple equilibria of some kind, and the diachronic problem, whereby the goal is to understand the mechanism of institutional evolution/change in a framework consistent with an equilibrium view of institutions, but allowing for the possibility of the emergence of novelty."

Chapter 2
Economic Theories of the Firm

2.1 General Remarks

Economic theories of the firm have provided much of the language and concepts of modern corporate governance and corporate law discourse.[1]

Alternative mechanism. According to economic theories of the firm, the default form of economic exchanges is through the market. The mechanism of market prices is assumed to allocate resources to their most effective uses. The firm is an alternative mechanism.

Variation. There are various competing theories of this alternative mechanism. This is partly caused by the nature of economics. Whereas law is normative and must be applied by people and firms in the complex circumstances of real life, economists have more discretion as economic theories are not applied in a normative way. The firms studied by economists are firms reduced to certain aspects. One can therefore say that economists study fictive rather than real firms.[2] This can contribute to the existence of large differences between the competing theories.

Categories. Economic theories of the firm can be categorised in various ways. If it is assumed that market contracting solves everything, there is no room for the firm. A theory based on such an assumption cannot tell us why firms exist.[3] There are nevertheless theories that go further.

---

[1] See, in particular, Bratton WW, The New Economic Theory of the Firm: Critical Perspectives from History, Stanford L Rev 41 (1989) pp 1471–1527.

[2] Demsetz H, The Structure of Ownership and the Theory of the Firm, J Law Econ 26(2) (1983) p 377: "It is a mistake to confuse the firm of economic theory with its real-world namesake. The chief mission of neoclassical economics is to understand how the price system coordinates the use of resources, not the inner workings of real firms."

[3] Foss NJ, Lando H, Thomsen S, 5610 The Theory of the Firm. In: Bouckaert B, De Geest G (eds), Encyclopedia of Law and Economics. Volume III. The Regulation of Contracts. Edward Elgar, Cheltenham (2000) pp 631–658.

P. Mäntysaari, *Organising the Firm*,
DOI 10.1007/978-3-642-22197-2_2,

One can broadly distinguish between theories of the existence of firms and theories of the limits of the firm. Theories of the existence of firms focus on market exchange and regard the firm as a production structure. Theories of the limits of the firm focus on internal exchange and regard the firm as a governance structure and an organisational construction. One can thus regard the firm as a production function or as an organisational structure.[4]

This distinction is also the distinction between (a) the *classical* or neoclassical theory of the firm and (b) the *institutional* theory or new institutional economics. The neoclassical theory started with the publication of two articles: Alchian and Demsetz (1972) and Jensen and Meckling (1976). Williamson (1981) is an example of the institutional theory of the firm. In addition, management theorists champion (c) the *resource-based* theory of the firm.[5]

2.2 Production Function

We will now discuss theories of the firm in more detail. The first theories of the firm studied the "*classical firm*". This firm is a *production function* personified by an *entrepreneur*. The main underlying assumption is that organising production within the firm is often more efficient than organising production through contracts between many independent parties.

Generally, theories that describe the firm as a production function are not actually theories of the firm but rather theories of markets in which firms are important actors. They customarily explain why firms exist but do not explain under what terms the firm is the superior form of organisation. For this reason, they are regarded as "black box constructions".[6]

Adam Smith (1776) is regarded as the most important pioneer. Smith identifies the benefits brought by division of labour and *specialisation* in society. According to Smith, firms exist to coordinate and motivate specialised people's economic activity.[7]

Coase (1937) explains the existence of firms by the existence of *transaction costs*: "The main reason why it is profitable to establish a firm would seem to be that there is a cost of using the price mechanism. The most obvious cost of 'organising' production through the price mechanism is that of discovering what the relevant

---

[4] See, for example, Williamson OE, The Modern Corporation: Origins, Evolution, Attributes, J Econ Lit 19 (1981) p 1539.

[5] See Wernerfelt B, The Resource-Based View of the Firm, Strat Man J 5(2) (1984) pp 171–180; Barney JB, Firm Resources and Sustained Competitive Advantage, J Man 17 (1991) pp 99–120; Peteraf MA, The Cornerstones of Competitive Advantage: A Resource-Based View, Strat Man J 14 (1993) pp 179–191.

[6] Jensen MC, Meckling WH, Theory of the Firm: Managerial Behavior, Agency Costs and Ownership Structure, J Fin Econ 3 (1976) pp 305–360.

[7] Smith A, The Wealth of Nations (1776).

prices are. This cost may be reduced but it will not be eliminated by the emergence of specialists who will sell this information. The costs of negotiating and concluding a separate contract for each exchange transaction which takes place on a market must also be taken into account."[8]

Theories based on the notion that the firm is just a *set of contracts* among factors of production are a radical departure from the earlier theories in other respects but still regard the firm as a production function.[9]

Ostrom (1990) mentions some firms (law firms and cooperatives) as examples of *common resource pools*. When the firm is studied as a common resource pool, it is implicitly assumed that it is a production function or a market. This brings the study of common resource pools close to the set-of-contracts theory of the firm (see below).[10]

2.3 Governance Structure or Organisational Construction

Whereas "black box constructions" do not explain under what terms the firm is the superior form of organisation, various theories that study the firm as an *organisational construction* or as a *governance structure* try to provide the answer.

Williamson (2002a, b) is an example of this approach.[11] According to Williamson, firms *exist* because all complex contracts are incomplete. The cost of completing transactions on the market increases, when their complexity increases, or when asset specificity increases (they involve assets that are worth more within a relationship between two parties than outside it). At some point, it makes sense to conduct transactions within the firm.

On the other hand, there are *limits* to the size of firms.[12] Williamson (1984, 1985) suggests that the transfer of transactions out of the market into the firm changes their governance (adaptability) and measurement (incentive) features. Three transaction characteristics are critical for the size of firms: frequency,

[8] Coase RH, The Nature of the Firm, Economica, New Series 4(14) (1937) pp 386–405.

[9] Alchian AA, Demsetz H, Production, Information Costs, and Economic Organization, Am Econ Rev 62 (1972) pp 777–795; Jensen MC, Meckling WH, Theory of the Firm: Managerial Behavior, Agency Costs and Ownership Structure, J Fin Econ 3 (1976) pp 305–360.

[10] Ostrom E, Governing the Commons. Cambridge U P, Cambridge (1990) pp 25 and 40.

[11] Williamson OE, The Lens of Contract: Private Ordering, Am Econ Rev 92(2) (2002) pp 438–443; Williamson OE, The Theory of the Firm as Governance Structure: From Choice to Contract. Journal of Economic Perspectives 16(3) (2002) pp 171–195.

[12] Arrow KJ, The Limits of Organization. Fels Lectures on Public Policy Analysis. Norton, New York (1974); Grossman SJ, Hart OD, The Costs and Benefits of Ownership: A Theory of Vertical and Lateral Integration, J Pol Econ 94 (1986) pp 691–719; Holmström B, Tirole J, The Theory of the Firm. In: Schmalensee R, Willig RD (eds), The Handbook of Industrial Organization. Volume 1. North-Holland, Amsterdam (1989) pp 61–133; Holmström B, Roberts J, The Boundaries of the Firm Revisited, J Econ Persp 12(4) (1998) pp 73–94.

uncertainty, and, in particular, asset specificity.[13] Williamson is regarded as the originator of modern transaction cost economics.

2.4 Personification of the Firm, Authority

2.4.1 General Remarks

The choice between the firm as a production function or as a governance structure is not the only fundamental choice one can make when studying firms. For the purposes of legal research, at least two questions are potentially relevant. They are only to a limited extent dependent on whether the firm is a production function or a governance structure.

The first relates to the *personification* of the firm. Do firms exist? Who is regarded as the firm? Should the firm be personified at all? These questions can be relevant from a legal perspective, because laws generally facilitate the balancing of conflicting interests. It is important to understand whose interests legal norms should protect. The existence of interests worthy of protection can explain the existence and contents of various legal rights and duties.

The second relates to *authority*. Is authority characteristic of the firm? Who decides or should decide? Even these questions can be relevant, because decision-making can be based on consensus (contract) or authority, and the existence and contents of various legal norms are also connected to the nature of decision-making.[14] For example, the default legal norm is that the amendment of contract terms requires the consent of all contract parties; in an authority relationship, however, one party has a legal right to give instructions unilaterally and the other party has a legal duty to follow the instructions, subject to legal constraints.

Unfortunately, economic theories of the firm do not provide sufficient answers for legal research.

2.4.2 Personification

Obviously, one does not need the concept of authority for the purpose of defining the firm at all, if one assumes that the firm does not exist in the first place. We can therefore begin with the question of personification.

There are at least six customary approaches to personification of the firm in present research: the non-existence of the firm; the owner-manager-entrepreneur

---

[13] Williamson OE, The Incentive Limits of Firms, Rev World Econ 120(4) (1984) p 741; Williamson OE, The Economic Institutions of Capitalism. The Free Press, New York (1985) p 137.

[14] See also Arrow K, The Limits of Organization. W. W. Norton & Company, New York (1974) pp 68–70 (on consensus and authority).

approach; the team approach; the legal entity approach; the absence of personification; and the principal–agent approach. They are not mutually exclusive and may be overlapping.

Owner-manager-entrepreneur. In classical economics, the firm is regarded as a production function and personified by an owner-manager-entrepreneur that directs production. The existence of an owner-manager-entrepreneur is central for the definition of the "classical firm".[15]

It does not necessarily matter whether the firm is characterised by authority or, as in neoclassical economics, regarded as a set of contracts (see below). The "classical firm" can often be found even in neoclassical economics. For example, Jensen and Meckling (1976) argue that it is misleading to personify the firm. They suggest that the behaviour of the firm is like the behaviour of the market.[16] However, even their starting-point is the existence of an owner-manager.[17]

Team. The firm can also be personified by a team. Alchian and Demsetz (1972) view the firm as a team whose members act from self-interest but realise that their destinies depend to some extent on the survival of the team in its competition with other teams.[18]

Legal entity. Some theories assume that the economic boundaries of the firm are defined by the legal boundaries of the legal entity. The firm and the legal entity are often used interchangeably. Jensen and Meckling (1976)[19] and Chandler (1977)[20] are examples of this approach.

---

[15] Alchian AA, Demsetz H, Production, information costs, and economic organization, Am Econ Rev 62(5) (1972) p 794: "The essence of the classical firm is identified here as a contractual structure with: 1) joint input production; 2) several input owners; 3) one party who is common to all the contracts of the joint inputs; 4) who has rights to renegotiate any input's contract independently of contracts with other input owners, 5) who holds the residual claim; and 6) who has the right to sell his contractual residual status. The central agent is called the firm's owner and the employer."

[16] Jensen MC, Meckling WH, Theory of the Firm: Managerial Behavior, Agency Costs and Ownership Structure, J Fin Econ 3 (1976) p 311: "The firm is not an individual. It is a legal fiction . . .".

[17] *Ibid*, p 312. For a critical view, see Fama EF, Agency Problems and the Theory of the Firm, J Pol Econ 88(2) (1980) pp 290–291.

[18] Alchian AA, Demsetz H, Production, Information Costs, and Economic Organization, Am Econ Rev 62 (1972) p 778. See also Jensen MC, Meckling WH, Theory of the Firm: Managerial Behavior, Agency Costs and Ownership Structure, *op cit*, pp 309–310; Simon HA, Organizations and Markets, J Econ Persp 5(2) (1991) p 36.

[19] Jensen MC, Meckling WH, *op cit*, p 310: "It is important to recognize that most organizations are simply legal fictions which serve as a nexus for a set of contracting relationships among individuals. This includes firms . . ." The authors define legal fiction in footnote 12: "By legal fiction we mean the artificial construct under the law which allows certain organizations to be treated as individuals."

[20] See Rajan RG, Zingales L, The Governance of the New Enterprise. In: Vives X (ed), Corporate Governance, Theoretical & Empirical Perspectives. Cambridge U P, Cambridge (2000) pp 201–227: "Summarizing, there are three main features of [what Chandler (1977) calls the modern business Enterprise (MBE)] that shaped the ensuing debate on corporate governance.

No personification. When the firm is regarded as an organisational construction or a governance structure, the firm is assumed to exist but is not necessarily personified at all.

For example, the behavioural approach represented by Simon (1991) does not require the personification of the firm. Simon discusses why people choose to work for the firm. What motivates them? Simon argues that managers and employees are motivated by authority, rewards, loyalty (identification with goals of the organisation), and coordination (standards and rules).[21]

Transaction cost economics represented by Williamson (1998, 2005) provides a further example of an approach that does not require the personification of the firm.[22]

No existence. In neoclassical economics, the starting point is that the firm as such does not exist. The firm is regarded as a production function and a means of transforming inputs into outputs.

For example, Fama (1980) rejects the notion of the "classical firm". He argues that a corporation does not have owners in any meaningful sense, and that a modern corporation does not have an entrepreneur. On the other hand, each factor in the firm is owned by somebody. The firm is just "the set of contracts covering the way inputs are joined to create outputs and the way receipts from outputs are shared among inputs".[23]

Another example is the study of the firm as a common resource pool (Ostrom 1990). The traditional problem with common resource pools is the so-called "tragedy of the commons"[24] or the fact that resources that do not belong to anyone are not used in a sustainable way since each individual acts according to his own self-interest. It used to be assumed that there are two alternative ways to address the problem: the use of property rights (if the problem is that "everybody's property is nobody's property", one can give the resources to somebody); or turning to an

First, the MBE was well defined by the ownership of assets. The legal boundaries of the corporation could be drawn around these assets and also coincided with its economic boundaries. Moreover, these boundaries did not change unless ownership changed. Since the boundaries were well defined, the main issue in corporate governance was how the surplus generated within these boundaries was to be allocated, and not on how to preserve and protect the boundaries. Second ... outsiders could obtain power by virtue of their ownership of the crucial assets. As a result, the MBE came to be owned by outsiders. Finally, the concentration of power at the top of the organizational pyramid, together with the separation between ownership and control, made the agency problem between top managers and shareholders the corporate governance problem."

[21] Simon HA, Organizations and Markets, Journal of Economic Perspectives 5(2) (1991) p 30.

[22] Williamson OE, Transaction Cost Economics: How It Works; Where It Is Headed, De Economist 146 (1998) pp 23–58; Williamson OE, Transaction Cost Economics. In: Menard C, Shirley MM (eds), Handbook of New Institutional Economics. Springer, Dordrecht (2005) pp 41–65.

[23] Fama EF, Agency Problems and the Theory of the Firm, J Pol Econ 88(2) (1980) p 290.

[24] Hardin G, The Tragedy of the Commons, Science 162 (1968) pp 1243–1248.

external authority. Ostrom identifying self-governance as a sustainable way to govern common resource pools.[25]

Principal–agent. The last approach identified here is the principal–agent approach.[26] According to this approach, one focuses on the interests of the party or parties chosen as "the principal". Once again, it does not matter whether the firm is regarded as a production function or as an organisational construction (governance structure). Neither does it matter whether the firm is assumed to exist or not.

For example, Fama (1980) distinguishes between management and risk-bearing and treats residual claimants as risk bearers and principals (no personification of the firm, the firm is a set of contracts).[27] When Jensen and Meckling (1976) define the agency costs of outside equity and debt, they assume that the firm has an owner-manager (personification, the owner-manager-entrepreneur approach).[28] Williamson (1985) treats shareholders as the principal in transaction cost economics (no personification). Alternatively, one can also choose other constituencies.[29]

2.4.3 Authority

The second question is the role played by authority. Like some of the questions relating to the personification of the firm, even this question is only to a limited extent influenced by the choice between the firm as a production function or as a governance structure.

Production function. Theories that regard the firm as a production function have different views about the role of authority. (a) According to Coase (1937), firms are defined by authority replacing the market pricing mechanism.[30] (b) In contrast, the notion that activities within the firm are governed by authority is rejected by the set-of-contracts theory of the firm.[31] (c) The modern property rights approach develops

---

[25] Ostrom E, Governing the Commons. Cambridge U P, Cambridge (1990) pp 24–25.

[26] Wilson R, On the Theory of Syndicates, Econometrica 36 (1968) pp 119–132; Arrow KJ, Essays in the Theory of Risk Bearing. Markham Publishing Co., Chicago (1971); Jensen MC, Meckling WH, Theory of the Firm: Managerial Behavior, Agency Costs and Ownership Structure, J Fin Econ 3 (1976) pp 305–360. For an overview, see Eisenhardt KM, Agency Theory: An Assessment and Review, Acad Man Rev 14 (1989) pp 57–74.

[27] Fama EF, Agency Problems and the Theory of the Firm, J Pol Econ 88(2) (1980) p 291.

[28] Jensen MC, Meckling WH, Theory of the Firm: Managerial Behavior, Agency Costs and Ownership Structure, J Fin Econ 3 (1976) p 312. See also Fama EF, Agency Problems and the Theory of the Firm, J Pol Econ 88(2) (1980) p 290–291.

[29] For a discussion of the role of constituencies, see Williamson OE, The Economic Institutions of Capitalism. The Free Press, New York (1985) pp 298–312.

[30] Coase RH, The Nature of the Firm, Economica, New Series 4(14) (1937) p 392.

[31] Alchian AA, Demsetz H, Production, Information Costs, and Economic Organization, Am Econ Rev 62 (1972) p 777; Jensen MC, Meckling WH, Theory of the Firm: Managerial Behavior, Agency Costs and Ownership Structure, J Fin Econ 3 (1976) p 310.

the set-of-contracts theory further: if the firm is regarded as a set of contracts and nothing else, the defining characteristic of firms is ownership of non-human assets (property rights) rather than authority.[32] (d) Authority is again important in the governance of common resource pools. One can solve the problem that "everybody's property is nobody's property" either by creating property rights or by allocating authority to an external regulator or the users of the common resource pool.[33]

Governance structure. Theories of the firm as a governance structure (behavioural and managerial theories of the firm) reject the classical model of an owner-manager in favour of theories that focus more on the motivations of a manager who controls but does not own.[34] However, this does not reduce the role of authority.

According to Simon (1991), it is characteristic of organisations that they use an authority mechanism. Through the authority mechanism, organisations provide a means for coordinating the activities of the groups of individuals that are its members.[35] The fact that firms exist for the purpose of coordination was identified already by Smith (1776) and the authority mechanism by Coase (1937).

2.5 Summary

Because of large variation, economic theories of the firm give little guidance for legal research. Economic theories of the firm seem to have different ideas about the most basic aspects of the firm. They can study the firm as a production function or as a governance structure. The firm can also be personified in different ways or not personified at all. Moreover, authority plays a different role depending on the theory.

Some things are nevertheless clear. First, regardless of the definition of the firm, *firms* are important (Sects. 4.2 and 7.3). Second, regardless of the definition of the firm, *people* are important (Sect. 7.2). For example, people can be regarded as the firm, as parties having authority, as members of an organisation, or as contract parties. Third, the firm is *not a legal entity*. The legal entity should not matter as far

[32] This approach was pioneered by Grossman SJ, Hart OD, The Costs and Benefits of Ownership: A Theory of Vertical and Lateral Integration, J Pol Econ 94 (1986) pp 691–719.

[33] Ostrom E, Governing the Commons. Cambridge U P, Cambridge (1990) pp 25 and 40.

[34] Baumol WJ, Business Behavior, Value and Growth. Macmillan, New York (1959); Simon HA, Theories of decision-making in economics and behavioral science, Am Econ Rev 49 (1959) pp 253–283; Cyert RM, March JG, A Behavioral Theory of the Firm. Prentice-Hall, Inc., Englewood Cliffs, NJ (1963); Williamson OE, The Economics of Discretionary Behavior: Managerial Objectives in a Theory of the Firm. Prentice-Hall, Englewood Cliffs, NJ (1964). See also Fama EF, Agency Problems and the Theory of the Firm, J Pol Econ 88(2) (1980) p 289.

[35] Simon HA, Organizations and Markets, J Econ Persp 5(2) (1991) pp 25–44.

as the definition of the firm is concerned (Sects. 4.2 and 4.6). Fourth, the scope of variation between different theoretical approaches probably implies that all economic theories cannot simultaneously be aligned with the reality of people, firms, and existing laws (Sect. 5.3). A legal theory of commercial law, corporate governance, or corporate law should *seek its own way*.

Chapter 3
Theory of Commercial Law: Past Approaches

3.1 Introduction

We can start seeking the new ways by studying the theory of commercial law first. We can begin with past approaches. A new theory will be proposed in Chap. 4.

Commercial law has something to do with firms. One might assume that there could be a connection between theories of commercial law and theories of the firm. Unfortunately, there has not been any such connection in the past. There are two reasons for this: the sorry state of commercial law theory; and the phenomena studied in commercial law research.

No theory. A few years ago, a law and economics journal published an issue containing papers presented at a conference on commercial law theory and the CISG.[1] The objective of the conference was to bring together commercial law scholars from the United States and Europe to explore different methodological approaches for analysing the CISG. But although the conference should also have been about commercial law theory, none of the papers spelled out the contents of such a theory or theories.

[1] The "Conference on Commercial Law Theory and the Convention on the International Sale of Goods (CISG)" was hosted by New York University School of Law in Florence, Italy, on October 14–16, 2004. The papers were published in 25(3) Int'l Rev L & Econ (2005). Related topics had already been discussed in Kraus JS, Walt SD (eds), The Jurisprudential Foundations of Corporate and Commercial Law. Cambridge Studies in Philosophy and Law. Cambridge U P, Cambridge (2000). In 2001, Harvard Law School hosted a symposium titled "Law, Knowledge, and the Academy". The papers presented at the symposium were published in 115 Harv L Rev (2002) pp 1277–1431. In Germany, related topics were discussed in Engel C, Schön W (eds), Das Proprium der Rechtswissenschaft. Recht – Wissenschaft – Theorie. Mohr Siebeck, Tübingen (2007). One can also mention "Beyond the State – Rethinking Private Law", a joint conference of the American Journal of Comparative Law and Rabels Zeitschrift. For conference reports, see Flohr M, Beyond the State? Rethinking Private Law. Symposium in Hamburg am 12. Und 13. Juli 2007, RabelsZ 72 (2008) pp 391–396; for articles, see 56 Am J Comp L (2008) pp 527–844.

P. Mäntysaari, *Organising the Firm*,
DOI 10.1007/978-3-642-22197-2_3, © Springer-Verlag Berlin Heidelberg 2012

The absence of a commercial law theory in papers presented at a conference on commercial law theory might seem odd but reflects the fact that the work of academic lawyers is, to a very large extent, "untheorised".[2] There is no commercial law theory.

One could, therefore, say that commercial law is not scientific enough and that it is just a "discursive formation" which has crossed neither the threshold of positivity nor the threshold of science.[3]

The perspective. There is a connection between the lack of a commercial law theory and the perspective chosen by commercial law academics. Obviously, it is impossible to formulate a theory of any kind without generalisations concerning the occurrence or non-occurrence of certain phenomena under investigation, and it is impossible to formulate meaningful generalisations, unless the phenomena have been defined narrowly. It is argued here that the root and cause of the problem is that mainstream commercial law research is *norm-based*. Norm-based research cannot lead to a meaningful theory of commercial law, because virtually any legal rules can, in a market economy, influence the behaviour of firms in one way or another.

Moreover, one cannot expect any meaningful connection between commercial law theory and theories of the firm, unless both study the same phenomena. But this is not the case, as norm-based research focuses on legal rules rather than the firm.

Purpose. The purpose of this chapter is to give a brief overview of present approaches to research in the extremely wide area of commercial law and discuss some of the reasons for the absence of a general commercial law theory. The purpose of Chap. 4 is to propose a commercial law theory that chooses the perspective of the firm and is management-based rather than norm-based.

3.2 Research Perspectives and Approaches

For obvious reasons, most legal research has as its starting point legal rules and can thus be described as *norm-based*. This applies even to commercial law. Commercial law is often broadly defined as a group of loosely connected rules, norms or customs governing trading and commercial activities. It is understood to mean roughly the same thing as business law. In some countries, commercial law in the narrow sense means the rules and norms contained in a particular commercial code. In most countries, however, commercial law is a vast subject, drawing on all streams of private and public law.[4]

---

[2] Posner RA, Legal Scholarship Today, Harv L Rev 114 (2002) pp 1314–1326; Engel C, Schön W (eds), Das Proprium der Rechtswissenschaft. Recht – Wissenschaft – Theorie. Mohr Siebeck, Tübingen (2007).

[3] Foucault M, L'Archéologie du Savoir. Éditions Gallimard, France (1969).

[4] See Goode RM, Commercial Law in the Next Millenium. The Hamlyn Lectures. Forty-ninth Series. Sweet & Maxwell, London (1998) p 8.

Theories. The mainstream paradigm is that legal research must be norm-based. As a result, there has never been a general theory of commercial law setting out the principles that describe legal phenomena in the context of commercial exchanges (*commercial law theory in the narrow sense*).[5]

In commercial law research, it is customary to use theories developed in other fields of law, or in other areas of social sciences (*imported theories*). To use theories imported from social sciences is characteristic of legal science in the US. After the realist revolution of the 1930s, US legal scholarship became specialised according to the separate social sciences. The resulting position has been described as follows: "It is accepted today, virtually universally, that the legal system can be best understood with the methods and theories of the social sciences."[6]

Research approaches. Different imported theories tend to be combined with different research approaches. One can distinguish between five broad mainstream research approaches in commercial law, each with its own imported theories: analysis of the history of commercial law; the doctrinal analysis; comparative law and the approximation of laws; philosophy of law; and economic analysis.[7] (One can also add proactive law as the sixth research approach, see below.)

Research methodologies. There are also a number of research methodologies. Legal phenomena can be studied from many disciplinary perspectives ranging from history to economics. The customary research methodologies developed in other areas of social sciences can be used even in the study of legal phenomena.

Research perspectives. In addition to the choice of a theory, a research approach, and a research methodology, commercial law research is, of course, limited by the choice of research questions. This choice is greatly influenced by four choices relating to the *perspective*: the audience and purpose of commercial law research;

[5] See also Druey JN, The practitioner and the professor – is there a theory of commercial law? In: Tison M, De Wulf H, Van der Elst C, Steennot R (eds), Perspectives in Company Law and Financial Regulation: Essays in Honour of Eddy Wymeersch. International Corporate Law and Financial Market Regulation. Cambridge U P, Cambridge (2009).

[6] Priest GL, Social Science Theory and Legal Education: The Law School as University, J Legal Educ 33 (1983) pp p 437. Moreover, Priest writes: "In 1930, prior to the realist revolution, future specialization in legal scholarship might have suggested increasingly detailed and narrow treatises addressing traditional legal subjects. Today, authorship of the legal treatise has been cast off to practitioners. The treatise is no longer even a credit to those competing on the leading edge of legal thought. Instead, legal scholarship has become specialized according to the separate social sciences."

[7] Each article published in 25(3) Int'l Rev L & Econ (2005) represented at least one of those research approaches (with the exception of philosophy of law). For a collection of articles with different research approaches, see also Gillette CP (ed), The Creation and Interpretation of Commercial Law. The International Library of Essays in Law and Legal Theory. Ashgate, Dartmouth (2003). The articles contained in Kraus JS, Walt SD (eds), *op cit*, mainly represented the areas of philosophy of law and economic analysis of law. The articles published in 56 Am J Comp L (2008) pp 527–844 mainly focused on the philosophy of law.

and the users and use of commercial law.[8] These choices are interrelated and very important for the purposes of the proposed theory of MBCL.

As the term implies, the *audience* of commercial law research means the category of people to whom the research is directed (addressed) and whose information needs the researcher tries to satisfy (clients of law firms, university professors, drafters of state laws, judges, or other parties).[9]

The audience is chosen for a certain *purpose*, the purpose of the research (provision of legal advice, writing a doctoral thesis, amendment of state laws, drafting a reasonable precedent, obtaining a favourable judgment, and so forth).

The *user* of commercial law means the category of people applying information about commercial law for the purposes of their own decision-making. Users of commercial law range from judges and arbitrators, who act as external adjudicators in legal proceedings, to lawyers, who try to assess the outcome of legal proceedings, and to in-house counsel, who try to manage the legal framework of the firm.

Users are not the same thing as the audience (the addressees). For example, a lawyer can write a memo on the interpretation of section 3 of a certain Act to a client firm. In this case, the client firm is the audience. A first-instance court can be chosen as the user, as state law is interpreted according to the rules and practices applied by the court. We can take another example. A junior researcher can write her doctoral thesis about the "efficiency" of section 3 of the same Act. The primary audience of the research is the researcher's university. The user of law is typically the legislator or the courts of the researcher's country. A third example would be an in-house counsel writing an internal memo on a compliance program made necessary by section 3. In this case, the firm is both the audience of the research and the user of commercial law.

The users of law need information about law for a certain *purpose*. The question of the user of commercial law is therefore linked to the question of the *use* of commercial law. The main distinction here is the distinction between the normative, simulated and non-normative use of law. (a) Law has traditionally been used in a *normative* way. For example, public authorities adopt legal rules and define them as binding for the parties to whom they apply (legislation). Courts are bound by these legal rules. Courts use information about norms to interpret them and to apply them to the facts of the case (enforcement). Firms use law in a normative way by trying to comply with it, and by trying to make others comply with it (regulatory compliance, contractual compliance, conflict resolution). (b) Such normative use of law can also be *simulated*. It is simulated by legal scholars, lawyers, and other parties who

[8] Compare Wendehorst CC, The State as a Foundation of Private Law Reasoning, Am J Comp L 56 (2008) p 602 distinguishing between different forms of legal reasoning: "Legal reasoning can take four different basic perspectives, which may be described as the internal, the external, the sovereign, and the subordinate perspective. Each of them has its own goals, its own patterns of argumentation, and its own tools for coping with plural and fragmented sources."

[9] See also Cheffins BR, Using Theory to Study Law: A Company Law Perspective, CLJ 58(1) (1999) p 199.

interpret norms without being bound by them themselves.[10] (c) In addition, information about normative rules can be used in a *non-normative* way. Typically, legal rules are used in a non-normative way when legal phenomena are studied in non-legal sciences such as economics or history, or for non-doctrinal research purposes in legal sciences. Public authorities can, in a non-normative way, design internal processes for the management of legislation, assess the quality of existing legislation, and plan new legislation. Firms can gather information about legal rules and practices in order to design internal processes for the management of legal affairs, assess the effect of legal rules on cash flow and risk, and plan the legal framework for their activities. The non-normative use of rules is often followed by their normative use.

Traditional norm-based commercial law research customarily chooses one or two categories of *users* of commercial law: (a) external *adjudicators* such as judges and arbitrators, and parties who deal with them (and simulate how external adjudicators would use norms) (*de lege lata*, what the law is); and (b) external *rule-makers* such as the state or private organisations (*de lege ferenda*, what the law ought to be). Typically, both user-categories *use* rules in a *normative* way.[11]

Traditional commercial law research does not typically choose *firms* as users of law. This is even where firms form its intended audience. Simply put, norm-based commercial law research focuses on legal rules that are, or should be, applied by the court. Only in rare cases does commercial law research deal with the *non-normative* use of legal things by firms; there is relatively little research on the legal objectives of firms and on the use of legal tools and practices in the management of firms.[12]

Now, the absence of a theory of commercial law and the choice of the perspective of external adjudicators or rule-makers are likely to have increased the variation of mainstream research approaches. In the following, the strikingly heterogeneous mainstream research approaches will be discussed briefly. Although well-known, studying the main points of the mainstream approaches is necessary for pedagogical reasons and because it will help to understand:

- The lack of a reasonably exact definition of commercial law
- The path-dependency[13] of commercial law research and its focus on "law"

[10] See already Wendell Holmes O Jr, The Path of the Law. Harv L Rev 10 (1897) pp 457–478 (prediction theory).

[11] Eidenmüller H, Effizienz als Rechtsprinzip. Die Einheit der Gesellschaftswissenschaften 90. Mohr Siebeck, Tübingen (2005) p 1 arguing that the two perspectives are that of the legislator and that of the judge: "Recht kann man insbesondere aus zwei Perspektiven betrachten: aus derjenigen des *Gesetzgebers* und aus derjenigen des *Richters*." For similar views, see Posner RA, Frontiers of Legal Theory. Harvard U P, Cambridge, Mass (2001); Engel C, Schön W, Vorwort. In: Engel C, Schön W (eds), *op cit*, p XII.

[12] See also Epstein RA, Let "The Fundamental Things Apply": Necessary and Contingent Truths in Legal Scholarship, Harv L Rev 115 (2002) p 1288 stating: "Nothing that we say or write here will, or should, alter the brute fact that much academic scholarship services the internal operations of the legal profession."

[13] Posner RA, Frontiers of Legal Theory. Harvard U P, Cambridge, Mass. (2001) p 145 (finding the legal profession the most "past dependent" of the professions). See also Mestmäcker EJ, A Legal

- That mainstream research approaches are interrelated
- The failings of mainstream commercial law research
- The need to design a theory of commercial law
- The differences between mainstream commercial law research and the theory proposed in Chap. 4

Past research perspectives and approaches, embedded and non-embedded. There are currently six important research approaches in commercial law. Five of them can be described as norm-based. They focus on: the history of commercial law; doctrinal analysis; comparative law and the approximation of laws; the philosophy of law; and the economic analysis of law. The sixth is not norm-based but focuses on the practices of firms. It is called preventive or proactive law.

Past research approaches have been regarded as embedded or non-embedded depending on the choice of the theoretical framework. "Embedded" means embedded in theories of legal science. "Non-embedded" means embedded in the theories of other social sciences.[14] One can see this distinction in a new light when one takes into account the purpose of the research.

The distinction seems to be a matter of degree depending on the purpose of the research. (a) When the purpose of the research is to simulate the normative use of law, the research is customarily embedded in the interpretation rules of the chosen jurisdiction. This is the core of embedded research and traditional jurisprudence.[15] However, such research can also be embedded in the theories of other social sciences. For example, quantitative methods can be used to predict the behaviour of judges. (b) When law is used in a normative way, it is customarily embedded in theories of legal science, but it can also be embedded in theories of other social sciences depending on the user. For example, economic theories customarily influence legislative reforms in company and securities markets law.[16] However, economic theories tend to play a lesser role when judges apply rules adopted by the legislator. (c) When the purpose of the research is the non-normative use of law,

---

Theory without Law. Walter Eucken Institut, Beiträge zur Ordnungstheorie und Ordnungspolitik 174. Mohr Siebeck, Tübingen (2007) p 56.

[14] Rakoff TD, Introduction to Symposium: Law, Knowledge, and the Academy, Harv L Rev 115 (2002) p 1279 (distinguishing between "embedded" and "non-embedded" legal scholarship); Fleischer H, Gesellschafts- und Kapitalmarktrecht als wissenschaftliche Disziplin – Das Proprium der Rechtswissenschaft. In: Engel C, Schön W (eds), *op cit*, pp 52–53 (commenting on the distinction made by Rakoff); Fleischer H, Zur Zukunft der gesellschafts- und kapitalmarktrechtlichen Forschung, ZGR 4/2007 pp 501–502.

[15] Wendell Holmes O Jr, The Path of the Law. Harv L Rev 10 (1897) pp 457–478. See also Larenz K, Über die Unentbehrlichkeit der Jurisprudenz als Wissenschaft. Walter de Gruyter, Berlin (1966) p 12: "Die Aufgabe der Rechtswissenschaft ... ist eine dreifache. Sie legt die Gesetze aus, sie bildet das Recht gemäß den der Rechtsordnung immanenten Wertmaßstäben und den in ihr liegenden gedanklichen Möglichkeiten fort und sie sucht immer aufs neue die Fülle des Rechtsstoffes unter einheitlichen Gesichtspunkten zu erfassen."

[16] See, for example, Fleischer H, Zur Zukunft der gesellschafts- und kapitalmarktrechtlichen Forschung, ZGR 4/2007 p 504.

theories of other social sciences can sometimes prevail, but legal research will always be embedded in theories of legal science.

3.3 Analysis of the History of Commercial Law

One of the perspectives from which one can study commercial law is to examine its historical origins. Legal history is a science with its own specific tools. Sources in legal history range from texts to other data such as archives, statistics, or even inscriptions. The mix of sources depends on the context, and the use of each source can require a different methodology.

Time frame, area of commercial law. Studies in the history of commercial law can be limited to a certain period of time, a certain area of commercial law, or both.

The classic work in this area is Goldschmidt (1891),[17] a presentation of the general history of commercial law – and so far the only one of its kind. Most works focus on particular aspects of the history of commercial law and choose a shorter time frame. For example, Goldschmidt was the supervisor – Doktorvater – of Max Weber's doctoral thesis.[18] Weber discussed the history of commercial partnerships in the Middle Ages. He became later known as one of the founders of sociology. Of recent works, one can mention Goetzmann and Rouwenhorst (2005),[19] which focuses on financial instruments and contracts that have survived through history, as well as Skeel (2001) and Mann (2002), which study the history of American bankruptcy laws.[20]

Law, commercial practices. "Law" can be defined in various ways, and studies in the history of commercial law can focus on different aspects of "law". It is customary to study rules and regulations that are *enforceable* ex post by the state or other third parties in an organised way and by using socially acceptable procedures (legal enforceability). It is also possible to focus on the history of *international* commercial law such as foreign trade laws, commercial treaty law, international conventions, maritime laws, and lex mercatoria.

Early commercial law. It is not the purpose of this book to study the history of commercial law as such. Because of the path-dependency of notions of commercial law, it is nevertheless useful to discuss some main points.

---

[17] Goldschmidt L, Handbuch des Handelsrechts. Erste Band. Erste Abtheilung. Universalgeschichte des Handelsrechts. Erste Lieferung. Ferdinand Enke, Stuttgart (1891). For a discussion of the impact of Goldschmidt's work, see Whitman J, Note, Commercial Law and the American Volk: A Note on Llewellyn's German Sources for the Uniform Commercial Code, Yale L J 97 (1987) pp 156–175.

[18] The thesis formed part of Weber M, Zur Geschichte der Handelsgesellschaften im Mittelalter. Nach südeuropäischen Quellen. Eure, Stuttgart (1889).

[19] Goetzmann WN, Rouwenhorst KG (eds), The Origins of Value. OUP, Oxford (2005).

[20] Skeel DA Jr, Debt's Domain. A History of Bankruptcy Law in America. Princeton U P, Princeton Oxford (2001); Mann BH, Republic of Debtors. Bankruptcy in the Age of American Independence. Harvard U P, Cambridge London (2002).

Generally, one could say that the roots of commercial law can be traced back to the roots of civilisation itself. Specialisation and the loss of self-sufficiency meant that people needed to exchange goods and services. In Mesopotamia, this led to the invention of writing, credit, and interest.[21] Later, parts of the Code of Hammurabi laid down rules designed to regulate commercial exchanges.

Research in the history of commercial law customarily starts with *Roman law*, in particular classical Roman law, and Justinian's Corpus iuris civilis, which codified classical Roman law. Both provided for an advanced law of obligations. After centuries of decline, the study of Roman law was revived in Italy in the twelfth century. Bologna scholars known under the name of Glossators developed a civil law system called ius commune, the common learned law of the whole of the West. In the nineteenth century, von Savigny, the most famous representative of the Historical School or Pandectistic School, interpreted Roman law and showed how it lived on in local German customs.[22]

However, the Roman and Byzantine economies were agrarian, and Roman law was not designed for commercial practice. Most of commercial law was developed much later.

Lex mercatoria. Commercial law started to develop independently of Roman law in the Middle Ages as *lex mercatoria.*[23]

Chronologically, lex mercatoria was divided into three stages,[24] although the stages may be a matter of taste.[25] The first was the period of *customary* commercial law from the twelfth to the fifteenth centuries. The driving force was the Italian mercantile community. The second was the period of *incorporation* of lex mercatoria into the various municipal or state systems of law. As a result, lex mercatoria was, to a large extent, replaced by national commercial codes and the regulation of commercial exchanges by the state.[26] The third stage was the modern

[21] Van de Mieroop M, The Invention of Interest. Sumerian Loans. In: Goetzmann WN, Rouwenhorst KG (eds), The Origins of Value. OUP, Oxford (2005) pp 17–18.

[22] von Savigny FC, Das System des heutigen römischen Rechts (1840–1849).

[23] See, for example, Van Caenegem RC, Johnston DEL, An Historical Introduction to Private Law. Cambridge U P, Cambridge (1992) 83–85.

[24] Schmitthoff CM, International Business Law: A New Law Merchant. In: Chia-Jui Cheng (ed), Clive M. Schmitthoff's Select Essays on International Trade Law. Martinus Nijhoff Publishers / Graham & Trotman, Dordrecht (1992) pp 21–22. Originally published as Schmitthoff CM, International Business Law: A New Law Merchant. In St J MacDonald R (ed), 2 Current Law and Social Problems. University of Toronto Press, Toronto (1961).

[25] See, for example, Michaels R, The True Lex Mercatoria: Law Beyond the State, Ind J Global Legal Stud 14:2 (2007) p 448.

[26] See, for example, Trakman LE, The Law Merchant: The Evolution of Commercial Law. Fred B. Rothman & Co., Littleton, Colorado (1983). See also Scott HS, The Risk Fixers, Harv L Rev 91 (1978) p 738: "In any case, statutory rules are principally designed to alter rather than to 'codify' the existing legal regime. They reflect concern with the ability of various transactors, whether merchants or consumers, to protect themselves in the marketplace, and they are ultimately distributional in character. Since they are designed to alter the existing order or to remedy market failure or inefficiency, statutory commercial rules are unlikely to be optional - mere backstops for existing merchant practices."

lex mercatoria characterised by the existence of large multinational firms, international rule-making organisations, and other *global players*.

We can have a closer look at the second stage as the stage that explains much of the absence of a commercial law theory (for the third stage, see Sects. 3.4 and 3.5).

Codification. From the sixteenth century, there were attempts to systematise the body of first-stage rules according to jurisprudential criteria. The first national commercial code was the French Ordonnance sur le Commerce (1673). It was complemented by Ordonnance sur la Marine (1681). In these ways, customs and usages of merchants were embodied in French law.[27] In addition to French law, Dutch commercial laws and practices played an important role in continental Europe.

Continental European countries can thank France for laying the foundations for much of the legislation and doctrinal research in this area. After the French revolution, five legal codes ("les cinq codes") were adopted under Napoléon I between 1804 and 1810. Code civil, the 1803 civil code, was complemented by Code de commerce, the 1807 commercial code. Code civil and Code de commerce shaped commercial law in continental Europe in four main ways. First, they were adopted in countries ruled by the French: Italy, the Netherlands, Belgium, Spain, Portugal, and the left bank of the Rhine. Second, they were used as a model in German codifications (1896 BGB and 1897 HGB). Third, German law was used as a model in countries such as Austria, Switzerland, and the Nordic countries (and even in Asian countries such as Japan and China). Fourth, Code civil and Code de commerce determined the distinction between general private law and commercial law still applied in continental Europe.

On the other hand, the French-German model also means that commercial law lacks general principles and does not exist as an independent field of law. Whereas Code civil contained provisions of general application, Code de commerce provided for exceptions applicable to merchants (commerçant) or to particular commercial contracts. In France, the general principles are based on Code civil rather than Code de commerce. In Germany, the general principles are based on the 1896 BGB, which codified the general private law, rather than the 1897 HGB, which provides for exceptions applicable to merchants (Kaufmann).[28] In both countries, one can distinguish between commercial law in the narrow sense (questions regulated by the commercial code) and in a broad sense (commercial questions regulated outside the commercial code). The legal developments in France and Germany were representative of what happened in continental Europe.[29]

[27] Trakman LE, *op cit*, p 25.

[28] This can be contrasted with the earlier 1861 Allgemeines Deutsches Handelsgesetzbuch (ADHGB) of the German Federation. As the ADHGB was not complemented by a general private law code, it regulated many questions belonging to general private law.

[29] Trakman LE, *op cit*, p 25.

In England, the use of medieval lex mercatoria was restricted in various ways. Commercial practices had to comply with rules of positive law.[30] Lord Mansfield is regarded as the founder of English commercial law.[31] He pioneered the reception into English law of the practices of continental and British merchants (international lex mercatoria). However, there is no commercial code in England. The concept of commercial law can therefore be used in an open and flexible way.[32] The history of commercial law may have influenced even recent views on its role.[33]

3.4 Doctrinal Analysis

Judging by commercial law textbooks, commercial law research is predominately *doctrinal*. It is about *interpreting* certain parts of law. One can distinguish between national commercial law, private international commercial law, lex mercatoria, public international commercial law, transnational commercial law, and EU law.

National commercial law. Most commercial law research is about interpreting national law. Such doctrinal research does not help to develop a global commercial law theory.

First, the choice of the legal issues that fall within what is regarded as commercial law is jurisdiction-specific and depends to a large extent on convention. There is thus a difference between the doctrinal approach (which is jurisdiction-specific and not functional) and the comparative approach (which is functional and not jurisdiction-specific to the same extent, see Sect. 3.5).

In countries that have adopted a particular commercial law code, the scope of commercial law in the narrow sense depends on the scope of the code (Code de commerce, Handelsgesetzbuch, the Uniform Commercial Code, and so forth). This also means that commercial law discourse can be jurisdiction-specific.

For example, the HGB contains rules on business forms, financial information (bookkeeping, accounting, auditing), and commercial contracts. The U.C.C. does not contain rules on business forms and financial information, but does focus more on financial contracts. From a functional perspective, HGB and the U.C.C. are not comparable (Table 3.1).

---

[30] *Ibid*, p 27.

[31] Especially for his work in cases such as: Pillans & Rose v Van Mierop & Hopkins [1765] 3 Burr 1663; and Carter v Boehm [1766] 3 Burr 1905. Lord Mansfield was born William Murray in Scotland in 1705.

[32] See Goode RM, Commercial Law in the Next Millenium. The Hamlyn Lectures. Forty-ninth Series. Sweet & Maxwell, London (1998) p 8.

[33] See Goode RM, The Wilfred Fullagar Memorial Lecture: The Codification of Commercial Law, Monash U L R 14 (1988) p 148 (arguing that the primary function of commercial law is "to accommodate the legitimate practices and expectations of the business community in relation to their commercial dealings").

Table 3.1 The HGB and the U.C.C.

HGB	U.C.C.
First book *Merchants*, second book *Business Entities and the Silent Company*, third book *Accounts*, fourth book *Commercial Contracts*, fifth book *Sea Trade*	Article 1 *General Provisions*, Article 2 *Sales*, Article 2A *Leases*, Article 3 *Negotiable Instruments*, Article 4 *Bank Deposit*, Article 4A *Funds Transfers*, Article 5 *Letters of Credit*, Article 6 *Bulk Transfers and Bulk Sales*. Article 7 *Warehouse Receipts, Bills of Lading and Other Documents of Title*, Article 8 *Investment Securities*, Article 9 *Secured Transactions*

Of course, commercial law discourse can spread across borders. The commercial law discourse of one country can be adopted in another country, and the classification of certain legal issues as commercial law issues in one country can become a legal transplant abroad. For example, the HGB has influenced commercial law discourse in countries that belong to the German legal family and in the Nordic countries.[34]

But if commercial law discourse is jurisdiction-specific and commercial law is not really the same thing in different jurisdiction, it is difficult to develop a general commercial law theory applicable in all jurisdictions.

Second, national conventions may prevent the development of jurisdiction-specific commercial law theories.

This can be illustrated with the French–German model. According to this model, commercial law in the narrow sense consists of "exceptions" to the regulation of dealings in general. As a result, it has virtually no general principles of its own. If it has such principles, they can relate to two things. They can relate to the scope of the commercial law exceptions, and define terms such as "merchant" (commerçant, Kaufmann), "commercial activity" (Gewerbebetrieb), "undertaking" (Unternehmen), and "consumer" (Verbraucher).[35] In addition, each particular

[34] Mäntysaari P, En teoretisk referensram för handelsrätten, TfR 2011.

[35] According to the French-German model, commercial law is basically defined as rules applicable to certain parties (according to German terminology, it as a "subject-based system") rather than rules applicable to certain categories of transactions generally (it is not an "object-based system"). For example, the German discussion about the definition of commercial law has focused on whether the commercial law exceptions should apply just to "merchants" or even to the wider category of "undertakings". See Zöllner W, Wovon handelt das Handelsrecht? ZGR 1/1983 pp 82–91 (generally). According to traditionalists, commercial law is "particular private law for merchants" ("Sonderprivatrecht für Kaufleute"). For the traditional view, see Canaris CW, Handelsrecht, 24. Auflage. C.H. Beck, München (2006). Some define commercial law as "external private law for undertakings" ("Außenprivatrecht der Unternehmen"). See Schmidt K, Vom Handelsrecht zum Unternehmens-Privatrecht? JuS 1985 pp 249–257; Schmidt K, Zerfällt das Handelsgesetzbuch? Eine Gedankenskizz zur Zukunft des Vierten Buchs. In: Berger KP, Borges G, Herrmann H, Schlüter A, Wackerbarth U (eds), Zivil- und Wirtschaftsrecht im Europäischen und Globalen Kontext / Private and Commercial Law in a European and Global Context: Festschrift für Norbert Horn zum 70. Geburtstag. de Gruyter Recht, Berlin (2006). See already

sector of commercial law can have its own set of general principles not shared by other sectors.

This means that commercial law in the narrow sense is not regarded as an independent branch of law. In the broad sense, it consists of various independent branches of law each with its own set of public policy objectives, sector-specific regulation, general principles, and terms. They are complemented by the general principles applied to all private-law or public-law transactions.

In common law countries, attempts have been made to define other kinds of general principles for commercial law. For example, Goode has proposed the following principles of commercial law: party autonomy; predictability; flexibility; good faith; the encouragement of self-help; the facilitation of security interests; the protection of vested interests; and the protection of innocent third parties.[36] However, such principles do not seem to differ from the legal principles that apply to private-law or public-law transactions in general.[37]

One can therefore say that the emergence of a commercial law theory has, in particular in continental Europe, been hampered by two things: the almost exclusive focus on rules applied by a state's courts and the notion that commercial law consists of "exceptions" applicable to certain parties. That notion was first adopted two centuries ago and has clearly become outdated.[38]

Private international commercial law. The doctrinal analysis of commercial law is not limited to the substantive provisions of a certain country's laws. Textbooks in international commercial law always discuss the matter of governing law and related questions such as prorogation agreements (choice-of-law clauses), the international jurisdiction of courts, and dispute resolution in international contracts. Compared with the interpretation of national commercial law, foreign materials and international materials such as international conventions and treaties play a more important role in the process of interpreting rules of private international commercial law.

Modern lex mercatoria. In addition to research in private international commercial law, there is a vast amount of research in what is called *modern lex mercatoria*

Raisch P, Geschichtliche Voraussetzungen, dogmatische Grundlagen und Sinnwandlung des Handelsrechts. C.F. Müller, Karlsruhe (1965); Raisch P, Die rechtsdogmatische Bedeutung der Abgrenzung von Handelsrecht und bürgerlichem Recht, JuS 1967 pp 533–542. In 2005, the latter view was adopted in Austria when the Austrian Handelsgesetzbuch (HGB) was amended and renamed Unternehmensgesetzbuch (UGB, Business Enterprise Code).

[36] Goode RM, The Wilfred Fullagar Memorial Lecture: The Codification of Commercial Law, Monash U L R 14 (1988) pp 135–157.

[37] Compare DCFR, Principles.

[38] See Zöllner W, Wovon handelt das Handelsrecht? ZGR 1/1983 pp 82–91; Baumann H, Strukturfragen des Handelsrechts, AcP 184 (1984) pp 45–66; Neuner J, Handelsrecht — Handelsgesetz — Grundgesetz, ZHR 157 (1993) pp 243–290.

(the third stage of lex mercatoria). Schmitthoff and Goldman are regarded as the founding fathers of lex mercatoria as a modern area of law.[39]

Modern lex mercatoria is to some extent codified. For example, the International Chamber of Commerce (ICC) has played an important part in the codification and unification of customs and usages in international trade and commerce: most commercial lawyers have used INCOTERMS, the Uniform Customs and Practices for Documentary Credits, and the Uniform Rules for Demand Guarantees in addition to other codified practices or model terms published by the ICC. There is also what is known as "creeping codification" through the drafting of lists of rules and principles of lex mercatoria.[40]

However, there is no international consensus on what modern lex mercatoria means, or how it should be defined, or whether it really exists in the first place.[41]

Most tend to agree on what lex mercatoria is not: It is not national legislation.[42] According to the least ambitious definition, lex mercatoria consists of usages and settled expectations that can be taken into account when interpreting contracts under the governing law. However, this definition would leave the concept of lex mercatoria rather meaningless, as any usages and expectations of the parties can be taken into account when interpreting contracts (in particular in civil law countries which do not apply the parol evidence rule).[43] According to a more ambitious view, it is a system of principles and rules generally accepted in international commerce, or even an autonomous legal order, created by parties involved in international commercial relations.

For the purposes of this book, it is neither necessary nor meaningful to discuss the possible definitions of this vague concept in more detail.[44] It suffices to say that lex mercatoria can be understood as certain kinds of *external rules* (state or non-state) that apply to contracts.

---

[39] Schmitthoff CM, The Unification of the Law of International Trade, JBL 1968 pp 105–119; Goldman B, Lex Mercatoria, Forum Internationale 3 (1983) pp 3–7. See also Hatzimihail NE, The Many Lives—And Faces—of Lex Mercatoria: An Essay on the Genealogy of International Business Law, Law & Contemp Probs 71 (2008) pp 169–190.

[40] Berger KP, International Economic Arbitration. Studies in Transnational Economic Law 9. Kluwer Law and Taxation Publishers, Deventer (1993) p 543; Berger KP, The Creeping Codification of the Lex Mercatoria. Kluwer Law International, The Hague (1999); Lando O, The Harmonization of European Contract Law through a Restatement of Principles. Centre for the Advanced Study of European and Comparative Law, University of Oxford (1997) p 20.

[41] See, in particular, Mustill MJ, The New Lex Mercatoria: The First Twenty-Five Years. In: Bos M, Brownlie I (eds), Liber Amicorum for the Rt. Hon. Lord Wilberforce, PC, CMG, OBE, QC. Clarendon Press, Oxford (1987). Published also as Mustill MJ, Arbitration International 4 (1988) pp 86–119.

[42] See Ramberg J, International Commercial Transactions. ICC, Kluwer Law International, Norstedts Juridik Ab, Stockholm (1998) p 20.

[43] See Articles 8 and 9 of the CISG.

[44] There is a vast amount of literature. See, for example, Michaels R, The True Lex Mercatoria: Law Beyond the State, Ind J Global Legal Stud 14:2 (2007) pp 447–468.

Public international commercial law. Many international organisations have played an important role in the development of international treaties and conventions in the area of commercial law. The interpretation of such treaties and conventions is a wide research area. Typically, public international law has its own methodology for the interpretation of international treaties and conventions. The principles of international treaty law are embodied in the 1969 Vienna Convention on the Law of Treaties. International trade law, Law of the Sea, international aviation law, and international environmental law are some of the branches of public international law.

EU Law. Finally, one should mention EU Law. The doctrinal analysis of the regulation of commercial transactions under Community law is an important area of commercial law. Although the Community Treaties are basically treaties under public international law, they create a new legal system, and the European Court of Justice has emphasised that they are not necessarily interpreted in the same way as ordinary treaties.[45] Some provisions of Community law have direct effect in the Member States.[46] Furthermore, the interpretation of primary and secondary Community law influences the interpretation of Member States' laws.[47]

3.5 Comparative Law and the Approximation of Laws

The third main research approach is that of comparative law and the approximation of laws. The comparative aspects of commercial law, the convergence of commercial laws, and the analysis of national provisions of law are closely connected in modern commercial law research. Modern commercial law research is increasingly comparative and functional rather than limited to the legal sources of just one country.[48]

Comparative law. One can distinguish between comparative law in the narrow and broad sense. Both remained rare for a long time, although comparative law does have long roots.[49]

In the broad sense, it is possible to take the contents of foreign law into account without applying the comparative legal method as such.[50] Foreign law is often

[45] See Case 270/80 Polydor [1982] ECR 329; Case 104/81 Kupferberg [1982] ECR 3641, paragraphs 28–31.

[46] Case 26/62 Van Gend en Loos [1963] ECR 1.

[47] See Case C-106/89 Marleasing [1991] ECR I–4135.

[48] Eidenmüller H, Forschungsperspektiven im Unternehmensrecht, ZGR 4/2007 p 486; Merkt H, Die Zukunft der privatrechtlichen Forschung im Unternehmens- und Kapitalmarktrecht, ZGR 4/2007 pp 540–541.

[49] See Hug W, The History of Comparative Law, Harv L Rev 45 (1932) pp 1027–1070.

[50] An early example of this approach in international law is Grotius H, De jure belli ac pacis libri tres (1625).

taken into account in the context of legal dogmatics or national rule-making for the purpose of improving local law.[51]

In the narrow sense, comparative law is a research area with its own methodology. Comparative law in the narrow sense is a relatively late phenomenon. It started to flourish in continental Europe in the 1920s. Lambert and Rabel belong to its pioneers.[52] In the field of commercial law, the first major comparative study was probably Rabel (1936 and 1957–1958).[53] European integration, Community law, and the approximation of Member States' laws have brought comparative aspects to mainstream commercial law research.[54]

The comparative legal method. One can distinguish between micro-comparison and macro-comparison in the field of traditional comparative law. In micro-comparison, the *functional method* is the mainstream legal method.[55] The purpose of the functional method is simply to facilitate the comparison of comparable things. It means the comparison of sets of all legal things that share the same chosen function. The functional method is not suitable for macro-comparison.

Comparative empirical study of law. Traditional comparative law is complemented by the comparative *empirical* study of law. Unlike the functional method of traditional comparative law that tries to include all legal factors that

---

[51] Kadner Graziano T, Die Europäisierung der juristischen Perspektive und der vergleichenden Methode – Fallstudien, ZVglRWiss 106 (2007) pp 248–249: "Seit Inkrafttreten der großen Kodifikationen im 19. und frühen 20. Jahrhundert diente der Blick auf ausländische Rechtsordnungen in erster Linien dem Zweck, Lücken der nationalen Kodifikationen zu schließen, Anregungen für die Auslegung des eigenen Rechts zu erhalten oder Defizite dieses Rechts zu beheben. Ausgangs- und Bezugspunkt für den Vergleich war jeweils das eigene nationale Recht, das auf diese Weise verbessert oder dessen Lücken geschlossen werden sollten."

[52] In 1920, Lambert founded the Institut de droit compare in Lyon. L'Académie internationale de droit comparé (the International Academy of Comparative law) was founded in 1924. In 1926, Rabel founded the Kaiser-Wilhelm-Institut für ausländisches und internationales Privatrecht in Berlin, now the Max Planck Institute for Comparative and International Private Law in Hamburg. In the same year, L'Institut international pour l'unification du droit privé (Unidroit, the International Institute for the Unification of Private Law) was set up in Rome as an auxiliary organ of the League of Nations. In 1931, Lévy-Ullmann and Capitant founded the Institut de droit compare of the University of Paris.

[53] Rabel E, Das Recht des Warenkaufs. Eine rechtsvergleichende Darstellung. Band I–II. de Gruyter, Berlin and Leipzig (1936) / Mohr, Tübingen (1957–1958). One can also mention Almén T, Das skandinavische Kaufrecht. Carl Winters Universitätsbuchhandlung, Heidelberg (1922).

[54] Kadner Graziano T, Die Europäisierung der juristischen Perspektive und der vergleichenden Methode – Fallstudien, ZVglRWiss 106 (2007) p 249: "Bei allen auf Europäisierung des Privatrechts gerichteten Initiativen kommt der rechtsvergleichenden Methode eine Schlüsselrolle zu."

[55] Zweigert K, Kötz H, Einführung in die Rechtsvergleichung auf dem Gebiete des Privatrechts, 3. Auflage. Mohr Siebeck, Tübingen (1996) is a standard work on comparative law and the functional method. For the functional method, see also Husa J, Farewell to Functionalism or Methodological Tolerance? RabelsZ 67 (2003) pp 419–447; De Coninck J, The Functional Method of Comparative Law: Quo Vadis? RabelsZ 74 (2010) pp 318–350.

share the same function, the empirical study of law means that legal phenomena are reduced to a small number of variables that can be given a numeric value.[56] It can also take the form of qualitative comparative analysis (QCA).[57]

Related concepts include law and economics, law and finance, and legal origins.[58] (a) The comparative empirical study of law and *law and economics* share the use of quantitative research methods. The difference is that law and economics focuses on the overall social welfare and does not need to compare different jurisdictions. (b) There is a bigger difference between the comparative empirical study of law and *law and finance*. Whereas the former means the use of particular numerical and statistical methods, law and finance is a research area. The best-known study in the area of law and finance is La Porta et al (1998).[59] (c) The *legal origins* approach is in the intersection point of comparative empirical study of law and law and finance.[60] There is a stream of research in law and finance explaining differences between the financial markets of different countries by the presumed quality of each country's legal system. In other words, "legal origins matter". In corporate governance research, this approach can suffer from a common law bias.[61]

Attempts to increase convergence. As indicated above, the comparative aspects of commercial law and attempts to increase the convergence of commercial laws are closely related. The laws of different countries are often compared in order to propose better rules or common rules, or to explain why divergence is the better alternative and why country A should not adopt the rules or concepts of country B.

[56] Lieder J, Legal Origins und empirische Rechtsvergleichung. Zur Bedeutung des Rechts für die Entwicklung von Kapitalmärkten und Corporate-Governance-Strukturen, ZVglRWiss 109 (2010) p 228.

[57] Herala N, Use of Qualitative Comparative Analysis (QCA) in Comparative Law. Acta Wasaensia 124, Universitas Wasaensis, Vaasa (2004) p 17: "Qualitative comparative analysis, or QCA, combines two ways of simplifying complexity. It both examines similarities and differences between a limited number of cases, and it inspects relations between variables (Ragin 1987:XIII). QCA could be described as a variable-oriented qualitative comparative method." See also Ragin CC, The Comparative Method: Moving Beyond Qualitative and Quantitative Strategies. U Cal P, Berkeley Los Angeles London (1987).

[58] Lieder J, Legal Origins und empirische Rechtsvergleichung. Zur Bedeutung des Rechts für die Entwicklung von Kapitalmärkten und Corporate-Governance-Strukturen, ZVglRWiss 109 (2010) pp 228–230; Eidenmüller H, Forschungsperspektiven im Unternehmensrecht, ZGR 4/2007 pp 486–495.

[59] La Porta R, Lopez-de-Silanes F, Shleifer A, Vishny RW, Law and Finance, J Pol Econ 106 (1998) pp 1113–1155. See also Djankov S, La Porta R, Lopez-de-Silanes F, Shleifer A, The law and economics of self-dealing, J Fin Econ 88 (2008) pp 430–465; Djankov S, Glaeser E, La Porta R, Lopez-de-Silanes F, Shleifer A, The New Comparative Economics, J Comp Econ 31 (2003) pp 595–619.

[60] Lieder J, Legal Origins und empirische Rechtsvergleichung. Zur Bedeutung des Rechts für die Entwicklung von Kapitalmärkten und Corporate-Governance-Strukturen, ZVglRWiss 109 (2010) pp 229–230.

[61] See *ibid*, pp 216–264.

There are constraints on the adoption of foreign rules, practices and other institutions. For example, foreign rules could become "legal irritants" because of complex linkages between institutions.[62] This contributes to path dependency.

However, rules applicable in one country are often adopted or used as a model in another country (reception of laws,[63] legal transplants[64]). This is customary in countries belonging to the same legal family (for example, the French, German, common law, or Nordic legal families). Depending on the area of law, rules applicable in one country may be used as a model even globally: "The reception of foreign legal institutions is not a matter of nationality, but of usefulness and need. No one bothers to fetch a thing from afar when he has one as good or better at home, but only a fool would refuse quinine just because it didn't grow in his back garden."[65] For example, Anglo-American rules and concepts have been transplanted into the laws of many countries in recent years, and many "legal platforms" are based on them.[66]

In addition, there can be common rules at the international level (international conventions, international model rules) or regional level (for example, Community law and legal co-operation between the Nordic countries). International attempts to unify commercial laws were first successful in the area of transport law, sale of goods, and commercial arbitration. There is now a large number of international conventions regulating commercial transactions.

In the European Union, the process of creating the internal market has required the approximation of selected parts of the Member States' laws. The acquis communautaire contains a vast amount of rules leading to the convergence of the regulation of business. Community law is particularly important in matters relating to access to markets, competition, consumer protection, intellectual property, labour law, and the integration of capital markets (financial reporting, financial disclosure obligations, corporate governance).

Transnational commercial law. Transnational commercial law is a broad concept related to the convergence of laws.[67] It means the body of law that governs

---

62 Aoki M, Toward a Comparative Institutional Analysis. The MIT Press, Cambridge, Mass. (2001) p 17.

63 See Watson A, Aspects of Reception of Law, Am J Comp L 44 (1996) pp 335–351.

64 Watson A, Legal Transplants: An Approach to Comparative Law. Scottish Academic Press, Edinburgh (1974); Watson A, Legal Transplants and European Private Law, 4.4 ELECTRONIC JOURNAL OF COMPARATIVE LAW, http://www.ejcl.org/ejcl/44/44-2.html (2000).

65 von Jhering R, Geist des römischen Rechts auf den verschiedenen Stufen seiner Entwicklung. Breitkopf & Härtel, Leipzig (1852–1865). Cited in Zweigert K, Kötz H, Einführung in die Rechtsvergleichung auf dem Gebiete des Privatrechts, 3. Auflage. Mohr Siebeck, Tübingen (1996) § 2 II. Translation from Xanthaki H, Legal Transplants in Legislation: Defusing the Trap, ICLQ 57 (2008) p 661.

66 For "legal platforms", see Mäntysaari P, The Law of Corporate Finance. Volume II. Springer, Berlin Heidelberg (2010) pp 9–12.

67 For the concept of transnational law, see Jessup PC, Transnational Law. Yale U P, New Haven (1956).

international commercial transactions and results from the convergence of national laws. In other words, it is law that is common to a number of jurisdictions because of international conventions, the adoption of uniform rules, or lex mercatoria.

3.6 Philosophy of Law (Jurisprudence)

Lex mercatoria, the existence of different categories of overlapping regulatory systems, the harmonisation of laws, and the problem of what to compare as functional equivalents in comparative law have given rise to two particular questions in the area of *philosophy of law* (jurisprudence). The first question belongs to *analytic* jurisprudence: What is law in this context? The second is a question of *normative* jurisprudence: What are the jurisprudential foundations of commercial law, or on what grounds should one regulate commercial phenomena?

Law. There is a large amount of literature particularly in the areas of comparative law and transnational commercial law on the nature of "law".[68] However, the nature of "law" has become a relevant issue even in mainstream research in private law,[69] and research in corporate and commercial law is no exception.

In comparative law, this question is linked to two things. The first is the functional method. What phenomena should one compare as "legal" phenomena? The second is socio-legal research in "legal pluralism", that is, the existence of overlapping legal systems which apply simultaneously.[70]

As regards substantive corporate and commercial law, the nature of law is a modern issue because of three simultaneous and overlapping trends.[71]

First, states have privatised or outsourced much of the regulation of business. Standard-setting by the FASB, IASB, and the Basel Committee on Banking Supervision are examples of outsourcing required or supported by laws.[72] The widespread use of corporate governance codes and the comply-or-explain principle is an example of flexible industry self-regulation.

Second, states have started to rely on non-traditional ways to adopt rules. For example, the EU uses the Lamfalussy process, a four-level, comitology-based

---

[68] One can refer to any textbook on comparative law or transnational commercial law.

[69] See also 56 Am J Comp L (2008) pp 527–844 ("Beyond the State – Rethinking Private Law").

[70] See, for example, Teubner G, Substantive and Reflexive Elements in Modern Law, Law & Soc'y Rev 17 (1983) pp 239–285; Teubner G, The Two Faces of Janus: Rethinking Legal Pluralism, Cardozo L Rev 13 (1992) pp 1443–1462; Teubner G, Global Bukowina: Legal Pluralism in the World-Society. In: Teubner G (ed), Global Law Without a State. Aldershot, Dartmouth (1997); de Sousa Santos B, Law: A Map of Misreading. Toward a Postmodern Conception of Law, J L & Soc'y 14 (1987) pp 279–302.

[71] See, for example, Kalss S, Maßgebliche Forschungsfelder in der nächsten Dekade im Bereich des Gesellschafts- und Kapitalmarktrechts, ZGR 4/2007 pp 523–526.

[72] Regulation 1606/2002 (IAS Regulation); Directive 2006/48/EC and Directive 2006/49/EC (the Capital Requirements Directive).

regulatory approach for financial services. Increased reliance on expert bodies (such as the Committee of European Banking Supervisors, the Committee of European Insurance and Occupational Pensions Supervisors, and the Committee of European Securities Regulators[73]) and documents with different normative qualities can raise questions of the nature of law.[74]

Third, there is a trend of pluralisation and internationalisation of sources of law.[75]

The jurisprudential foundations of commercial law. The jurisprudential foundations of corporate and commercial law are another matter. A US scholar wrote that you are likely to receive a blank stare if you ask a law professor about them.[76] There is hardly any literature.

One of the rare attempts to fill the void was to refer vaguely to "efficiency".[77] In the European context, it would nevertheless be wrong to accept "efficiency" as the normative goal for state law.

First, efficiency is too complex as a normative goal.[78] Efficiency is only relative or fictive efficiency as it can only be assessed by reducing complex phenomena to a small number of variables. What should one take into account when assessing efficiency?

Second, it is unclear what the efficiency of commercial law means. Virtually any legal rule can influence the behaviour of firms directly or indirectly in a market economy that upholds the rule of law. The relevant legal framework depends on the commercial context, and there is a vast amount of different commercial contexts. This means that there is a vast amount of relevant combinations of rules forming the legal framework of commercial transactions. Which combination of rules would one take into account when assessing efficiency?

Third, existing regulation of commerce cannot be explained by mathematically rational (Zweckrationalität) "efficiency" arguments alone. In the words of Goode, "the law cannot be concerned solely with economic efficiency as the yardstick by which to measure the success of social goals".[79] For example, the regulation of

---

[73] Commission Decisions 2001/527/EC, 2004/5/EC, and 2004/6/EC establishing CESR, CEBS, and CEIOPS, respectively.

[74] Eidenmüller H, Forschungsperspektiven im Unternehmensrecht, ZGR 4/2007 p 488; Kalss S, *op cit*, pp 523–525.

[75] Merkt H, Die Zukunft der privatrechtlichen Forschung im Unternehmens- und Kapitalmarktrecht, ZGR 4/2007 p 533.

[76] Posner EA, Book Review: Kraus, Jody S., and Walt, Steven D., eds., The Jurisprudential Foundations of Corporate and Commercial Law, Ethics 112 (2002) pp 626–628.

[77] Kraus JS, Walt SD, Introduction. In: Kraus JS, Walt SD (eds), *op cit*, p 1: "Efficiency is the dominant paradigm in contemporary corporate and commercial law scholarship. The jurisprudential foundations of corporate and commercial law, then are the foundations of efficiency analysis." For a critique, see Posner EA, *supra*.

[78] See also Kornhauser LA, Constrained Optimization. Corporate Law and the Maximization of Social Welfare. In: Kraus JS, Walt SD (eds), *op cit*, p 89.

[79] Goode RM, Commercial Law in the Next Millenium. The Hamlyn Lectures. Forty-ninth Series. Sweet & Maxwell, London (1998) p 29.

commerce has various and seemingly contradictory objectives in EU law. Most of them deal with what is regarded as reasonable or moral (Wertrationalität). The relative weight of different objectives depends on the context, the interests that regulation seeks to protect, and high-level goals such as sustainability, fairness, and high quality of life.[80] Another example is provided by the Draft Common Frame of Reference (DCFR). The DCFR distinguishes between "underlying principles", which are "all pervasive within the DCFR" and consist of freedom, security, justice, and efficiency, and "overriding principles", which are "of a high political nature".[81]

Fourth, the high-level objective of legal norms is often thought to be facilitating justice as fairness (Rawls 1971).[82]

The jurisprudential foundations of non-state law. The jurisprudential foundations of commercial law raise even more difficult questions in the case of non-state law. For example, they could include the following: "From where could legal rules and arguments derive their legitimacy, if not from the state's authority?"[83]

3.7 Economic Analysis

Doctrinal analysis and economic analysis are the two dominant research approaches in contemporary commercial law scholarship. In Europe, doctrinal analysis prevails. In the US, economic analysis of law has been extremely influential.[84]

Coase[85] and Calabresi[86] are regarded as the pioneers of modern law and economics. Posner (2007)[87] and Cooter and Ulen (2007)[88] can be mentioned as examples of standard textbooks in law and economics. There is also what can be

---

[80] See Article 2 of the Treaty on European Union and Articles 7–14 of the Treaty on the Functioning of the European Union.

[81] DCFR Intr. 14–16.

[82] Rawls J, A Theory of Justice. Harvard U P, Cambridge, Mass (1971).

[83] Jansen N, Michaels R, Private Law and the State. Comparative Perceptions and Historical Observations, RabelsZ 71 (2007) p 356.

[84] See Posner RA, The Decline of Law as an Autonomous Discipline: 1962–1987, Harv L Rev 100 (1987) pp 761–780; Dau-Schmidt KG, Brun CL, Lost in Translation: The Economic Analysis of Law in the United States and Europe, Colum J Transnat'l L 44 (2006) pp 602–621.

[85] Coase RH, The Problem of Social Cost, J Law Econ 3 (1960) pp 1–44.

[86] Calabresi G, Some Thoughts on Risk Distribution and the Law of Torts, Yale L J 70 (1961) pp 499–553.

[87] Posner RA, Economic Analysis of Law. Seventh Edition. Wolters Kluwer Law & Business, Austin, Texas (2007).

[88] Cooter R, Ulen T, Law and Economics. 5th International Edition. Pearson/Addison-Wesley, Boston, Mass. (2007).

described as a canon of law and economics articles and other works customarily referred to in legal education.[89]

In the economic analysis of commercial law, efficiency concerns predominate. Economic analysis of law is primarily a theory for law-makers.[90] However, a certain legal rule can influence a large number of decisions and different kinds of decisions. It can be difficult to develop a legal rule that is simultaneously efficient in different contexts.[91]

3.8 Preventive or Proactive Law

Finally, one can briefly mention preventive law and proactive law. Preventive law focuses on the prevention of legal risks and disputes.[92] Proactive law tries to promote what is desirable and prevent what is not desirable by doing something in advance.

However, both approaches are problematic. They are not based on theory. Neither do they have ambitions to formulate a theory. Moreover, the objectives of firms do not include the prevention of legal risks and disputes. On the contrary, firms manage risks in the normal course of business by avoiding, transferring, mitigating, or accepting them. To promote what is desirable and prevent what is not desirable is obviously too vague to give firms any guidance. There is nevertheless a Nordic School of Proactive Law, and the European Economic and Social Committee has given an opinion supporting the proactive law approach.[93]

3.9 The Reasons for the Absence of a General Theory of Commercial Law

The reasons for the absence of a general theory of commercial law can be summed up as follows: the fact that commercial law research is norm-based; the existence of many jurisdictions each with its own rules; the existence of many areas of law each

---

[89] See Whaples R, Morris AP, Moorhouse JC, What Should Lawyers Know about Economics? J Legal Educ 48 (1998) pp 120–124; Fleischer H, Grundfragen der ökonomischen Theorie im Gesellschafts- und Kapitalmarktrecht, ZGR 1/2001 pp 1–32.

[90] Eidenmüller H, Effizienz als Rechtsprinzip. Die Einheit der Gesellschaftswissenschaften 90. Mohr Siebeck, Tübingen (2005) p 13.

[91] See Kornhauser LA, Constrained Optimization. Corporate Law and the Maximization of Social Welfare. In: Kraus JS, Walt SD (eds), *op cit*, p 90.

[92] Louis M Brown was first to introduce the approach by this name in Brown LM, Manual of Preventive Law. Prentice-Hall, Inc., New York (1950).

[93] Opinion of the European Economic and Social Committee on 'The proactive law approach: a further step towards better regulation at EU level' (2009/C 175/05).

with its own legislative objectives; the existence of various research approaches each with its own imported research methodologies; and tradition.

Legal rules. If the starting point is rules applied and interpreted by the court, it becomes impossible to develop a general commercial law theory. There cannot be a "norm-based" theory of commercial law, because there are too many rules influencing the behaviour of firms.

Many areas of law. Furthermore, each traditional branch of commercial law is governed by its own rules, and rules belonging to different branches of commercial law are typically designed to further different public policy objectives. For example, one can easily see that rules governing consumer sales, company law matters, intellectual property, competition, international banking, electronic commerce, and business taxation can further very different legislative objectives. It can be difficult to find meaningful common denominators for all such rules even in just one jurisdiction.[94] The traditional branches of commercial law are likely to drift apart even more as the amount and sophistication of regulation increases (the legislator fine-tunes its sector-specific public policy objectives and adopts more sector-specific rules).

Many jurisdictions. It is even more difficult to design a norm-based commercial law theory that would make sense in all countries. The "bottom up" approach (inductive reasoning) would not work on a global scale in norm-based research, because each jurisdiction has its own rules and public policy objectives. The "top-down" approach (deductive reasoning) would not work, because there is no generally accepted global definition of commercial law and each jurisdiction has its own classification of rules as belonging to commercial law or other areas of law.

Research approaches. In practice, the path-dependency of commercial law research has contributed to the fact that the existing research approaches have been perceived as sufficient. Obviously, a scholar happy with one of the research approaches (and one of the general research methodologies imported from other areas of law or social sciences) does not simultaneously need any competing research approach (or research methodology) designed for commercial law in particular. Indeed, there is a vast amount of research in the area of commercial law although there is no particular generally accepted theory of commercial law.

---

[94] Compare Basedow J, The State's Private Law and the Economy–Commercial Law as an Amalgam of Public and Private Rule-Making, Am J Comp L 56 (2008) pp 714–718 arguing that state [commercial] law has the following functions: the provision of dispositive legal rules; assignment of property rights; protecting the market; and compensation for market failures. However, the functions listed by Basedow do not seem to explain the regulation of company law, tax law, and labour law matters sufficiently, although matters belonging to such areas of law are very important for commercial enterprises.

3.10 The Main Failings of the Mainstream Approaches

The mainstream research approaches are nevertheless inadequate. Some of their failings are obvious. First, norm-based research approaches have been unable to *define* commercial law, because there is a vast amount of rules applicable to firms belonging to various branches of law.[95] Second, norm-based approaches have been unable to *explain* on what grounds certain topics should fall within its scope. Third, focusing on legal rules adopted by external regulators such as the state for a large number of transactions has meant that the mainstream approaches have not been effective in explaining the *behaviour of firms* or giving an individual firm *guidance* about what to do in a particular situation.[96] Fourth, focusing on legal rules has made the mainstream approaches very *jurisdiction-specific*. Generally, one could say that the "strictly legal point of view"[97] has been too strict.

---

[95] See Goode RM, Commercial Law in the Next Millenium. The Hamlyn Lectures. Forty-ninth Series. Sweet & Maxwell, London (1998) p 8.

[96] See, for example, Eidenmüller H, Forschungsperspektiven im Unternehmensrecht, ZGR 4/2007 pp 484–499 in which the only information needs that seemed to matter were the information needs of the legislator.

[97] See, for example, Ernst W, Gelehrtes Recht – Die Jurisprudenz aus der Sicht des Zivilrechtslehrers. In: Engel C, Schön W (eds), *op cit*, pp 30–31.

Chapter 4
Theory of Commercial Law: Management-Based Commercial Law

4.1 General Remarks

The lack of a theory can be cured by using a management-based research approach and adopting a theory that we will call the theory of management-based commercial law (MBCL).

While there cannot be a "norm-based" theory of commercial law (there are too many legal norms influencing firms, the norms are too heterogenic, and the norms do not share the same public policy objectives), there can be a *management-based* theory of commercial law (firms can share the same objectives at a high level of generality).

The theory of MBCL recognises the existence of *firms* with one general goal: their own long-term *survival* in a competitive environment. Firms try to reach their commercial and legal *objectives* by using *legal tools and practices* in order to survive. Firms try to reach their objectives at many *levels* of corporate decision-making. One can distinguish between general MBCL and particular branches of MBCL depending on the commercial *context*.

The theory of MBCL is thus a framework that tries to explain the behaviour of various kinds of business organisations in different commercial contexts.[1] It can be applied to firms in the broad sense: family businesses, large listed firms, NGOs, and other firms.

[1] This can be contrasted with the German legal area of Unternehmensrecht (enterprise law or "law of the firm") which consists of normative legal rules. See, for example, Zimmer D, Internationales Gesellschaftsrecht. Schriftenreihe Recht der Internationalen Wirtschaft. Band 50. Verlag Recht und Wirtschaft GmbH, Heidelberg (1996), Zweiter Teil A III at p 136: "... als spezifisch unternehmensrechtlich werden hier diejenigen Normen bezeichnet, die die Privatautonomie der Eigentümer und der ihnen eingesetzten Geschäftsführer zugunsten solcher Anliegen beschränken, die ausserhalb des 'klassischen' gesellschafstrechtlichen Beziehungsdreiecks stehen."

P. Mäntysaari, *Organising the Firm*,

DOI 10.1007/978-3-642-22197-2_4,

One could say that MBCL is also an attempt to revisit the original ideas behind the great commercial law codifications of Europe, that is, Code de commerce and the German HGB. The CC and the HGB regulate, with minor variations, the following areas: business forms; financial information; commercial contracts in general; as well as the commercial exchange of goods. These areas are united by the requirements of the firm. Obviously, the firm needs a business form. It needs a large number of contracts for its operations. The contracts can be of various kinds. Many of them regulate sales, distribution channels, and logistics in the broad sense.

There is nevertheless a fundamental difference. As said above, mainstream legal research focuses on legal norms applied by the court. In MBCL, the starting point is the firm. The firm is regarded as the user of law with its own legal objectives. The management-based research approach thus means the study of the legal practices of firms, or how firms get things done by legal means. The scope of MBLC is not limited by the scope of existing regulation.

4.2 The Firm

The firm is a concept that has been defined in various ways in economics and management science (see Chap. 2). In legal science, however, the concept of the firm must be aligned with existing laws.[2]

Not a normative concept. We can first discuss what the firm is not. The firm is not used here as a normative concept that can be defined through the interpretation of laws. According to the theory of MBCL, the firm is a functional concept. There are nevertheless several related normative concepts.

First, there are norms that apply to all *firms*, business undertakings, or traders in the jurisdiction. Such norms customarily require registration, bookkeeping and accounting, and the payment of taxes.[3]

[2] Fleischer H, Zur Zukunft der gesellschafts- und kapitalmarktrechtlichen Forschung, ZGR 4/2007 pp 502–503: "Gefragt sind hier die Qualitäten des Gesellschafts- und Kapitalmarktrechtlers als eines *Interface Actor*. Wo ihm die benachbarten Disziplinen Teilergebnisse bereitlegen, beginnt seine eigentliche Aufgabe: Er darf sich nicht mit einer unreflektierten Teil- oder Vollrezeption fachfremder Theorien begnügen, sondern muss jedes Einzelargument auf der juristischen Ebene erneut prüfen und dem rechtswissenschaftlichen Zugriff zugänglich machen, sofern er es für überzeugungskräftig hält."

[3] For example, Article 3(1) of Directive 2009/101/EC (that applies to limited-liability companies): "In each Member State, a file shall be opened in a central register, commercial register or companies register, for each of the companies registered therein." § 1 HGB and § 238(1) HGB (on bookkeeping duties for traders): "Jeder Kaufmann ist verpflichtet, Bücher zu führen und in diesen seine Handelsgeschäfte und die Lage seines Vermögens nach den Grundsätzen ordnungsmäßiger Buchführung ersichtlich zu machen ..." Article 3(1)(c) of the OECD Model Tax Convention on Income and on Capital (on the definition of an enterprise).

Second, there are norms that apply to certain *activities* regardless of the legal form of the entity carrying out the activity. Many norms can thus apply to firms, undertakings, or the party that carries out the activity.[4]

Third, consumer laws customarily regulate the relationship between consumers and parties that act in a *commercial or professional capacity*.[5]

Fourth, there are a large number of norms that regulate the *attribution* of circumstances to legal entities. Circumstances that are connected to one legal entity can be attributed to another legal entity or both, when the legal entities belong to the same firm, undertaking, or group. The same can be said of circumstances that are connected to a person. (a) For example, some entities must prepare consolidated accounts.[6] Rules on the consolidation of accounts tend to be based on: the proprietary concept (also known as the ownership theory or the proportionate consolidation theory); the entity concept (the economic unit concept); or an intermediary concept (the parent company concept or the parent company extension concept).[7] (b) Furthermore, there are minimum capital requirements for banking groups under the Basel II/III Framework since all financial activities conducted within a banking group are captured through consolidation.[8] (c) EU competition law applies to undertakings.[9] According to the case-law of the ECJ, the concept of an undertaking "covers any entity engaged in an economic activity, regardless of its legal status and the way in which it is financed",[10] and "must be understood as designating an economic unit even if in law that economic unit consists of several persons, natural or legal".[11] The conduct of one legal entity may thus be attributed to another legal entity.[12] (d) Generally, the attribution of acts is an important issue in the area of contract law, tort law, and the criminal liability of companies.

Not the business form. Neither does the firm mean the business form of the organisation. MBCL distinguishes between the firm and the legal entity.

---

[4] For example, Article 3 of Directive 2000/12/EC: "The Member States shall prohibit persons or undertakings that are not credit institutions from carrying on the business of taking deposits or other repayable funds from the public ..." Article 1: "For the purpose of this Directive ... 1. 'credit institution' shall mean an undertaking whose business is to receive deposits or other repayable funds from the public and to grant credits for its own account ..."

[5] For example, Article 2 of Directive 97/7/EC (Directive on distance contracts) provides that the directive applies to certain contracts concluded between a supplier and a consumer. "Supplier" means "any natural or legal person who ... is acting in his commercial or professional capacity".

[6] See, for example, Article 1 of Directive 83/349/EEC (Seventh Company Law Directive).

[7] Küting K, Gattung A, Konzerntheorien in der nationalen und internationalen Konzernrechnungslegung, ZVglRWiss 102 (2003) pp 505–527.

[8] Paragraph 24 of the Basel II Framework.

[9] Articles 101 and 102 of the Treaty on the Functioning of the European Union.

[10] Case C-90/09 P, General Química and others v Commission, paragraph 34.

[11] Case C-90/09 P, General Química and others v Commission, paragraph 35.

[12] For subsdiaries, see Case C-97/08 P, Akzo Nobel and others v Commission [2009] ECR I–8237, paragraph 58. For merger control, see Article 5(4) of Regulation 139/2004 (EC Merger Regulation).

Legal entities are tools used by firms. This brings MBCL closer to continental European legal tradition and "legal realism" (Sect. 5.2.4).[13]

Not the market. The firm does not mean the market. This separates MBCL from the set-of-contracts theory of the firm according to which the firm does not exist and the "behaviour" of the firm is like the behaviour of the market.[14] In commercial law, the "perspective of the market" tends to mean a "norm-based" approach to commercial law (see Sect. 3.2).[15]

Exclusion of certain economic theories. While the firm is not used as a normative concept in MBCL, it cannot be used a purely economic concept either. This is because of the existence of many different economic theories of the firm, and because most of them are not aligned with existing laws.

For legal reasons, it is necessary to exclude the set-of-contracts theory and the property rights theory of the firm. First, these theories cannot be aligned with the separate legal existence of companies. Second, the set-of-contracts theory of the firm is not made up of contracts that are enforceable in the legal sense. For example, the employees and managers of a limited-liability company do not owe any contractual duties to the company's shareholders or creditors. They owe their contractual duties to the legal entity. Third, the property rights of the property rights theory are not necessarily enforceable in the legal sense. For example, the assets of a limited-liability company are owned by the legal entity. They are not owned by the entity's shareholders.

Organisational construction. We can now turn to how the firm can be defined in MBCL. To begin with, the theory of MBCL is based on the hypothesis that firms exist. Firms consist of people working as organised teams. The firm can thus be regarded as a particular kind of organisational construction competing against other teams in the market.[16]

---

[13] See also Bratton WW, The New Economic Theory of the Firm: Critical Perspectives from History, Stanford L Rev 41 (1989) pp 1504–1505 (on Chief Justice Marshall's opinion in Trustees of Dartmouth College v. Woodward, 17 U.S. (4 Wheat.) 518, 636 (1819)): "Since the corporation is not a natural person it has no ability to formulate its own purposes and follow them. Less than a person, it is only a means to prescribed ends." Traces of this approach can also be found in Bainbridge S, Director Primacy: The Means and Ends of Corporate Governance, Northw U L Rev 97 (2003) pp 550–551: ". . . director primacy treats the corporation as a vehicle by which the board of directors hires various factors of production." Other examples include Mäntysaari P, The Law of Corporate Finance Volume 1. Springer, Berlin Heidelberg (2010) PI and Robé JP, The Legal Structure of the Firm, Acc Econ L 1(1) (2011).

[14] Jensen MC, Meckling WH, Theory of the Firm: Managerial Behavior, Agency Costs and Ownership Structure, J Fin Econ 3 (1976) p 311.

[15] Compare Goode RM, Commercial Law in the Next Millenium. The Hamlyn Lectures. Forty-ninth Series. Sweet & Maxwell, London (1998) p 4: "Commercial law is about problem-solving, about fashioning the contract structures and other legal tools by which the legitimate needs of the market can be met." This definition is designed to lead to a rule-based approach to commercial law.

[16] Coase RH, The Nature of the Firm, Economica, New Series 4(14) (1937) pp 386–405; Alchian AA, Uncertainty, Evolution, and Economic Theory, J Pol Econ 58 (1950) pp 211–221; Arrow KJ, The Limits of Organization. Fels Lectures on Public Policy Analysis. Norton, New York (1974);

The firm has a value as an organisational construction. According to econonomics, it has a value as a mechanism to manage information, reduce transaction costs, and handle incentive and adaption problems. (a) The organisation of the firm is a way to handle *information*.[17] For individual members of the organisation and the firm, the designing of internal communication channels and investment in information are acts of irreversible investment. Each firm has its own "code". If the firm is broken up, such investments will be lost. If the firm is merged with another firm, new investment becomes necessary. (b) According to *transaction cost economics*, all complex contracts are unavoidably incomplete. The firm is regarded as an alternative mode of governance and as a way to handle this problem.[18] The firm can thus not always be replaced by the market without a cost. (c) Neither can the firm always be merged with another firm without a cost. This is because of the *costs of bureaucracy*. Large firms must find ways to mitigate the *incentive* and *adaptation* problem caused by an increase in firm size.[19] For example, the firm will try to manage its internal agency relationships, information flows, and decision-making processes. Changing the size of the organisation may affect the incentive and adaptation problem in many ways. Reducing firm size can reduce the problem. Merging the firm with another firm can increase the problem. An outsourcing network can enable the firm to grow while managing such problems.

The firm has a value also in MBCL. According to MBCL, members of the firm's organisation manage the firm's *cash flow and exchange of goods and services*, *risk*, *agency relationships*, and *information*. If the firm is broken up, the firm's investment in the particular tools and practices to handle these aspects will be lost. If the organisation is changed, the particular ways to handle them may have to be changed as well.

In practice, firms form the economically most important category of self-interested users of commercial law. One can regard firms – such as Facebook, Steiff, the small Othello bakery in the town of Vasa, Crédit Agricole, Goldman Sachs, FC Barcelona, Slaughter and May, and Ikea – as the most important market participants in capitalism (Weber 1922). Most goods and services are produced by firms, and most people in Western countries earn their living as their employees.[20]

Simon HA, Organizations and Markets, J Econ Persp 5(2) (1991) pp 25–44; Williamson OE, The Economic Institutions of Capitalism. The Free Press, New York (1985); Alchian AA, Demsetz H, Production, Information Costs, and Economic Organization, Am Econ Rev 62 (1972) pp 777–795; Holmström B, Moral Hazard in Teams, Bell J Econ 13 (1982) pp 324–340; Fama EF, Agency Problems and the Theory of the Firm, J Pol Econ 88(2) (1980) pp 288–307; Fama EF, Jensen MC, Separation of Ownership and Control, J Law Econ 14(2) (1983) pp 301–325; Fama EF, Jensen MC, Agency Problems and Residual Claims, J Law Econ 14(2) (1983) pp 327–349.

[17] Arrow KJ, The Limits of Organization. W. W. Norton & Company, New York (1974) pp 53–55.

[18] See, for example, Williamson OE, The Economic Institutions of Capitalism. Free Press, New York (1985) pp 30–31.

[19] Williamson OE, The Incentive Limits of Firms: A Comparative Institutional Assessment of Bureaucracy, Rev World Econ 120(4) (1984) pp 736–763.

[20] See also Simon HA, Organizations and Markets, J Econ Persp 5(2) (1991) pp 25–44.

The survival and growth of firms is very important for a very large number of stakeholders and society at large.[21]

4.3 The Rational Decision-Making of the Firm

It is assumed here that the firm's decision-making should be rational. But "the firm" has neither brains nor a mind of its own as a mere governance structure or organisational construction. Can the firm's decision-making be rational? The answer is yes, to the extent that human decision-making can be rational in the first place (bounded rationality, Simon 1957).

We assumed that firms are organisational constructions or teams competing against other teams in the market. The people that belong to the firm's organisation can take more or less rational decisions on the firm's behalf. Because of patterns of human behaviour, this is what managers and employees normally do unless the firm is governed by a pathological corporate of social culture.

It is customary for people to comply with social expectations. The behaviour of people is, in general, influenced by their instinctive need to belong to groups or teams.[22] Once they have become members, it is also influenced by the expectations of other team members. Team membership can influence the behaviour of its members for the better or for the worse (Freud 1921; Simon 1991).[23]

Some teams will survive in the short term, and a small number of teams even longer. A firm will not be able to survive unless its employees and managers voluntarily try to further its interests in a rational way. Firms try to hire such people. Firms generally do not want to hire people that are expected to act randomly (in any way whatsoever), to further nobody else's interests but their own, or to further the interests of somebody else instead of those of the firm.

4.4 The Ultimate Goal of the Firm

But what is rational in this context? What is the ultimate goal of the firm's decision-making, the Grundnorm (Kelsen) of business organisations?

---

[21] For the stakeholder concept, see Freeman RE, Strategic Management. A Stakeholder Approach. Cambridge U P, Cambridge (originally published in 1984) pp 25, 31–33, and 46.

[22] Freud S, Massenpsychologie und Ich-Analyse. Internationaler Psychoanalytischer Verlag, Wien (1921), Chapter IX pp 98–99: "Getrauen wir uns also, die Aussage Trotter's, der Mensch sei ein Herdentier, dahin zu korrigieren, er sei vielmehr ein Hordentier, ein Einzelwesen einer von einem Oberhaupt angeführten Horde." Freud discusses even Gustave Le Bon's Psychologie des foules (1985), William MacDougall's The Group Mind (1920), and Charles Darwin's The Descent of Man, and Selection in Relation to Sex (1871).

[23] See Freud S, *supra*, Chapter III pp 33–35 (discussing when the behavior of the group can change for the better according to McDougall).

If we assume that firms exist, that they can take rational decisions in one way or another, and that they can have their own objectives, the highest objective of a firm must be its own survival. The choice of efficient ways to ensure the long-term survival of the firm in a competitive environment is likely to increase the firm's long-term survival chances compared with choices that do not serve that purpose.[24]

Depending on the circumstances, different methods may help the firm to survive. It is nevertheless clear that most firms must make a profit and create value over a long period of time in order to survive.[25] Profitability requires investments, operational efficiency, risk-taking, and growth. Few firms can rely on the benevolence of a sponsor who can be expected to cover losses in the long term, although there may be firms whose business model can temporarily be based on access to such funding (football clubs, state-owned companies, non-profit organisations sponsored by billionaires, banks sponsored by taxpayers).

4.5 The Legal Objectives of the Firm

It is not enough to choose the perspective of the firm as the user of law. The perspective of the firm should also be defined. What does the perspective of the firm mean in the context of MBCL?

To begin with, it seems reasonable to assume that the firm has the same rational approach to non-legal and legal decision-making. Firms are not interested in legal aspects as such. One could also say that there is no such thing as non-legal decision-making. The firm's rational decision-making always incorporates the legal point of view.

In the financial sense, rational decision-making is based on *expected return and perceived risk*. Typically, return and risk should be quantifiable for the purposes of financial decision-making. There is also *a social dimension*. The firm expects members of its organisation, its contract parties, and many other parties to further its interests in various ways. These relationships can be described as *principal-agency* relationships. There is a large number of relationships with the firm as principal and many other parties as the firm's agents.[26] For example, employees are

[24] Alchian AA, Uncertainty, Evolution, and Economic Theory, J Pol Econ 58 (1950) pp 211–221. See also Freeman RE, Strategic Management. A Stakeholder Approach. Cambridge U P, Cambridge (originally published in 1984) p 33.

[25] Alchian AA, *supra*; Friedman M, The Social Responsibility of Business is to Increase its Profits, The New York Times Magazine, September 13, 1970.

[26] For principal-agent relationships, see Jensen MC, Meckling WH, Theory of the Firm: Managerial Behavior, Agency Costs and Ownership Structure, J Fin Econ 3 (1976) pp 305–360; Alchian AA, Demsetz H, Production, Information Costs, and Economic Organization, Am Econ Rev 62 (1972) pp 777–795; Fama EF, Jensen MC, Separation of Ownership and Control, J Law Econ 14 (2) (1983) pp 301–325; Fama EF, Jensen MC, Agency Problems and Residual Claims, J Law Econ 14(2) (1983) pp 327–349.

agents that belong to the firm's internal organisation. Suppliers, customers, investors, and stakeholders are examples of external agents. Outsource providers can have the characteristics of both internal and external agents. Moreover, rational decision-making is always based on *information*.[27]

It would be rational and reasonable for the firm to manage such aspects. The use of legal tools and practices is an important way to manage them in a market economy that upholds the rule of law.

This leads to the conclusion that all firms regardless of the jurisdiction share the same *generic legal objectives*. Their generic legal objectives consist of the management, by legal tools and practices, of: (1) cash flow and the exchange of goods and services; (2) risk; (3) principal-agency relationships; and (4) information.[28] These four aspects and various related concepts (such as "signalling") have been defined in economics and management sciences and are thus based on imported theories.

4.6 The Legal Tools and Practices of the Firm

We have identified one general goal and four generic objectives for the firm's rational decision-making. The firm will try to manage the four issues in some way or another.

All firms use legal tools and practices to reach their generic legal objectives. Legal tools and practices belong to "institutions" in the broad sense, that is, rules, norms, and strategies used by humans in repetitive situations. Such legal tools and practices can be classified as institutions in various ways (North 1990; Ostrom and Crawford 2005).[29]

For our purposes, we can identify five generic legal tools and practices used simultaneously in most transactions in one way or another: (a) choice of a business form (which facilitates the organising of production within the firm and helps to regulate asset ownership and other matters); (b) contracts (promises complemented by a particular sanction system enforceable by the state); (c) regulatory compliance and organisation of the firm's internal activities[30]; (d) generic ways to manage

[27] For a historical survey, see Stiglitz JE, Information and the change in the paradigm of economics, Am Econ Rev 92 (2002) pp 460–501.

[28] See, for example, Mann RJ, Explaining the Pattern of Secured Credit, Harv L Rev 110 (1997) pp 625–680.

[29] North DC, Institutions, Institutional Change and Economic Performance. Cambridge U P, Cambridge (1990) pp 3–4; Ostrom E, Crawford S, Classifying Rules. In: Ostrom E, Understanding Institutional Diversity. Princeton U P, Princeton Oxford (2005), Chapter 7, pp 190–191 (rules can be position, boundary, choice, aggregation, information, payoff, or scope rules).

[30] For regulatory compliance as a legal tool, see, for example, Mäntysaari P, The Law of Corporate Finance. Volume I. Springer, Berlin Heidelberg (2010) pp 52–62. For the statutory regulation of the firm's processes as a corporate governance tool, see Merkt H, Die Zukunft der privatrechtlichen Forschung im Unternehmens- und Kapitalmarktrecht, ZGR 4/2007 pp 535–536; Binder JH, „Prozeduralisierung" und Corporate Governance, ZGR 5/2007 pp 745–788.

principal-agency relationships[31]; and (e) generic ways to manage information.[32] This means, for example, that all commercial contracts are ways to manage cash flow and the exchange of goods and services, risk, agency, and information at different levels of the decision-making of the firm.[33] Contracts work in this way because of the existence of contract-enforcement institutions.[34]

Many tools can be used actively or passively. There is a trend of increasing active use of legal tools and practices by firms (self-regulation by each firm), increasing use of non-state rule-making (in particular, industry self-regulation and routinised practices), and decreasing reliance on state law. This is caused by many factors which have increased legal risk, made the management of risk more important, or made the management of risk easier. Such factors include: the globalisation of business and firms; the need to adapt the firm's business to a multitude of jurisdictions and cultures; various information related-questions (global reach of information, global access to information, digitalisation, the Internet); increased regulation that forces firms to adapt; increased sophistication of financial markets; and increased legal sophistication of so-called global players.

4.7 Levels of Decision-Making

The firm tries to reach its legal objectives at the strategic, operational, and transaction level.[35] Strategic management typically includes issues that relate to: strategic direction; strategic programme formulation; budgeting; control; as well as structures and systems.[36] At the operational level, the firm typically manages its business processes.

---

[31] For legal ways to manage agency, see Mäntysaari P, The Law of Corporate Finance. Volume I. Springer, Berlin Heidelberg (2010) pp 99–114.

[32] For legal ways to manage information, see *ibid*, pp 335–469.

[33] Generally, see Mäntysaari P, The Law of Corporate Finance. Volume II. Springer, Berlin Heidelberg (2010). For example, it would be easy to apply the principles even to "the interprofessional agreement of 1988 on the market for cattle above 6 months old" discussed in Mazé A, Ménard C, Private ordering, collective action, and the self-enforcing range of contracts, Eur J Law Econ 29 (2010) p 143, Table 1.

[34] See, for example, Greif A, Commitment, coercion, and markets: The nature and dynamics of institutions supporting exchange. In: Menard C, Shirley MM (eds), Handbook of New Institutional Economics. Springer, Dordrecht (2005) p 730.

[35] See, for example, Mäntysaari P, The Law of Corporate Finance. Volume I. Springer, Berlin Heidelberg (2010) pp 48, 120, and 123. For a different research stream on "legal strategies", see Masson A, Shariff MJ, Through the Legal Looking Glass: Exploring the Concept of Corporate Legal Strategy, EBLJ 2011 pp 51–77.

[36] See Freeman RE, Strategic Management. A Stakeholder Approach. Cambridge U P, Cambridge (originally published in 1984) p 44. Strategic direction: "What is the direction or mission of the organization?" Strategic programme formulation: "What paths or strategies will achieve such a mission?" Budgeting: "What resource allocations or budgets must be made for the strategies to be

This can be illustrated with the following situations. (a) The choice of the *business form* can be a strategic choice or an operational decision. For example, corporate structure (one entity or several entities), the place of incorporation of the parent (say, Russia, Finland, or the US) and the business form of the parent (co-operative, partnership, public limited-liability company) belong to the most important legal decisions at the strategic level. The choice of business form and corporate structure will also influence the firm's administrative costs and tax burden (cash flow) at the operational level, and influence the firm's exposure to risk. Special purpose vehicles are often used as risk management tools at the operational level (they are employed to ring-fence assets or to make them bankruptcy remote). (b) Like the business form, *contracts* can be used at different levels of corporate decision-making. Outsourcing contracts with outsource providers can be a way to manage principal-agent, information, and cost problems caused by large firm size. This can be an operational decision or a strategic choice.[37] (c) The third illustration relates to *compliance and organisation* in the field of emission regulation. Future restrictions on CO^2 emissions may force the firm to mitigate risk by changing its business areas (strategic level). The firm may adopt internal guidelines for its contracts for trading in emission rights (operational level). The firm may also insist on a certain contract term to be included in a particular contract for the purchase of emission rights in order to give its contract party an incentive to fulfil its obligations (transaction level).

4.8 Branches of Management-Based Commercial Law

The choice of the perspective of the firm, the study of the legal objectives of the firm, the study of the legal tools and practices used to reach those objectives, and the distinction between various levels of management are characteristic of *general MBCL*. Such aspects are taken into account by firms generally, that is, regardless of the nature of the transaction. In addition, one can distinguish between

implemented?" Control: "How can we be sure the strategies are on track or in control?" Structure and systems: "What are the macro-systems and structures necessary for implementation?"

[37] Geis GS, The Space Between Markets and Hierarchies. Virginia L Rev 95 (2009) pp 99–154: "... I argue that business outsourcing ... can add value ... by allowing firms to fashion an efficient governance compromise between markets and hierarchies. This can be true for four reasons. First, business outsourcing helps firms reintroduce some market discipline into production decisions. Second, it can reduce the hold-up problem that arises with market transactions. Third, it can mitigate the corporate agency cost problem. And fourth, it can allow firms to better attune their capital structures to underlying asset characteristics. The decision to pursue a hybrid outsourcing transaction can therefore be seen as an attempt to compromise among each (or all) of these four dimensions."

general MBCL and particular *branches of MBCL*. The branches of MBCL are functional.[38]

Functional questions depending on the commercial context. The firm will manage cash flow and the exchange of goods and services, risk, principal-agency relationships, and information in some way or another regardless of the transaction, but the particular payments, goods, services, risk, principal-agency relationships, and information-related issues that firms tend to manage depend on the commercial *context*. Furthermore, the firm will use the generic legal tools and practices regardless of the transaction in some way or another, but the particular manner of using them depends again on the context. As virtually any legal norm can influence the behaviour of firms in some way or another in a market economy that enforces the rule of law, the firm can also use a large number of particular legal tools and practices depending on the context.

If one identifies a particular commercial context, the particular aspects of the objectives of firms, the particular manner of reaching them with generic legal tools and practices, and the particular legal tools and practices used by firms in that context, one can identify a functional branches of MBCL.

This can be illustrated by the law of corporate finance. Obviously, the firm must manage its finances. We can therefore identify a commercial context. The firm must address four fundamental issues in this context: How should the firm invest (the investment decision)? How should the firm raise funding (the funding decision)? How should funds be returned to investors (the exit decision)? How should the firm manage situations that threaten its existence (the existential decision)? The study of the management of the particular legal aspects of investment, funding, exit, and existential decisions from the perspective of the firm can be called *the law of corporate finance*.

Like the law of corporate finance, the law of corporate governance can be defined as a functional branch of MBCL. This will be done in Chap. 7. Both will influence corporate law theory. This will be discussed in Chap. 8.

Generic objectives and generic legal tools and practices v branches of MBCL. One can ask whether the generic legal objectives (such as risk management) or the generic legal tools and practices (such as the use of contracts or the particular ways to manage information) can be regarded as branches of MBCL.

Of course, this is a matter of taste. However, the former are functional as objectives, and the latter are functional as ways to reach those broad objectives. It is, in both cases, possible to define the particular aspects that will need to be managed by the firm. One could therefore define the management of each of

---

[38] For functional branches of commercial law, see Eidenmüller H, Forschungsperspektiven im Unternehmensrecht, ZGR 4/2007 p 486; Fleischer H, Gesellschafts- und Kapitalmarktrecht als wissenschaftliche Disziplin – Das Proprium der Rechtswissenschaft. In: Engel C, Schön W (eds), *op cit*, p 50; Mäntysaari P, The Law of Corporate Finance. Volume I. Springer, Berlin Heidelberg (2010) pp 1 and 165.

those generic legal objectives and the use of each of the generic legal tools and practices as broad branches of MBCL. Collectively, they form the general MBCL.

4.9 Management-Based Commercial Law and Transaction Cost Economics

As a branch of legal science, MBCL is clearly different from neoclassical economics. However, there are some similarities between MBCL and the new institutional economics, in particular transaction cost economics (TCE). For example, MBCL uses partly the same terminology when discussing the management of agency and information and generally the organisation of the firm. The similarities and differences can help to understand the nature of MBCL better.

The following are probably the most important *similarities*. First, whereas neoclassical economics describes the firm as a production function (which is a technological construction), TCE describes the firm as a *governance structure* (which is an organisational construction). So does MBCL. This helps to paint a more realistic picture of the firm compared with neoclassical economics.[39] Second, TCE maintains that the *transaction* is the unit of analysis and insists that *organisation form* matters.[40] Both are important in MBCL as well. Third, TCE studies economic phenomena through the lens of *contract*, and contracts belong to the generic legal tools used by the firm according to the theory of MBCL.[41] Fourth, TCE and MBCL have partly similar approaches to *rationality*. Whereas neoclassical economics maintains a "maximising orientation", TCE relies on the cognitive assumption of "bounded rationality".[42]

There are also important *differences* between MBCL and TCE. Simply put, MBCL and TCE answer different questions.

---

[39] Bratton WW, The New Economic Theory of the Firm: Critical Perspectives from History, Stanford L Rev 41 (1989) p 1481.

[40] Williamson OE, The Economic Institutions of Capitalism. The Free Press, New York (1985) p 18.

[41] *Ibid*, pp 17–18: "As compared with other approaches to the study of economic organization, transaction cost economics (1) is more microanalytic, (2) is more self-conscious about its behavioral assumptions, (3) introduces and develops the economic importance of asset specificity, (4) relies more on comparative institutional analysis, (5) regards the business firm as a governance structure rather than a production function, and (6) places greater weight on the ex post institutions of contract, with special emphasis on private ordering (as compared with court ordering)." Williamson OE, Transaction Cost Economics: How It Works; Where It Is Headed, De Economist 146 (1998) pp 23–58; Williamson OE, Transaction Cost Economics. In: Menard C, Shirley MM (eds), Handbook of New Institutional Economics. Springer, Dordrecht (2005) pp 51–65.

[42] Williamson OE, The Economic Institutions of Capitalism. The Free Press, New York (1985) p 44: "Three levels of rationality are usefully distinguished. The strong for contemplates maximizing. Bounded rationality is the semistrong form. The weak form is organic rationality."

First, whereas TCE studies economic phenomena, MBCL focuses on legal phenomena, that is, the attainment of relevant objectives by legal tools and practices.

Second, MBCL distinguishes more clearly between the firm and the legal entity. Legal entities are legal tools used by firms and other market participants.

Third, MBCL studies a wider range of behaviour. In TCE, the underlying viewpoint is that transaction costs are economised by assigning transactions to governance structures in a discriminating way.[43] In MBCL, the firm is assumed to manage not only costs (cash flow and the exchange of goods and services) but even risk, principal-agency relationships, and information (which all can even be sources of transaction costs).

Fourth, MBCL studies a wider range of legal tools and practices. Whereas both the neoclassical theory of the firm and TCE study economic phenomena through the lens of contract,[44] MBCL identifies five categories of generic legal tools and practices of which contracts are one. MBCL takes into account even special legal tools and practices depending on the commercial context of firms.

Fifth, MBCL tries to be even more micro-analytic. Whereas TCE explains the assigning of transactions to governance structures in general (the make or buy decision), MBCL tries to explain the detailed terms of transactions and the contents of governance structures.

Sixth, there are differences regarding rationality. Whereas TCE is limited to what is rational in a technical or mathematical way (Zweckrationalität), MBCL takes into account also what is reasonable (Wertrationalität).[45]

Seventh, such and other differences regarding rationality are connected to differences regarding the choice of the relevant actors and their self-interest orientation. Although both TCE and MBCL rely on the cognitive assumption of bounded rationality, the relevant actors are "intendedly rational"[46] in slightly different ways, because TCE and MBCL focus on the rational decision-making of different actors and MBCL places greater weight on what is reasonable. (a) MBCL studies the decision-making of the firm. It is assumed that the firm can have a self-interest orientation.[47] The most fundamental objective of the firm is its own long-term survival in a competitive environment. It is also assumed that firms that adapt to their competitive environment by doing whatever it takes to survive in the long term are more likely to survive than firms that do other things. For example, the firm

[43] *Ibid*, p 18.

[44] See, for example, Bratton WW, The New Economic Theory of the Firm: Critical Perspectives from History, Stanford L Rev 41 (1989) pp 1480–1482.

[45] See, for example, Mäntysaari P, The Law of Corporate Finance. Volume I. Springer, Berlin Heidelberg (2010) p 165.

[46] According to Simon, economic actors are assumed to be "intendedly rational, but only limitedly so".

[47] For a contrary view, see Fama EF, Agency Problems and the Theory of the Firm, J Pol Econ 88 (2) (1980) pp 288–307 (arguing that the firm is just a set of contracts, a market).

should make a profit.[48] For such reasons, the relative importance of "organic rationality" is higher in MBCL compared with TCE.[49] (b) In TCE, transaction costs are economised by assigning transactions to governance structures in a discriminating way.[50] Although it is recognised that the firm exists as a governance structure, it is not necessary for TCE to assume that the firm would have any particular objectives of its own. Only its "constituencies",[51] that is, non-firm actors have objectives. They are defined in relation to the firm and as three levels of self-interest seeking (opportunism, simple self-interest seeking, and obedience).[52]

4.10 Management-Based Commercial Law and Traditional Branches of Law

The use of legal tools and practices to reach the firm's legal objectives is a legal exercise that requires specialised legal know-how. For this reason, MBCL can be regarded as a field of law rather than a particular area of management science or economics. Typically, business consultants and investment bankers who have received an education in management or economics do not possess the necessary legal know-how but turn to external law firms or in-house counsel for advice. On the other hand, economic objectives are the cause of commercial transactions, and economic arguments can help to choose between alternative legal tools and practices.[53]

There are fundamental differences between MBCL and the traditional research approaches and branches of norm-based commercial law. They have already been discussed above but can be summed up here.

Research approaches. Whereas *legal norms* (state law and non-state law) applied by the court are the starting point of the mainstream research approaches,

---

[48] Alchian AA, Uncertainty, Evolution, and Economic Theory, J Pol Econ 58 (1950) p 213: "Realized positive profits, not *maximum* profits, are the mark of success and viability. It does not matter through what process of reasoning or motivation such success was achieved. The fact of its accomplishment is sufficient. This is the criterion by which the economic system selects survivors: those who realize *positive profits* are the survivors; those who suffer losses disappear."

[49] Williamson OE, The Economic Institutions of Capitalism. The Free Press, New York (1985) p 47.

[50] *Ibid*, p 18.

[51] *Ibid*, p 298: "labor, capital, suppliers, customers, the community, and management".

[52] *Ibid*, p 47: "The strongest form, the one to which transaction cost economics appeals, is opportunism. The semistrong form is simple self-interest seeking. Obedience is the weak (really null) form."

[53] See already Holmes OW, The Path of the Law, Harv L Rev 10 (1897) pp 457–490: "For the rational study of the law the black-letter man may be the man of the present, but the man of the future is the man of statistics and the master of economics."

the management-based research approach has as its starting point the *management objectives* of firms.

As management objectives can be determined functionally, the management-based research approach is related to the functional approach used in *comparative law*.[54] This means also that studies based on the management-based research approach can be useful in comparative legal research. In practice, some comparative lawyers have found client memos and articles written by practicing lawyers surprisingly useful compared with academic studies written by law professors.

The management-based research approach often studies functional questions that are studied even in economic sciences,[55] but it is separate from *law and economics*. Simply put, it does not ask: "Why should lawyers study economics? Why should economists study law?"[56] Instead, it asks: "Why should managers study law?"[57]

The management-based research approach incorporates *doctrinal analysis*. Obviously, management can use legal rules better if it has information about them. However, it is more than doctrinal analysis, because it contains more layers of analysis.[58] One could also say that there is a difference between legal research which is doctrinal with a functional twist[59] and legal research which is management-based and functional by definition. Doctrinal research cannot be perfectly functional, because the legal tools and practices employed by firms to achieve a certain objective are to a very large extent chosen and designed by firms rather than the state or other external rule-makers.

Branches of commercial law. One can also distinguish special *branches* of MBCL on the basis of the *functional* questions that must be addressed by firms depending on the context. The branches of MBCL are thus functional and modern rather than dogmatic and traditional.

The traditional branches of traditional commercial law are a loose bunch and do not necessarily have much in common. This is because state law reflects the preferences of the legislator and is designed to further various public policy

---

[54] See Mäntysaari P, Comparative Corporate Governance. Springer, Berlin Heidelberg (2005) pp 16 and 30; Mäntysaari P, The Law of Corporate Finance. Volume I. Springer, Berlin Heidelberg (2010) p 165 (for the definition of corporate governance as an example of the similarities of the functional method and MBCL).

[55] See also Mattei U, Comparative Law and Economics. U Michigan P, Ann Arbor (1997) p ix: "... comparative law may gain theoretical perspective by using the kind of functional analysis employed in economic analysis of law."

[56] See Cooter R, Ulen T, Law and Economics. 5th International Edition. Pearson/Addison-Wesley, Boston, Mass. (2007).

[57] For an example of this approach, see Bagley CE, Winning Legally. Harv Bus School P, Boston, Mass. (2005).

[58] JP Morgan (1837–1913) famously put it this way: "I don't ... want a lawyer to tell me what I cannot do. I hire him to tell me how to do what I want to do."

[59] For an example of such an approach, see Ferran E, Principles of Corporate Finance Law. OUP, Oxford (2008).

objectives.[60] Typically, rules that belong to different areas of state law have been designed to further different public policy objectives. Furthermore, the choice of the branches of commercial law and the scope of each branch are both jurisdiction-specific and path-dependent: they are influenced by the legal family to which the jurisdiction belongs, convention, other areas of law, and other things. Although it may be beneficial to call the loose bunch of certain branches of law "commercial law" for educational purposes or to identify those branches of law that are particularly important for firms, one could just as well regard them as independent branches of law. The existence or absence of a particular commercial law code is unlikely to change this.[61]

The branches of MBCL have more in common. By definition, the branches of MBCL should choose the firm (rather than the court) as the user of legal tools and practices, and branches of MBCL can be defined on the basis of the firm's management objectives or functions (rather than on the basis of public policy objectives).

Unlike the branches of traditional commercial law, the branches of MBCL do not have to be jurisdiction-specific. Firms are – at least at a very high level of generality – relatively homogeneous regardless of the jurisdiction. Typically, firms tend to have similar generic objectives when managing legal questions in similar commercial contexts.

The choice of the perspective of the firm as the user of legal norms also means that the distinction between private law and public law, or between any traditional branches of law, is basically irrelevant in MBCL. Obviously, when a firm tries to design a proper legal framework in order to make a profit and survive, it is not interested in law professors' rather philosophical discussions about the structure of the legal system.

Because of fundamental differences in the perspective, the branches of traditional commercial law do not "belong" to MBCL. For example, "company law" cannot be regarded as a branch of MBCL, although some branches of MBCL such as the law of corporate finance or the law of corporate governance can address many traditional questions of company law and the tools used by firms are governed by rules belonging to traditional branches of commercial law. The same can be said of all the other branches of traditional norm-based commercial law.

Management-based commercial law and "law". Firms are not interested in the definition of "law" as such, or on the jurisdictional foundations of "law". From the perspective of the firm, the distinction between various categories of "law" (various categories of state law, non-legal institutionalised normative systems, or the firm's own self-practices) is irrelevant, unless there is a difference in the perceived

---

[60] For the reasons of regulation, see, for example, Goode RM, Commercial Law in the Next Millenium. The Hamlyn Lectures. Forty-ninth Series. Sweet & Maxwell, London (1998) p 44–47.

[61] Compare *ibid*, p 102 (arguing that a code "integrates ... a disparate collection of statutes, unconnected to each other, replacing them with provisions which cover the field as a whole, in which each part is linked to the others and which are bedded down on a set of general provisions governing all transactions to which the code applies").

usefulness (information, content, addressee, impact, cost, risk) of norms belonging to different categories. Typically, the firm can use many overlapping "legal" layers to regulate the same context.

4.11 Concluding Remarks

It takes a theory to beat a theory.[62] However, there is hardly any commercial law theory to beat, because the mainstream research paradigm makes it virtually impossible to design one. Changing the research paradigm from norm-based to management-based makes it easier to formulate a theory for global use.

One can distinguish between general management-based commercial law and its branches.

At the general level, the theory of MBCL recognises the existence of firms that try to increase the likelihood of their own long-term survival in a competitive environment. For this reason, they have legal objectives. Their legal objectives consist of the management, by legal tools and practices, of: (1) cash flow and the exchange of goods and services; (2) risk; (3) principal-agency relationships; and (4) information. They always use five categories of legal tools and practices: (1) choice of the business form; (2) contracts; (3) regulatory compliance and organisation of internal processes; (4) particular legal ways to manage agency relationships; and (5) particular legal ways to manage information. The objectives are managed by the legal tools and practices at all three levels of corporate decision-making: (1) the strategic level; (2) the operational level; and (3) the transaction level.

One can also distinguish particular branches of management-based commercial law on the basis of the functional questions that must be addressed by firms in different commercial contexts. The branches are therefore functional rather than dogmatic.

[62] Kuhn TS, The Structure of Scientific Revolutions, Second Edition. U Chicago P, Chicago (1970) p 77.

Chapter 5
Theories of Corporate Law and Corporations: Past Approaches

5.1 Introduction

We can now move on to theories of corporate law. Corporate law belongs to the traditional branches of commercial law in continental Europe. Both the Napoleonic Code de commerce and the German Handelsgesetzbuch address company law issues. Whereas norm-based commercial law is largely untheorised as a much too heterogenic branch of law, there is more discussion on the theoretical foundations of corporate law. The purpose of this chapter is to explain the main theories and explain why they are unsatisfactory. A new theory will be proposed in Chap. 8 after analysing corporate governance theory in Chaps. 6 and 7.

Legal theories v economic theories. To begin with, it is important to keep in mind that there is a fundamental difference between legal theories and economic theories such as theories of the firm.

Law is normative. As a normative discipline, law must be applied, and it must be complied with by a very large number of real firms and real people. Its contents should be predictable and regarded as fair and reasonable (Rawls 1971). This also means that law and legal theories tend to be conservative. Legal theories face a reality check every day when enforced in practice. As a result of the connection between law and real life, law can also give valuable information about the behaviour of real people and firms and about how society works.

Economic theories are not law. It should take some time before an economic theory of the firm can be accepted in corporate law, and the number of theories that can be accepted is limited. One should think twice before aligning legal norms designed to be applied by real people and firms with an economic theory based on a few aspects of fictive people or firms.

P. Mäntysaari, *Organising the Firm*,
DOI 10.1007/978-3-642-22197-2_5, © Springer-Verlag Berlin Heidelberg 2012

Economic theories of the firm have nevertheless influenced theories of corporate law.[1] The role of the former depends on the nature of the latter. There are different kinds of corporate law theories.

Theory of corporate law, theory of corporations. A legal theory may broadly address questions relating to language, existence, scope, contents, structure, and interaction.[2] For the purposes of this book, these aspects can relate to corporate law or corporations. One can therefore distinguish between legal theories of corporate law and legal theories of corporations.[3]

Theory of corporate law. A legal theory of corporate law can seek to define corporate law. This may require a common language, that is, common concepts and terminology. The theory could explain the existence, purpose, contents, scope, and effects of corporate law. It could provide a structural framework that helps to describe and analyse its contents. It could also explain the relationship of corporate law and other areas of law or society.

Theory of corporations. A legal theory of corporations can address similar questions in the more limited context of corporations. It can provide a common language. It can try to define corporations. It can explain their existence and purpose, their structure and organisation, and their interaction with corporate insiders and third parties.

Dogmatics v economics. Existing legal theories of corporate law and corporations have addressed all such questions.

The earliest theories were theories of corporations. In Europe, legal theories of corporations still predominate. This is partly caused by the dogmatic nature of mainstream European research in corporate law. Legal theories of corporations are jurisdiction-specific, connected to the normative purpose of corporate law, and applied in the context of the interpretation of legal rules.

A need for theories of corporate law emerged at a later stage. There is more demand for theories of corporate law in the US compared with Europe. This is partly caused by the more prominent role of economic sciences in US legal

[1] See Bratton WW, The New Economic Theory of the Firm: Critical Perspectives from History, Stanford L Rev 41 (1989) pp 1471–1527.

[2] Von der Pforten distinguishes between the following characteristics of "something": (1) Reale, mereologische, raumzeitliche Bestimmung. (2) Kausale Bestimmung. (3) Funktionale Bestimmung. (4) Qualitative Bestimmung. (5) Begriffliche Bestimmung. (6) Sprachlich-semantische Bestimmung. (7) Intentionale Bestimmung. In short: real (something in space and time); causal; functional; qualitative, conceptual, linguistic, and intentional. See von der Pforten D, Was ist Recht? Eine philosophische Perspektive. In: Brugger W, Neumann U, Kirste S (eds), Rechtsphilosophie im 21. Jahrhundert. Suhrkamp Verlag, Frankfurt am Main (2008) pp 261–285.

[3] Compare Bratton WW, The New Economic Theory of the Firm: Critical Perspectives from History, Stanford L Rev 41 (1989) p 1474. Bratton distinguishes between "traditional legal theories of the corporate firm", "managerialism", and "the new economic theory of the firm". Traditional legal theories of the corporate firm are here regarded as examples of theories of corporations. Managerialism and the new economic theory of the firm are examples of theories of corporate law.

research. It is customary to apply theories developed in economic sciences even when interpreting provisions of corporate law in US courts.

Differences. There are characteristic differences between theories of corporate law and theories of corporations caused by the choice of perspective and the level of abstraction. Like theories of the firm, theories of corporate law or corporations tend to be limited to certain aspects. Theories of corporations tend to be based on existing corporate forms (inductive reasoning). This makes them more detailed and concrete. Theories of corporate law are based on general concepts (deductive reasoning). As a result, there is a risk that they fail to connect with the existing regulation of corporations.

5.2 Legal Theories of Corporations

5.2.1 General Remarks

Legal theories of corporations tend to be limited to certain aspects of the corporation. They are not designed to show the whole picture. As a result, the 1976 view was that "the general principles governing the legal structure of the corporation have never been well articulated".[4]

The most common legal theories of corporations focus on: the formation and general nature of corporations; the listing of the characteristics of corporations; the legal personality of corporations; their capacity; their purpose and objects; and the separation of corporate functions. Theories of supranational or international corporate forms focus on the particular legal aspects of such corporate forms.

5.2.2 Formation and General Nature

Theories on the formation and general nature of corporations seek to explain how corporations come to existence and how corporations are classified in the legal system.

Numerus clausus or party freedom. To begin with, one may ask whether only certain types of corporations should be permitted to exist (numerus clausus) or whether parties should have discretion to design corporations as they wish.

[4] Eisenberg MA, The Structure of the Corporation. Beard Books, Washington, D.C. (1976) p 1. See nevertheless Bratton WW, The New Economic Theory of the Firm: Critical Perspectives from History, Stanford L Rev 41 (1989) p 1508: "By 1976, traditional theory of the firm concepts had fallen so far from view that theoretically ambitious works on corporate structure omitted any mention of them."

The main rule is that there is a numerus clausus of corporations in substantive law[5] but not in international private law.[6]

The founding of corporations. Corporations can nevertheless be created in different ways. In substantive law, the founding of a corporation can require: a contract; filing of the corporation with a registry; a charter or a similar authorisation; a statute; or a treaty. A corporation can thus be regarded as a contract, a private law entity, a public law entity, or an international law entity in legal dogmatics.

One can also distinguish between concession systems (the concession theory), normative systems as intermediate systems, and contractual systems as the opposite of concession systems.

A *concession* system means that the incorporation of a company requires consent by the state. There can be various degrees of the concession system. (a) First, the existence of a corporation can be in the discretion of the state (stronger form). This form of concession system was common in the past. For example, the Bubble Act prohibited incorporation without a Royal Charter or Act of Parliament in English law.[7] The Bubble Act was replaced by the 1844 Act. In the German Reich, incorporation was not liberalised until 1870.[8] (b) Second, incorporated entities may need a concession to do business (weaker form).[9] This system is likely to be found in branches that are regulated in the public interest, economies that are controlled by a state bureaucracy, and dictatorships.

A *normative* system means that the incorporation of a company and the carrying out of business is a legal right provided that all the legal requirements are met.[10]

---

[5] See, for example, Article 530(2) of the Swiss Code of Obligations (OR). If an entity cannot be regarded as a corporation, it is deemed to be a partnership.

[6] See Article 150(2) of the Swiss Federal Act on Private International Law (IPRG). See Guillaume F, The Law Governing Companies in Swiss Private International Law. In: Sarcevic P, Volken P, Bonomi A, Yearbook of Private International Law, Volume 6 (2004). Sellier, München / Staempfli Publishers, Berne / Swiss Institute of Comparative Law (2005) pp 253–255.

[7] In the US, Chief Justice Marshall's opinion on the nature of the corporation in the famous corporate law case of Trustees of Dartmouth College v. Woodward, 17 U.S. (4 Wheat.) 518, 636 (1819) reflects the concession theory: "A corporation is an artificial being, invisible, intangible, and existing only in contemplation of law. Being the mere creature of law, it possesses only those properties which the charter of its creation confers upon it, either expressly, or as incidental to its very existence."

[8] Article 208 of Allgemeines Deutsches Handelsgesetzbuch: "Aktiengesellschaften können nur mit staatlicher Genehmigung errichtet werden ..." Article 249: "Den Landesgesetzen bleibt vorbehalten, zu bestimmen, daß es der staatlichen Genehmigung zur Errichtung von Aktiengesellschaften im Allgemeinen oder von einzelnen Arten derselben nicht bedarf ..."

[9] Bratton WW, The New Economic Theory of the Firm: Critical Perspectives from History, Stanford L Rev 41 (1989) p 1475. See also pp 1483–1484 (for American corporate law's special charter phase).

[10] See, for example, Priester HJ, Beginn der Rechtsperson – Vorräte und Mäntel, ZHR 168 (2004) p 255.

In English company law, for example, the Act of 1844[11] represented a shift from the privilege of incorporation to the right of incorporation provided that the statutory conditions were fulfilled.[12] The normative system is the default system in the EU[13] and the system likely to be found in countries that enforce the rule of law and have a low level of corruption.

The *contractual* system means that individuals should have a right to incorporate entities and carry out business without state interference.[14] This system is rather rare in developed countries.

The regulation of corporations. There can also be a connection between the general nature of corporations and the regulation of corporations, in particular the balance between mandatory and dispositive provisions of law. If one wants to increase the discretion of the parties and limit the scope of state regulation, one can regard the corporation as something similar to a contract and argue that freedom of contract should prevail. Alternatively, one can argue that the corporation is not a contract and that mandatory standardisation reduces transaction costs and benefits the society as a whole.

5.2.3 Characteristics of the Corporation

The characteristics of the corporation depend on its general nature. For example, a corporation based on a statute or a treaty shares some of its characteristics with capitalist limited-liability corporations, but not necessarily all characteristics.

In substantive law, it is nowadays customary to describe the structural characteristics of capitalist limited-liability corporations roughly as follows: (1)

---

[11] The Joint Stock Companies Act of 1844 and the Limited Liability Act of 1855.

[12] Hurst JW, The Legitimacy of the Business Corporation in the Law of the United States 1780–1970. The U P of Virginia, the USA (1970) pp 5–6: "The shift in English policy from a focus upon political considerations to a focus upon economic utility anticipated a much later analogous course of policy in the United States."

[13] Article 10 of Directive 68/151/EEC (First Company Law Directive): "In all Member States whose laws do not provide for preventive control, administrative or judicial, at the time of formation of a company, the instrument of constitution, the company statutes and any amendments to those documents shall be drawn up and certified in due legal form." Article 3(1): "In each Member State a file shall be opened in a central register, commercial register or companies register, for each of the companies registered therein." Article 2(1): "Member States shall take the measures required to ensure compulsory disclosure by companies of at least the following documents and particulars: (a) The instrument of constitution, and the statutes if they are contained in a separate instrument ..."

[14] Bratton WW, *op cit*, p 1475: "The contractual response locates the source of all firms' economic energy in individuals. Stated most strongly, this view holds that the individuals' freedom of contract implies a right to do business as a corporation without state interference. A variant of this discussion suggests that the corporation is not a suitable subject for regulation because its activities have a 'private' rather than a 'public' nature."

legal personality; (2) indefinite duration; (3) the limited liability of shareholders; (4) freely transferable shares; (5) the separation of functions between corporate bodies; (6) majority rule; and (7) profit orientation.

Examples of studies that discuss such structural characteristics include Bergström and Samuelsson (1997),[15] Clark (1986),[16] and Kraakman et al. (2004).[17] There have also been much earlier attempts to describe the characteristics of the corporation. In the US, Angell and Ames (1871) defined the corporation by drawing on definitions from prominent earlier works.[18]

We can take a closer look at the structural characteristics of corporations and start with legal personality.

5.2.4 Legal Personality

Theories on legal personality focus on one of the most fundamental aspects of corporations. Although these theories are important and have influenced corporate law in surprisingly many ways, they have a narrow scope. There are issues relating to legal personality in substantive law and in international private law. We can first have a look at developments in substantive law.

Substantive law – fiction or realist theory. In Europe, the most important early theories were the nineteenth century realist theory of Otto von Gierke and the fiction theory of Friedrich Carl von Savigny and Bernhard Windscheid. The question was which of the theories should prevail. Is a legal person just a fiction (von Savigny and Windscheid)? Or should one assume that it exists and apply, by analogy, rules applicable to actions by individuals (von Gierke)?[19]

---

[15] Bergström C, Samuelsson P, Aktiebolagets grundproblem. En rättsekonomisk analys. Nerenius & Santérus Förlag, Stockholm (1997) p 48.

[16] Clark RC, Corporate Law. Little, Brown & Co., Boston, Mass (1986). For an analysis of Clark's theory, see Klausner MD, The Contractarian Theory of Corporate Law: A Generation Later, J Corp L 31 (2006) pp 779–797.

[17] According to Kraakman et al., the characteristics are: (1) legal personality; (2) limited liability; (3) transferable shares; (4) centralised management under a board structure; and (5) shared ownership by contributors of capital. Kraakman R, Davies P, Hansmann H, Hertig G, Hopt KJ, Kanda H, Rock EB, The Anatomy of Corporate Law: A Comparative and Functional Approach. OUP, Oxford (2004) p 5.

[18] Bratton WW, The New Economic Theory of the Firm: Critical Perspectives from History, Stanford L Rev 41 (1989) pp 1502–1503: "One definition came from Kent's Commentaries, but had origins going as far back as the writings of Pope Innocent. The second came from Kyd's late eighteenth century British treatise on corporate law. The third was the famous description of the corporation in Chief Justice Marshall's opinion in the Dartmouth College case."

[19] This discussion was relevant even in the US. See Bratton WW, *op cit*, p 1475: "Here one line of responses holds the corporation to be at most a reification—a construction of the minds of the persons connected with the firm and those who deal with them and their products. A conflicting line holds the corporate firm to be a real thing having an existence, like a spiritual being, apart from the separate existences of the persons connected with it."

The latter theory (von Gierke) was adopted by German law and in continental Europe.[20] This explains, for example, why continental European companies have traditionally been represented by their "organs" (the organic theory).[21] German legal science also distinguishes between the legal entity and the firm. The firm (das Unternehmen) has interests (Unternehmensinteresse, see below) and belongs at law to a legal entity that acts as the "carrier of the firm" (Unternehmensträger).[22] This makes it also easier to recognise that the business of modern firms is not limited to the confines of one legal entity. For example, the regulation of company groups (Konzernrecht) and the duties of good faith ("Treu und Glauben", § 242 BGB) between group members make it easier to manage a firm that uses a fleet of legal entities.[23] In France, the "Rozenblum" doctrine serves the same purpose.[24]

English law chose a different path. In English law, the question of legal personality was discussed in the landmark case of *Salomon v Salomon*.[25] After this case, the question of legal personality has customarily been discussed in the context of the limited liability of shareholders.[26] It is rare to discuss the nature of legal personality or the relationship between the company and the firm. As a result, the company and the firm are terms that tend to be used interchangeably in corporate law scholarship (such as Keay 2008). This is reflected in the absence of group law.

---

[20] See Larenz K, Allgemeiner Teil des deutschen Bürgerlichen Rechts, Ein Lehrbuch. 7. Auflage. Verlag C.H. Beck, München (1988) § 9 I; Teubner G, Enterprise Corporatism: New Industrial Policy and the "Essence" of the Legal Person, Am J Comp L 36 (1988) pp 130–155; Foster NHD, Company Law Theory in Comparative Perspective: England and France, Am J Comp L 48 (2000) pp 573–621; Mäntysaari P, The Law of Corporate Finance. Volume II. Springer, Berlin Heidelberg (2010) p 193.

[21] See also Article 10 of Directive 2009/101/EC, previously Article 9 of Directive 68/151/EEC (First Company Law Directive).

[22] One can see evidence of this also in § 3(1)(2) GmbHG and § 23(2)(2) AktG. See, for example, Priester HJ, Beginn der Rechtsperson – Vorräte und Mäntel, ZHR 168 (2004) p 252.

[23] Mäntysaari P, Comparative Corporate Governance. Springer, Berlin Heidelberg (2005) p 363.

[24] See Hofstetter K, Parent Responsibility for Subsidiary Corporations: Evaluating European Trends, ICLQ 39 (1990) pp 576–598.

[25] Salomon v A Salomon & Co Ltd [1897] AC 22.

[26] Easterbrook and Fischel regard limited liability as *the* distinguishing figure of corporate law in the US. Easterbrook FH, Fischel DR, The Economic Structure of Corporate Law. Harvard U P, Cambridge, Mass. (1991) p 40. Blair nevertheless provides a very different view. Blair argues: "While [the ability to amass large amounts of capital, limited liability, and the centralization of control] were important in many situations, it was a fourth factor that turned out to be the critical advantage of the corporate form: the ability to commit capital, once amassed, for extended periods of time ... [T]he chartering of a corporation legally transformed the business enterprise in ways that would have been impossible or extremely difficult to achieve through ... contract law ... The first way was that incorporation gave the enterprise 'entity' status under the law, and the second was that incorporation required governance rules that legally separated business decisionmaking from contributions of financial capital." Blair MM, Locking in Capital: What Corporate Law Achieved for Business Organizers in the Nineteenth Century, UCLA L Rev 51 (2003) p 390.

Different companies do not belong to the same firm. Each company is expected to pursue its own interests.[27]

In the US, von Gierke's theory – the theory adopted in German law – inspired a theory called corporate realism. Its most prominent advocate was Ernst Freund.[28] Corporate realism survived into the 1920s as the theory that, unlike the classical model with an owner-manager-entrepreneur, could describe complex, capital-intensive corporate entities, offered a theory of groups, and suited the interests of the management.[29] Corporate realism and the management corporation rose together.[30] Corporate realism disappeared in the mid 1920s as managerialist concepts made popular by Berle and Means (1932) prevailed in legal research:[31] the "enduring ideas came from contemporary American economics rather than from nineteenth century European jurisprudence".[32] The classical model lived longer in economic theories of the firm.[33]

International private law – recognisability. In international private law, the question of legal personality can be rephrased, in a situation that has connections to two or more jurisdictions, as a question of (a) the governing law and (b) whether entities are recognised as legal entities.[34] States customarily apply a system of rules grounded in the real seat theory, the incorporation theory, or a combination of both theories.[35] Case-law of the European Court of Justice[36] in effect forces Member

[27] See, for example, Mäntysaari P, Comparative Corporate Governance. Springer, Berlin Heidelberg (2005) p 217.

[28] Freund E, The Legal Nature of Corporations. U Chicago P, Chicago (1897) § 6 pp 13–14 (discussing von Gierke's organic theory).

[29] Bratton WW, The New Economic Theory of the Firm: Critical Perspectives from History, Stanford L Rev 41 (1989) pp 1490–1491 (with references in footnote 90).

[30] *Ibid*, p 1511 commenting on Horwitz MJ, Santa Clara Revisited: The Development of Corporate Theory, W Virginia L Rev 173 (1986) pp 173–224.

[31] *Ibid*, pp 1490–1491; Bainbridge S, Director Primacy: The Means and Ends of Corporate Governance, Northw U L Rev 97 (2003) pp 549 and 561–563. For a critique of the theory, see Dewey J, The Historic Background of Corporate Legal Personality, Yale L J 35 (1926) p 672: "... the entire discussion of personality, whether of single or corporate personality, is needlessly encumbered with a mass of traditional doctrines and remnants of old issues."

[32] Bratton WW, *op cit*, p 1512.

[33] See Alchian AA, Demsetz H, Production, information costs, and economic organization, Am Econ Rev 62(5) (1972) p 794.

[34] See, for example, Großfeld B, Zur Geschichte der Anerkennungsproblematik bei Aktiengesellschaften, RabelsZ 38 (1974) pp 344–371; Zimmer D, Grenzüberschreitende Rechtspersönlichkeit, ZHR 168 (2004) pp 355–368; Roth WH, From Centros to Überseering: Free Movement of Companies, Private International Law, and Community Law, ICLQ 52 (2003) pp 177–208.

[35] For the benefits of the real seat doctrine, see Schmidt K, Sitzverlegungsrichtlinie, Freizügigkeit und Gesellschaftsrechtspraxis. Grundlagen, ZGR 1999 pp 23–24.

[36] Case C-212/97 Centros [1999] ECR I–459; Case C-208/00 Überseering [2002] ECR I–9919; Case C-167/01 Inspire Art [2003] ECR I–10155; Case C-411/03 SEVIC Systems [2005] ECR I–10805; Case C-196/04 Cadbury Schweppes [2006] ECR I–7995; and the opinion of advocate general Poiares Maduro in Case C-2010/06 Cartesio.

States of the EU to apply, in a non-discriminatory way, the incorporation theory to EU companies.[37]

5.2.5 *Capacity*

A distinction can be made between legal personality (Rechtspersönlichkeit, personnalité juridique) and legal capacity (Handlungs- und Geschäftsfähigkeit, capacité juridique). A company that is regarded as a legal person customarily possesses legal capacity. Entities can nevertheless possess legal capacity without being regarded as legal persons,[38] and the legal capacity of an entity may be limited although the entity is regarded as a legal person. The common law doctrine of ultra vires is an example of the latter (see below).

5.2.6 *Purpose and Object*

Even where a corporation is regarded as a legal person, its actions may be constrained by its purpose or objects. Theories on the purpose and objects of corporations can be connected with other theories.

First, they can be connected with theories on the *capacity* of the corporation. (a) The doctrine of ultra vires provides an example. This doctrine used to pay an important role in common law systems. It meant that actions that fell outside the company's objects clause were "ultra vires" and not binding on the company.[39] As a result, the objects clause used to be very detailed and cover a long list of activities. The ultra vires doctrine has lost much of its relevance due to EU company law,[40] the UK Companies Act of 2006,[41] and developments in US company law.[42] (b) Like

---

[37] Articles 49 and 54 TFEU.

[38] Fleischer describes one such case. Fleischer H, Supranational Corporate Forms in the European Union: Prolegomena to a Theory on Supranational Forms of Association, CMLR 47 (2010) p 1704: "Article 1(2) EEIG Regulation grants legal personality ... to the EEIG, while Article 1 (3) leaves it up to each Member State to decide whether or not groups registered there will have legal personality. In most Member States – the marked exceptions being Germany and Italy – the EEIG is a legal person, although in the United Kingdom it is generically classified as a body corporate." For the German version of this paper, see Fleischer H, ZHR 174 (2010) pp 385–428.

[39] Ashbury Railway Carriage and Iron Co Ltd v Riche (1875) LR 7 (House of Lords) 653.

[40] Originally Article 9 of Directive 68/151/EEC (First Company Law Directive), now Article 10 of Directive 2009/101/EC.

[41] Section 31(1) of Companies Act 2006: "Unless a company's articles specifically restrict the objects of the company, its objects are unrestricted." Section 39(1): "The validity of an act done by a company shall not be called into question on the ground of lack of capacity by reason of anything in the company's constitution." The doctrine's relevance was reduced already by section 35A of the Companies Act 1985 inserted by the Company Act 1989.

[42] § 3.01(a) of the Revised Model Business Corporation Act: "Every corporation incorporated under this Act has the purpose of engaging in any lawful business unless a more limited purpose is

the doctrine of ultra vires, the French doctrine of spécialité statutaire has lost much of its earlier importance due to EU company law.[43]

Second, they can be connected with the *interests* to be served. The purpose of the corporation can influence the legal duties of corporate bodies and the allocation of power between shareholders and corporate bodies. This question will be discussed in Sect. 6.3.

Third, they can also be connected with theories on the *separation* of corporate functions (see below).

5.2.7 Separation

Theories on the separation of corporate functions have long roots. The leading countries are Germany and the US.

In Germany, the separation of corporate functions with a management board, supervisory board, and general meeting of shareholders was made mandatory for large companies by the Commercial Code of 1897.[44] Rathenau (1917a) described how share ownership had changed in large companies, how the responsibility for the affairs of the firm had moved from the supervisory board to the management board, and how the new structures contributed to conflicts between the general meeting and management.[45]

set forth in the articles of incorporation." Compare this with Chief Justice Marshall's opinion in the famous corporate law case of Trustees of Dartmouth College v. Woodward, 17 U.S. (4 Wheat.) 518, 636 (1819) on the nature of the corporation: "Being the mere creature of law, it possesses only those properties which the charter of its creation confers upon it, either expressly, or as incidental to its very existence."

[43] Zimmer D, Internationales Gesellschaftsrecht. Schriftenreihe Recht der Internationalen Wirtschaft. Band 50. Verlag Recht und Wirtschaft GmbH, Heidelberg (1996), Dritter Teil C I 1 b at pp 243–244.

[44] § 239 HGB 1897 and § 246 HGB 1897. There were exemptions for small companies – GmbH – combined with restrictions on the transferability of shares and an increased liability of shareholders. See, for example, Cosack K, Lehrbuch des Handelsrechts. Sechste Auflage. Verlag von Ferdinand Enke, Stuttgart (1903) § 122.

[45] Rathenau W, Vom Aktienwesen. Eine geschäftliche Betrachtung. Berlin (1917) p 13; Riechers A, Das "Unternehmen an sich". Die Entwicklung eines Begriffes in der Aktienrechtsdiskussion des 20. Jahrhunderts. Beiträge zur Rechtsgeschichte des 20. Jahrhunderts 17. Mohr Siebeck, Tübingen (1996); Laux F, Die Lehre vom Unternehmen an sich. Walther Rathenau und die aktienrechtliche Diskussion in der Weimarer Republik. Schriften zur Rechtsgeschichte RG 74. Duncker & Humblot, Berlin (1998) p 7.

In the US, the separation of ownership and control was recognised as a modern phenomenon in the 1920s.[46] It was later made popular by Berle and Means (1932) who explained that the separation of ownership from control is one of the characteristics of the modern corporation.[47] The work of Berle and Means was influential (see below).

Eisenberg (1976) builds on the work of Berle and Means. He discusses both closely-held and publicly-held corporations.

Eisenberg analyses the separation of functions in *closely-held* corporations on the basis of the fair expectations of "owners". He argues that there are matters that "owners" would expect to decide by themselves, and matters they would expect the managers to decide.[48] However, he does not explain on what grounds "owners" can be assumed to have such expectations, and he discusses their expectations only in the context of the founding of the company.

In *publicly-held* corporations, he distinguishes between different categories of decisions. *Structural changes* should be decided on by shareholders, because, first, "management is likely to be deeply self-interested in structural decisions"[49] and, second, neither judicial review nor approval by a government agency would work as alternative decision-making mechanisms.[50] Managers should take care of most *management matters*. Eisenberg argues that the main function of the board of a publicly-held corporation is the selection and removal of the *chief executive*.[51] He discusses boards composed of independent directors, boards with a clear majority of independent directors, the statutory two-tier system, and de facto two-tier systems of American corporations.[52]

5.2.8 Supranational or International Corporate Forms

Some corporate forms can be regarded as supranational or international. International companies are founded on the basis of a private or public law treaty between

[46] Brandeis LD, On Industrial Relations (testimony before the United States Commission on Industrial relations, January 23, 1915, see Bruner CM, The Enduring Ambivalence of Corporate Law, Alabama L Rev 59 (2008) p 1390); Veblen T, Absentee Ownership and Business Enterprise in Recent Times: The Case of America. B.W. Huebsch, New York (1923); Riechers A, *op cit*, p 183.

[47] Berle AA, Means GC, The Modern Corporation and Private Property. Transaction Publishers, New Brunswick, New Jersey (1968). Originally published in 1932. See also Mark Roe, Strong Managers, Weak Owners (1994). According to Roe, the emergence of dispersed share ownership was not entirely dictated by economics.

[48] Eisenberg MA, The Structure of the Corporation. Beard Books, Washington, D.C. (1976) pp 12–13, 16.

[49] *Ibid*, p 33.

[50] *Ibid*, pp 34–36.

[51] *Ibid*, pp 162–170.

[52] *Ibid*, pp 172–185.

several States.[53] Supranational corporate forms are different. In the EU, supranational corporate forms include the European Economic Interest Grouping (EEIG),[54] the European Company (Societas europaea, SE),[55] and the European Cooperative Society (Societas cooperativa europaea, SCE),[56] and may include the European Private Company (Societas privata europaea, SPE) in the future.[57]

It is characteristic of such corporate forms that they are not created by a national legislator. A theory of supranational or international corporate forms must therefore explain their creation and the interaction of international/supranational law and national law.[58] Such corporate forms nevertheless share most of their characteristics with similar national corporate forms. Their cross-border nature does not really set them apart from national corporate forms as the business of firms has become increasingly international or global.[59] In principle, supranational or international corporate forms could nevertheless have characteristic elements not shared by other corporate national corporate forms.

5.2.9 Problems

Existing theories of corporations raise certain problems. First, a list of characteristics does not explain why the company has exactly those and not other characteristics. Neither does it explain the relationship between the different characteristics. This could be achieved by identifying the bigger idea behind all the characteristics, that is, the main objectives of the legal framework that governs corporations, and the particular functions that must be regulated. In practice, such

---

[53] Fleischer H, Supranational Corporate Forms in the European Union: Prolegomena to a Theory on Supranational Forms of Association, CMLR 47 (2010) pp 1680–1681 citing, in particular, Marty G, Les Sociétés Internationales, RabelsZ 27 (1962) pp 73–88; Wiedemann H, Gesellschaftsrecht. Vol. I. C.H. Beck, München (1980), § 15 IV p 881.

[54] Regulation 2137/85 (EEIG Regulation).

[55] Regulation 2157/2001 (SE Regulation).

[56] Regulation 1435/2003 (SCE Regulation).

[57] Commission, Proposal for a Council Regulation on the Statute for a European private company, COM(2008) 396 final. See, for example, Bormann J, König DC, Der Weg zur Europäischen Privatgesellschaft, RIW 3/2010 pp 111–119; Teichmann C, Die Societas Privata Europaea (SPE) als ausländische Tochtergesellschaft, RIW 3/2010 pp 120–127.

[58] Fleischer H, Supranational Corporate Forms in the European Union: Prolegomena to a Theory on Supranational Forms of Association, CMLR 47 (2010) p 1717: "As far as the interaction of supranational and national law is concerned, two types of legislative techniques may be distinguished: the referential model (paradigm: the SE Regulation) and the complete statute (paradigm: the draft SPE Regulation)."

[59] *Ibid*, p 1717 (on a theory of European supranational corporate forms): "Some distinguishing features which may play a role in furthering the doctrinal assessment of European corporate law are: legal personality; corporate purpose and company object; cross-border involvement; registered and head offices; and company members from third countries."

theories must be complemented by theories of corporate law (see below) or other theories. Second, although separate legal personality and the separation of functions are characteristic of companies, there must be other factors explaining the details of corporate law. For example, what are the factors explaining how functions are separated?

5.3 Legal Theories of Corporate Law

5.3.1 General Remarks

The most important theories of corporate law are probably the contractarian theory of corporate law, applications of the agency theory, and the team-production theory of corporate law.[60]

5.3.2 Contract

The *contractarian* theory of corporate law was the next big thing after Berle and Means (1932) in mainstream corporate law research. It is still the mainstream approach in Anglo-American legal science. This theory analyses corporate law as a set of standard form contracts. The "corporate contract" consists of the terms of a corporation's articles of association (charter) and the corporate law the firm selects by virtue of incorporating in a particular jurisdiction.

The contractarian theory of corporate law is influenced by the set-of-contracts theory of the firm but it has much longer historical roots in English company law.[61] English law treats articles of association as a "statutory contract".[62] American law was greatly influenced by English law,[63] and economic sciences were influenced by the existing legal framework (path dependency). One could say that the set-of-contracts theory of the firm "confirms and repeats legal history" when it asserts that the corporation is a contract.[64]

---

[60] See, for example, Bruner CM, The Enduring Ambivalence of Corporate Law, Alabama L Rev 59 (2008) p 1396.

[61] See already Berle AA, Means GC, The Modern Corporation and Private Property (1932), Chapter IV.

[62] Section 33 of the Companies Act 2006; section 14 of the Companies Act 1985. See also Mäntysaari P, Comparative Corporate Governance. Springer, Berlin Heidelberg (2005) pp 105–113.

[63] See Berle AA, Means GC, *op cit*, Book Two, Chapter I.

[64] Bratton WW, The New Economic Theory of the Firm: Critical Perspectives from History, Stanford L Rev 41 (1989) p 1513.

As a result, it was relatively easy to adopt the set-of-contracts theory of the firm in American economic sciences,[65] and it is relatively easy to explain the theory's success in corporate legal theory in common law countries.[66]

The contractarian theory of corporate law contains a political agenda. The representatives of this theory argue: that the corporation is a set of contracts; that the main principle in contract law is party autonomy; and that company law should, therefore, be enabling and without mandatory provisions. This means that the contractarian theory does not reflect existing corporate law.[67] Although not its originators, Easterbrook and Fischel belong to the best-known modern representatives of the set-of-contracts theory in corporate law.[68]

In economic sciences, the set-of-contracts theory of the firm is complemented by the property rights approach. This has led to attempts to describe the *proprietary* foundations of corporate law.[69]

The set-of-contracts theory of corporate law is very problematic.[70] It cannot help to define corporate law and its relevant issues. The most fundamental problems are caused by its failure to reflect the contents of the law.[71]

First, the set-of-contracts theory of corporate law relies on fictive rather than legal contracts. Whereas legal contracts (the real contracts) are legally enforceable, the fictive contracts of economic theory and the set-of-contracts theory of corporate law are not. This is recognised even by its representatives.[72] There is also a difference between the "statutory contract" created by English company law and contracts governed by contract law: the statutory contract binds members in their capacity as members only; normal remedies for breach of contract do not

---

[65] See Fama EF, Jensen MC, Separation of Ownership and Control, J Law Econ 26 (1983) pp 301–325.

[66] Bratton WW, *op cit*, p 1473.

[67] See also *ibid*, p 1517: "While the doctrinal theory always takes cognizance of contractual elements, it never makes contract the essence. The doctrinal theory balances contract against the corporate entity and a sovereign presence ... Selection of the applicable theoretical paradigm—managerialist or contractual—will occur in the particular context as a quasi-political decision."

[68] See Easterbrook FH, Fischel DR, The Economic Structure of Corporate Law. Harvard U P, Cambridge, Mass. (1991) p 15.

[69] Armour J, Whincop MJ, The Proprietary Foundations of Corporate Law, OJLS 27 (2007) pp 429–465 (http://ssrn.com/abstract=1150625).

[70] See Clark RC, Corporate Law. Little, Brown & Co, Boston, Mass. (1986); Clark RC, Contracts, Elites, and Traditions in the Making of Corporate Law, Columbia L Rev 89 (1989) pp 1703–1747; Klausner MD, The Contractarian Theory of Corporate Law: A Generation Later, J Corp L 31 (2006) pp 779–797.

[71] See also Bratton WW, *op cit*, p 1513: "This absolute contractualism makes problematic the new theory's practical application in the law." See also p 1517: "Contractual notions will be entertained, but any move to foreclose wider discussion by the assertion that contract should govern as a function of the intrinsic nature of the corporation will fail."

[72] Demsetz H, The Structure of Ownership and the Theory of the Firm, J Law Econ 26(2) (1983) p 377; Easterbrook FH, Fischel DR, The Economic Structure of Corporate Law. Harvard U P, Cambridge, Mass. (1991) pp 15–16.

necessarily apply; and the statutory contract can be altered by special resolution. Such "statutory contracts" are thus fictive rather than real.

Second, the set-of-contracts theory of corporate law is not compatible with separate legal personality, one of the most fundamental characteristics of corporations. For example, an employee does not owe any real contractual duties to a shareholder. An employee owes contractual duties to the employer, the legal entity. A CEO seldom owes contractual duties to a shareholder but does customarily owe them to the legal entity.

Third, freedom of contract is not characteristic of corporate law in the broad sense. There is an extensive *mandatory* regulatory regime for securities markets and corporate insolvency, there is an extensive *mandatory* regulatory regime for the disclosure of financial information, and there is an increasing amount of *mandatory* regulation of corporate governance. It is fair to assume that the regulation of securities markets, corporate insolvency, disclosure of financial information, and corporate governance can fall within the scope of corporate law in the broad sense.[73] The political agenda of the contractarian theory of corporate law has clearly failed.

5.3.3 Agency

The contractarian theory is combined with the agency theory. Of course, corporate law does not have its roots in the agency theory. Corporate law has existed for hundreds of years (or longer),[74] but the origins of the agency theory can be traced to the 1960s and early 1970s.[75] The agency theory nevertheless became the most popular theory in corporate governance research (see below) and started to influence corporate law scholarship in general. It has very slowly started to influence even other areas of law. That its penetration of legal science is very slow in Europe can be illustrated by a 2006 book published by the Stockholm Institute for

[73] Klausner MD, The Contractarian Theory of Corporate Law: A Generation Later, J Corp L 31 (2006) p 785. The scope of "corporate law" or "company law" can also have normative implications. See, for example, Case C–167/01 Inspire Art [2003] ECR I–10155, paragraph 138; Article 1(2)(f) of Regulation 593/2008 (Rome I).

[74] Malmendier U, Roman Shares. In: Goetzmann WN, Rouwenhorst KG (eds), *op cit*, p 32: "While the idea of offering shares in enterprises may date back further, most papers and monographs on the history of the corporation identify the East and West India Companies, which emerged during the early seventeenth century as the world's first business corporations . . . I argue that over two thousand years earlier the Roman *societas publicanorum*, or 'society of publicans' anticipated the modern corporation and, in particular, the use of fungible shares with limited liability."

[75] Wilson R, On the Theory of Syndicates, Econometrica 36 (1968) pp 119–132; Arrow KJ, Essays in the Theory of Risk-Bearing. Markham Publishing Co., Chicago (1971); Ross SA, The Economic Theory of Agency: The Principal's Problem, Am Econ Rev 63(2) (1973) pp 134–139; Jensen MC, Meckling WH, Theory of the Firm: Managerial Behavior, Agency Costs and Ownership Structure, J Fin Econ 3 (1976) pp 305–360.

Scandinavian Law which contained 25 articles on "a proactive approach" in law without mentioning the agency theory even once.

In their book "Aktiebolagets grundproblem" (The Fundamental Problems of the Corporation), Bergström and Samuelsson study the characteristics of the corporate form and how Swedish company law regulates conflicts of interest between managers and shareholders, between majority and minority shareholders, and between shareholders and creditors.[76] In their book "The Anatomy of Corporate Law. A Comparative and Functional Approach", a number of leading corporate law scholars (Kraakman et al. 2004) suggest that the central issue for corporate law in every jurisdiction is how to mediate such agency conflicts. In addition, the authors develop a typology of ten different strategies divided by operational and temporal criteria.[77] The authors then apply their scheme to related party transactions, control transactions, investor protection, and a variety of other key corporate law issues. This book has gained much influence.[78]

The mainstream agency model or "anatomy model" is nevertheless problematic. Like the contractarian theory, it fails to reflect the contents of existing law. Moreover, it fails to explain fundamental questions. The core failings of the anatomy model are: (1) that it does not explain why the limited-liability company has many of its basic legal characteristics (such as separate legal personality and shareholders with limited liability and freely transferable shares); [79] (2) that it does not explain why something should be done in the first place;[80] and (3) that there are various categories of potential principals with potentially conflicting interests.

The last of the three issues partly contributes to the other two issues. If shareholders, minority shareholders, and various kinds of third parties can all be

[76] Bergström C, Samuelsson P, Aktiebolagets grundproblem. En rättsekonomisk analys. Nerenius & Santérus Förlag, Stockholm (1997).

[77] Kraakman R, Davies P, Hansmann H, Hertig G, Hopt KJ, Kanda H, Rock EB, The Anatomy of Corporate Law: A Comparative and Functional Approach. OUP, Oxford (2004) p 23.

[78] See Skeel DA Jr., Corporate Anatomy Lessons, Yale L J 113 (2004) pp 1519–1577; Wiedemann H, Auf der Suche nach den Strukturen der Aktiengesellschaft. The Anatomy of Corporate Law, ZGR 2006 pp 240–258.

[79] Kraakman R, Davies P, Hansmann H, Hertig G, Hopt KJ, Kanda H, Rock EB, *op cit*, pp 1–2: "These characteristics are ... induced by the economic exigencies of the large modern business enterprise. Thus, corporate law everywhere must, of necessity, provide for them. To be sure, there are other forms of business enterprise that lack one or more of these characteristics. But ... almost all large-scale business forms adopt a legal form that possesses all five of the basic characteristics ... Self-evidently, a principal function of corporate law is to provide business enterprises with a legal form that possesses these five core attributes." Kraakman et al. nevertheless fail to explain why the limited-liability company has its basic legal characteristics. See also Williamson OE, The Modern Corporation: Origins, Evolution, Attributes, J Econ Lit 19 (1981) pp 1538–1539 (on the focus of the essay): "Key legal features of the corporation – limited liability and the transferability of ownership – are taken as given. Failure to discuss these does not reflect a judgment that these are either irrelevant or uninteresting. The main focus of this essay, however, is on the internal organization of the corporation."

[80] Skeel DA, Jr., Corporate Anatomy Lessons, Yale L J 113 (2004) pp 1543–1544.

regarded as principals depending on the circumstances, whose interests should prevail and why?[81] This argument is customarily used against stakeholder theories (Sect. 6.3). The mainstream view attempts to solve this problem by choosing shareholders as the most important principal. However, it uses weak arguments (Sect. 6.4).

Generally, the mainstream view defends the choice of shareholders as the most important principal by weak moral arguments,[82] arguments that should rather apply to other principals (shareholders are not the main source of capital, shareholders do not necessarily have the biggest risk exposure), or arguments that can make sense only in economic theory (the firm of economic theory exists only in economic theory;[83] it is clear that shareholders do not own the assets of a separate legal person;[84] and there is a difference between legally enforceable contracts and the fictional contracts of economic theory).

The choice of shareholders as the most important principal does not explain their existence as a class. Why are there claimants called shareholders in the first place? For example, the limitation of investors' liability cannot explain the existence of shareholders, because the limited liability of investors is "an attribute of most investment, not just of corporate law".[85] And if the cause of their existence could be explained, the choice of real shareholders as the principal would still be particularly problematic. Real shareholders can have different interests and are most likely to have very different interests in a company with a dispersed share ownership structure.[86] What are the real interests of a corporation's real shareholders? Of course, one could decide that the interests of real shareholders do not count and use the fictive interests of fictive shareholders instead. But fictive shareholders do not exist, and both corporate law and corporate decision-making must address issues caused by the real interests of shareholders that do exist.

5.3.4 Team Production

The team production theory is one of the attempts to solve the problem caused by the existence of many agency relationships. Blair and Stout (1999) argue that the

---

[81] An example of this approach is Keay A, Ascertaining The Corporate Objective: An Entity Maximisation and Sustainability Model, MLR 71(5) (2008) pp 676–677.

[82] Like Berle AA, Property, Production and Revolution. A Preface to the Revised Edition. In: Berle AA, Means GC, *op cit.*

[83] Demsetz H, The Structure of Ownership and the Theory of the Firm, J Law Econ 26(2) (1983) p 377.

[84] For a landmark case in English company law, see Salomon v A Salomon & Co Ltd [1897] AC 22.

[85] Easterbrook FH, Fischel DR, *op cit*, p 40.

[86] For example, they have very different political interests. See Bebchuk LA, Jackson RJ, Corporate Political Speech: Who Decides? Harv L Rev 124 (2010) pp 83–117.

essential economic function of the public corporation is not to address principal-agent problems at all. Instead, they suggest that the unique legal rules governing publicly-held corporations are primarily designed to address the team production problem identified by Holmström (1982). In particular, Blair (2003) points out that corporate law facilitates locking in capital.[87]

The team production problem arises when a number of individuals must invest firm-specific resources to produce a non-separable output. In such situations, team members may find it difficult or impossible to draft explicit contracts distributing the output of their joint efforts, and, as an alternative, might prefer to give up control over their enterprise to an independent third party charged with representing the team's interests and allocating rewards among team members.

According to Blair and Stout, the public corporation is a vehicle through which potential corporate stakeholders can jointly relinquish control over their firm-specific resources to a board of directors. Blair and Stout suggest that directors of public corporations should seek to maximise the joint welfare of all the firm's stakeholders who contribute firm-specific resources to corporate production.

Blair and Stout thus regard the firm as a production function. What makes their model problematic is that it gives little guidance on what should be done and how. There is a long list of potential contributors of firm-specific resources. How should the contributors of firm-specific resources be chosen? Is there a way to measure their joint welfare in any reasonable way? Whose interests should prevail?

5.4 Summary

One can distinguish between theories of corporations and theories of corporate law. These theories tend to be limited to certain questions. Of the two categories, theories of corporations tend to be narrower. Because of their inductive nature, they also tend to reflect the regulation of corporations better. The broader theories of corporate law seem to be problematic and flawed. In particular, they do not seem to reflect the reality of the regulation of corporations. This can partly be explained by their deductive nature.

[87] Blair MM, Stout LA, A Team Production Theory of Corporate Law, Virginia L Rev 85 (1999) pp 247–328; Blair MM, Locking In Capital: What Corporate Law Achieved for Business Organizers in the Nineteenth Century, UCLA L Rev 51(2) (2003) pp 433–434; Holmström B, Moral Hazard in Teams, Bell J Econ 13(2) (1982) pp 324–340.

Chapter 6
Legal and Economic Theories of Corporate Governance: Past Approaches

6.1 Introduction

Theories of the firm and theories of corporate law or corporations provide the basis for the study of corporate governance. One can say that all such theories address at least some questions that are interesting in this context. The purpose of this chapter is to provide a critique of the existing theories. A new theory will be proposed in the next chapter.

Theories of corporate law/corporations, theories of corporate governance. One should make a distinction between theories of corporate law/corporations and theories of corporate governance. They describe different phenomena.

Unlike corporate law, corporate governance is not a normative system consisting of legal rules. Corporate governance tends to be defined in various ways and studied in various disciplines in social sciences. It can be regarded as an economic, social, or organisational phenomenon (something happening), or as an organisational or management function (something to be organised or managed). There are many theories of corporate governance in economics and management science.

Corporate governance can also be regarded as a context that raises legal questions. There could therefore be one or more legal theories of corporate governance.

However, the mainstream approaches are typically applications of the mainstream theories of the firm (economic approaches) and corporate law/corporations (legal approaches). For this reason, one could say that there are not really any mainstream theories of corporate governance in particular.

Economic and legal theories of corporate governance. There is no clear dividing line between economic and legal theories of corporate governance, because economic theories have been influenced by legal theories and vice versa. In the following, legal and economic theories are therefore discussed generally as theories of corporate governance.

Four big questions. Unfortunately, the existing theories are rather narrow and fail to explain even the most fundamental issues of corporate governance.

P. Mäntysaari, *Organising the Firm*,
DOI 10.1007/978-3-642-22197-2_6,

A general theory of corporate governance should be able to answer at least four fundamental questions: (1) Why is the *legal entity* with its characteristic governance model chosen in the first place? (2) Whose *interests* should the people acting as or on behalf of the legal entity further? (3) Why does a legal entity have a *board*? (4) Why does a legal entity have *shareholders*? For example, one cannot explain the function of shareholders and the board unless one can explain why they exist and the general objective of their activities.

Most research approaches take the existence of a legal entity for granted and assume that a legal entity has shareholders and a board. Typically, most of them discuss just the second question: the corporate objective.[1] We can nevertheless study the question of choice first.

6.2 Choice of Business Form and Governance Model

The corporate governance model used by firms is governed and constrained by the external legal framework. On the other hand, the external legal framework that provides for the default corporate governance model is not static. The legal framework and the default model depend on several choices.

The choices relate to: the governing law (the legal framework of one country rather than the legal framework of another country)[2]; the business form (one business form facilitated by the governing law rather than another business form facilitated by the same governing law); and the combination of business forms (a certain combination of business forms rather than another combination). For example, a German legal entity with a governance model governed by German law can functionally be changed into a French legal entity whose governance model is governed by French law.[3] If this is what one wants, one will also choose between alternative French business forms each with a different legal framework. The governance structure could be based on the use of just one legal entity or a combination of two or more different or similar legal entities.

What explains the choices? A theory of corporate governance should be able to explain why a certain business form and its characteristic governance model are chosen in the first place.

---

[1] For an example of such an approach, see Keay A, Ascertaining The Corporate Objective: An Entity Maximisation and Sustainability Model, MLR 71(5) (2008) pp 663–698. Bainbridge S, The New Corporate Governance in Theory and Practice. OUP, Oxford (2008) studies this question and the question why there are boards.

[2] See, for example, Kahan M, Kamar E, The Myth of State Competition in Corporate Law, Stanford L Rev 55 (2002) pp 679–749.

[3] See, for example, Mäntysaari P, The Law of Corporate Finance. Volume I. Springer, Berlin Heidelberg (2010) pp 86–92.

Although there are examples of research that seek to explain the choices,[4] mainstream research approaches do not seem to recognise the existence of choice. Their corporate governance model is static in the sense that the choice of the governing law and the default governance model (usually that of a large public limited-liability company) are taken for granted.

For example, mainstream approaches do not explain why firms do not move more to jurisdictions whose laws are perceived as "better",[5] and they do not explain why firms choose incorporation in Delaware.[6] The path dependency of statutory corporate governance models cannot be the explanation.[7] The more discretion market participants have to choose between the corporate governance models of different states and the various corporate governance models available under the laws of a certain state, the less the path dependency of national corporate governance models should matter.

Neither do mainstream approaches explain why firms still use business forms that do not require the existence of shareholders with freely transferable shares. Most firms in the world are small private businesses without freely transferable shares.

6.3 Interests

6.3.1 General Remarks

The interests that the people acting as or on behalf of the legal entity should further depend on the chosen approach. In recent research, it is customary to distinguish between two mainstream approaches: the interests of shareholders (shareholder primacy) and the interests of stakeholders (the stakeholder approach).[8]

---

[4] See Aoki M, Jackson G, Understanding an emergent diversity of corporate governance and organizational architecture: an essentiality-based analysis, Ind Corp Change 17 (2008) pp 1–27 (studying equilibrium modes of linkage between assets held by basic stakeholders: managers' human assets, workers' human assets, and investor-supplied nonhuman (physical/financial) assets); Christensen JF, Corporate strategy and the management of innovation and technology, Ind Corp Change 11 (2002) pp 263–288 (studying the choice between the U-form and the M-form or various types of the M-form).

[5] See, for example, La Porta R, López de Silanes F, Shleifer A, Vishny R, Investor Protection and Corporate Governance, J Fin Econ 58(1) (2000) pp 3–27; Daines R, Does Delaware Law Improve Firm Value? J Fin Econ 62 (2001) pp 525–558.

[6] Kahan M, Kamar E, The Myth of State Competition in Corporate Law, Stanford L Rev 55 (2002) pp 679–749; Klausner MD, The Contractarian Theory of Corporate Law: A Generation Later, J Corp L 31 (2006) p 787.

[7] For path dependency in general, see Bebchuk L, Roe MJ, A Theory of Path Dependence in Corporate Ownership and Governance, Stanford L Rev 52 (1999) pp 127–170.

[8] Generally, see Freeman RE, Harrison JS, Wicks AC, Parmar BL, de Colle S, Stakeholder Theory. Cambridge U P, Cambridge (2010). Eisenberg assumed that the internal allocation of power and the interests furthered by company law should go hand in hand. He identified three mainstream

As far as the corporate objective is concerned, the most important problems with the mainstream views are: (1) that they fail to give the board and managers sufficient guidance; (2) that they, by design or in effect, force the board and managers to further conflicting interests; and (3) that it is difficult to align them with separate legal personality.

We will now discuss these problems in detail. The approach that can provide the answer will be discussed in Sect. 6.3.6.

6.3.2 Guidance

6.3.2.1 General Remarks

Problems with failing guidance relate not only to the school of thought called managerialism and the stakeholder approach but even to the shareholder primacy approach (Sect. 5.3.3 and 6.3.3). The notion of "efficiency" does not provide the answered.

6.3.2.2 Managerialism

Managerialism means a school of thought according to which managers should run the corporation in the public interest. This is said to require the balancing of several interests. Managerialism is the school of thought advocated, for example, by Berle and Means (1932).[9]

However, managers cannot reasonably be given a duty to maximise general welfare benefits.[10] This would require information managers cannot possess, or third-party acts beyond their control. One of the proposed solutions was that managers should choose growth (instead of profit or general welfare benefits) as the objective and "satisficing" (instead of maximising) as the behaviour pattern.[11]

---

approaches: "shareholder democracy" (also known as the shareholder primacy model, shareholders are given the right to decide); "client-group participation" (client-groups are given a formal role); and "managerialism" (management should run the company in the public interest). Eisenberg MA, The Structure of the Corporation. Beard Books, Washington, D.C. (1976) pp 28–29.

[9] Berle AA, Means GC, *op cit*, Book Four, Chapter IV. See also Eisenberg MA, The Structure of the Corporation. Beard Books, Washington, D.C. (1976) p 25.

[10] See also Eisenberg MA, *op cit*, p 25: "… the managerialists seem to greatly exaggerate the inclination and ability of management to serve as instruments of national policy."

[11] Baumol WJ, On the Theory of the Expansion of the firm, Am Econ Rev 52 (1962) pp 1078–1087; Cyert RM, March JG, A Behavioral Theory of the Firm. Prentice-Hall, Inc., Englewood Cliffs, NJ (1963). Cited in Bratton WW, The New Economic Theory of the Firm: Critical Perspectives from History, Stanford L Rev 41 (1989) pp 1494–1495.

This school of thought largely disappeared from mainstream corporate governance and corporate law research.[12] Instead, it became customary to: question the motivation and incentives of managers; assume that managers are not motivated by profit-seeking, but "by drives for power, prestige, and job security"; and study management performance.[13] Whereas managerialism was based on the idea that the corporation is and should be controlled by its managers, later corporate governance and corporate law research that was influenced by neoclassical economics adopted the view that there is and should be a "market for corporate control" (Manne 1965).[14]

In modern corporate governance research, managerialism has merged with the stakeholder approach and the corporate social responsibility debate (see below).

6.3.2.3 Mainstream Approaches and Efficiency

The mainstream approaches fail to give sufficient guidance even when they seek to foster "efficiency" as the most fundamental paradigm in economics. First, there can be different mainstream approaches based on different notions of economic efficiency. Second, mere economic efficiency is too vague as a regulatory objective in law.[15] Third, the firm's board and managers are not in a position to maximise welfare to the extent that this would require information that they cannot possess or acts beyond their control. Fourth, the mainstream approaches fail to solve the problem of conflicting intrests (Sect. 6.3.3). It is thus unclear what one should take into account when assessing efficiency.

Modern efficiency-based approaches. In modern corporate governance research, the efficiency-based approaches include: the disciplinary approach (the interests that should be served); the knowledge-based approach; and various combinations (synthetic approaches).[16] The choice of the approach influences the choice of the

---

[12] Bainbridge S, Director Primacy: The Means and Ends of Corporate Governance, Northw U L Rev 97 (2003) pp 549 and 561–563.

[13] Bratton WW, The New Economic Theory of the Firm: Critical Perspectives from History, Stanford L Rev 41 (1989) p 1494 (citing Means GC, The Corporate Revolution In America. The Crowell-Collier Press, New York (1962) pp 50–51) and pp 1508–1509.

[14] Manne HG, Mergers and the Market for Corporate Control, J Pol Econ 73 (1965) pp 110–120. See also Bratton WW, *op cit*, pp 1518–1521 on the acceptance of Manne's theory and the market for corporate control that appeared after 1980.

[15] See Eidenmüller H, Effizienz als Rechtsprinzip. 3. Auflage. Die Einheit der Gesellschaftswissenschaften. Band 90. Mohr Siebeck, Tübingen (2005); Farber DA, Economic Efficiency and The Ex Ante Perspective. In: Kraus JS, Walt SD (eds), *op cit*, pp 55–86; Kornhauser LA, Constrained optimization. Corporate law and the Maximization of Social Welfare. In: Kraus JS, Walt SD (eds), *op cit*, pp 87–117.

[16] See Charreaux GJ, Corporate Governance Theories: From Micro Theories to National Systems Theories, Working Papers FARGO 1041202, December 2004, http://ideas.repec.org/p/dij/wpfarg/1041202.html.

Table 6.1 Examples of the definition of corporate governance systems (Charreaux 2004)

Governance theories	Disciplinary: shareholder	Disciplinary: stakeholder	Knowledge-based
Theories of the firm:	Mainly agency theory (normative and positive).	Mainly agency theory (normative and positive) extended to numerous stakeholders.	Behavioural theory. Evolutionary theory. Resources and competence theory.
Efficiency criteria:	Shareholder value.	Stakeholder value.	Ability to create a sustainable organisational rent through innovation in particular.
Definition of corporate governance systems:	All mechanisms that secure financial investments.	All mechanisms that maintain the nexus of contracts and optimise the managerial latitude.	All mechanisms possessing the best potential for value creation through learning and innovation.

theory of the firm, efficiency criteria, and the definition of corporate governance systems.

Disciplinary approaches. As Table 6.1 (part of a more complete table published in Charreaux 2004) shows, there are different ideas about the interests that should be served. For example, one can distinguish between: the manager-oriented model; the labour-oriented model; the state-oriented model; stakeholder-oriented models; and the shareholder-oriented model.[17] It is customary to pick either the stakeholder approach or the shareholder primacy model in corporate governance research. We will therefore have a closer look at these two models first.

6.3.2.4 The Stakeholder Approach

Early corporations existed by virtue of a charter or concession granted when incorporation was believed to serve the interests of the crown or the state. The first approach to prevail was thus the *stakeholder* approach. This approach ruled for a long time in the regulation of companies.

For example, incorporation was not liberalised in the German Reich until 1870.[18] After that, the *shareholder* primacy model took over in

[17] Hansmann H, Kraakman R, The End of History for Corporate Law, Georgetown L J 89(2) (2001) pp 439–468.

[18] Article 208 of Allgemeines Deutsches Handelsgesetzbuch: “Aktiengesellschaften können nur mit staatlicher Genehmigung errichtet werden ...” Article 249: “Den Landesgesetzen bleibt vorbehalten, zu bestimmen, daß es der staatlichen Genehmigung zur Errichtung von Aktiengesellschaften im Allgemeinen oder von einzelnen Arten derselben nicht bedarf ...”

Germany.[19] This was most evident in small limited-liability companies (GmbH).[20] Shareholder primacy was confirmed by the Reichsgericht.[21]

The growing power of shareholders also contributed to social unrest.[22] In the Weimar Republic, the doctrine of the firm in itself - *Unternehmen an sich* - emerged as an alternative to the shareholder primacy model. The most important representative of this doctrine was Walter Rathenau.[23] According to this doctrine, large firms had de facto become an important way to further the interests of the public. This had also contributed to the increased independence of firms from shareholders.[24] The doctrine of the firm in itself was further influenced by the views of several leading American managers who supported social capitalism.[25]

The thinking of Rathenau inspired Berle and Means, who recommended a *stakeholder* approach in the US in 1932.[26] This was to be achieved by increasing public share ownership and making everybody a shareholder in big corporations; management should therefore focus on the distribution of profits to shareholders or all Americans.[27] Riechers (1996) explains that the opposite view was that firms

---

[19] See Flume W, Allgemeiner Teil des bürgerlichen Rechts, Band 1. Teil 2. Springer, Berlin Heidelberg (1983) § 2 IV.

[20] Cosack K, Lehrbuch des Handelsrechts. Sechste Auflage. Verlag von Ferdinand Enke, Stuttgart (1903) § 122 I 1: "Die Gesellschaft mit beschränkter Haftung ist zum Teil von der Bevormundung befreit, der die gewöhnliche Aktiengesellschaft unterliegt: keine Kontrolle durch einen Aufsichtsrat oder gar durch Revisoren, Formlosigkeit der Generalversammlung und ihrer Beschlüsse, größere Freiheit bei Aufstellung der Bilanz, geringere Förmlichkeiten bei der Gesellschaftsgründung, Zulassung eines beweglichen, durch Nachschüsse der Gesellschafter gebildeten Geschäftskapitals neben dem starren Grundkapital."

[21] RGZ 107, 72, 202.

[22] See, in particular, Marx K, Das Kapital (1872), Chapter 13.

[23] The term Unternehmen an sich was coined by Fritz Hausmann. Hausmann F, Vom Aktienwesen und vom Aktienrecht, Mannheim 1928 (criticising Rathenau). See, for example, Flume W, *op cit*, § 2 III–IV; Riechers A, *op cit*, pp 8–9 and 16; Laux F, *op cit*; von Hein J, Die Rezeption US-amerikanischen Gesellschaftsrechts in Deutschland. Beiträge zum ausländischen und internationalen Privatrecht 87. Mohr Siebeck, Tübingen (2008) pp 138–140.

[24] Rathenau W, Vom Aktienwesen. Eine geschäftliche Betrachtung. Berlin (1917) pp 38–39: [D]ie Großunternehmung ist heute überhaupt nicht mehr lediglich ein Gebilde privatrechtlichen Interessen, sie ist vielmehr, sowohl einzeln wie in ihrer Gesamtheit, ein nationalwirtschaftlicher, der Gesamtheit angehöriger Faktor, der zwar aus seiner Herkunft, zu Recht oder zu Unrecht, noch die privatrechtlichen Züge des reinen Erwerbsunternehmens trägt, während er längst und in steigendem Maße öffentlichen Interessen dienstbar geworden ist . . .

[25] In particular: Henry Ford; Owen D. Young (General Electric Corporation); Robert S. Brookings; John D. Rockefeller; and Herbert Hoover. See Riechers A, *op cit*, pp 181–182; Brookings RS, Die Demokratisierung der amerikanischen Wirtschaft, Berlin (1925).

[26] Berle AA, Means GC, *op cit*, Book Four, Chapter IV, citing Rathenau W, Von Kommenden Dingen, first published by D. Fischer, Berlin (1917). See also Nörr KW, Ein Gegenstand der Reflexion: Die Aktiengesellschaft in den Schriften Franz Kleins, Rudolf Hilferdings, Walther Rathenaus, ZHR 172 (2008) pp 133–143.

[27] Berle AA, Corporate Powers as Powers in Trust, Harv L Rev 44 (1931) pp 1049–1074; Berle AA, For Whom are Corporate Managers Trustees? Harv L Rev 45 (1932) pp 1365–1372.

provide a "national social service" and management should further the interests of the firm.[28]

The duty to further the interests of not only the company but even the society at large became mandatory for large German companies by virtue of the Aktiengesetz of 1937 which required the two boards of the AG to "direct the company in accordance with the requirements of the enterprise and its working force and the common benefit to the people and the empire".[29]

Since 1965, however, all board members of large German companies have had a duty to act in the interests of *the firm* (Unternehmensinteresse, see below)[30] and not in the interests of stakeholders or society as a whole.

Once again, the stakeholder approach emerged as an alternative in German *Unternehmensrecht* ("enterprise law"). Enterprise law can be described as a theoretical and political programme the purpose of which was to recognise the important role of the workforce and to empower employees in the governance of companies,[31] or as an area of law that is applied to companies but seeks to further interests that fall outside the classic company law "triangle" of shareholders, corporate bodies, and creditors.[32] However, the main rule is that the board must act in the interests of the firm.[33] This is reflected even in the German Corporate Governance Code.[34]

After the Second World War, the work of Berle and Means influenced *théorie institutionelle de l'enterprise* (the institutional theory of the firm) in France. The main representatives of the theory are Durand and Ripert. According to this theory,

[28] See Dodd EM, For Whom are Corporate Managers Trustees? Harv L Rev 45 (1932) pp 1145–1163; Dodd EM, Is Effective Enforcement of the Fiduciary Duties of Corporate Managers Practicable? University of Chicago Law Review 2 (1935) pp 194–207. See also Riechers A, *op cit*, pp 182–183.

[29] § 70(1) AktG 1937: "... wie das Wohl des Betriebs und seiner Gefolgschaft und der gemeine Nutzen von Volk und Reich es fordern".

[30] § 93(1) AktG. See, for example, Teubner G, Corporate Fiduciary Duties and Their Beneficiaries. In: Hopt K, Teubner G, Corporate Governance and Directors' Liabilities. de Gruyter, Berlin (1994) pp 149–177; Mäntysaari P, Comparative Corporate Governance. Springer, Berlin Heidelberg (2005) p 340.

[31] See Ballerstedt K, GmbH-Reform, Mitbestimmung, Unternehmensrecht, ZHR 135 (1971) pp 479–510; Raiser T, The Theory of Enterprise Law in the Federal Republic of Germany, Am J Comp L 36(1) (1988) pp 111–129; Klages P, Die Wiederentdeckung schlafender Alternative in der Rechtslehre, Berliner Debatte Initial 18 (2007) pp 75–82.

[32] Zimmer D, Internationales Gesellschaftsrecht. Schriftenreihe Recht der Internationalen Wirtschaft. Band 50. Verlag Recht und Wirtschaft GmbH, Heidelberg (1996), Zweiter Teil A pp 131–136.

[33] BGHZ 64, 325, 329 = NJW 1975, 1412 (Bayer); BVerfGE 50, 290 = NJW 1979, 833. See nevertheless the discussion about the KonTraG.

[34] Section 4.1.1 of the German Corporate Governance Code: "The Management Board is responsible for independently managing the enterprise in the interest of the enterprise, thus taking into account the interests of the shareholders, its employees and other stakeholders, with the objective of sustainable creation of value."

"the firm is autonomous in relation to its members, and the objective defined by its management must be to satisfy the general interest" (Aglietta and Rebérioux 2005).[35]

The approach that management should run the corporation in the public interest is also called "managerialism" (see above).[36] This term is slightly misleading, since the fact that managers customarily take into account various interests in the normal course of business does not necessarily mean that managers would run the corporation in the public interest.

The emergence of managerial theories of the firm after the Second World War happened roughly at the same time as the move from the classical growth theory of political economy (that stressed the importance of the accumulation of capital; Smith 1776) to the neo-classical growth model (that stressed the role of technological change; Solow 1957).

The neo-classical theory was later followed by the new growth theory or the endogenous growth theory (that stresses the importance of human capital; Romer 1986). The recognition of the importance of human capital has so far had a relatively minor impact on mainstream corporate governance theory,[37] but it played an important role in Unternehmensrecht even before the emergence of the new growth theory.

Variations of the stakeholder approach have contributed to management literature in recent years. They range from "putting employees first" to "customer-driven capitalism".[38] In economics, the stakeholder approach has influenced Tirole (2001) who defines corporate governance as "the design of institutions that induce or force management to internalize the welfare of stakeholders".[39] Generally,

---

[35] See Aglietta M, Rebérioux A, Corporate Governance Adrift. A Critique of Shareholder Value. Edward Elgar, Cheltenham (UK) Northampton (Mass.) (2005) pp 41–43.

[36] Eisenberg MA, The Structure of the Corporation. Beard Books, Washington, D.C. (1976) pp 24–25. In the Nordic area, examples of studies that have adopted a similar approach include Tolonen JP, Der allgemeine Erklärungshintergrund der wirtschaftlichen Ordnung und seine Anwendung auf das Aktiengesellschaftsrecht. Rechtsvergleichende Untersuchung. Suomalainen Tiedeakatemia, Helsinki (1974) and Sjåfjell B, Towards a Sustainable European Company Law. A Normative Analysis of the Objectives of EU Law, with the Takeover Directive as a Test Case. European Company Law Series 3. Wolters Kluwer, Alphen Aan Den Rijn (2009).

[37] The importance of human capital was pointed out in Rajan RG, Zingales L, The Governance of the New Enterprise. In: Vives X (ed), Corporate Governance, Theoretical & Empirical Perspectives. Cambridge U P, Cambridge (2000) pp 201–227: "... even if an agent sells her labor, she cannot sell it irrevocably for a long period. Thus the individual cannot pledge the residual control rights over her human capital to someone else for any significant length of time through contract. Control over valuable human capital would seem then to be a greater source of power than control over physical assets since almost all control rights over it are residual, i.e., not allocable through contract."

[38] See Shareholders v stakeholders. A new idolatry, The Economist, April 2010; Martin R, The Age of Customer Capitalism, HBR 1/2010.

[39] Tirole J, Corporate Governance, Econometrica 69 (2001) p 4.

representatives of the stakeholder approach regard it as "a genre of management theory" rather than a specific theory.[40]

6.3.2.5 The Shareholder Primacy Approach

Modern theories of corporate governance are customarily based on agency theory and the set-of-contracts theory of the firm.[41] Such theories are aligned with traditional English law - and therefore also with the fiction theory of von Savigny (see above) - rather than German law. The origins of the mainstream view could already be seen in Berle (1931, 1932) and Berle and Means (1932).

According to the mainstream view, the company and the firm are basically one and the same thing: a fiction which can neither be regarded as a party nor have its own interests. The mainstream view has, for various reasons, adopted the *shareholder primacy* model.[42] Managers should thus further the interests of *investors*, in particular the interests of *shareholders* as "residual claimants" and "the most important principal". The "director primacy" model (Bainbridge 2003) is an application of the shareholder primacy model. It is designed to reflect existing US laws. Director primacy "accepts shareholder wealth maximization as the proper corporate decisionmaking norm, but rejects the notion that shareholders are entitled to either direct or indirect decisionmaking control".[43]

The following is an example of an influential modern mainstream definition of corporate governance: "Corporate governance deals with the ways in which suppliers of finance to corporations assure themselves of getting a return on their investment. How do the suppliers of finance get managers to return some of the profit to them? How do they make sure that managers do not steal the capital they supply or invest it in bad projects? How do suppliers of finance control managers?"[44] Shortly put: "Corporate governance is, to a large extent, a set of

[40] Freeman RE, Harrison JS, Wicks AC, Parmar BL, de Colle S, Stakeholder Theory. Cambridge U P, Cambridge (2010) pp 63–64.

[41] Fama EF, Agency Problems and the Theory of the Firm, J Pol Econ 88(2) (1980) pp 288–307; Fama EF, Jensen MC, Separation of Ownership and Control, J Law Econ 26 (1983) pp 301–325.

[42] Hansmann H, Kraakman R, The end of history for corporate law. In: Jeffrey N. Gordon, Mark J. Roe, Convergence and Persistence in Corporate Governance. Cambridge U P, Cambridge (2004) p 33: "There are, broadly speaking, three ways in which a model of corporate governance can come to be recognized as superior: by force of logic, by force of example, and by force of competition ... There is no longer any serious competitor to the view that corporate law should principally strive to increase long-term shareholder value."

[43] Bainbridge S, Director Primacy: The Means and Ends of Corporate Governance, Northw U L Rev 97 (2003) p 563.

[44] Shleifer A, Vishny RW, A Survey of Corporate Governance, J Fin 52(2) (1997) p 737.

mechanisms through which outside investors protect themselves against expropriation by the insiders."[45]

However, the shareholder primary approach fails to give sufficient guidance as it does not solve the problem of conflicting intrests and relies on too many fictions (see below).

Transaction cost economics has not brought about any change. In transaction cost economics, potential principals include shareholders and other constituencies of the firm.[46]

6.3.3 The Problem of Conflicting Interests

Both the stakeholder approach and shareholder primacy give rise to two problems: How can one deal with conflicting interests? How can one combine the chosen approach with separate legal personality? We can start with the Formes.

Stakeholder approach. If the stakeholder approach means that the board and managers are asked to serve many masters with conflicting interests, it fails to provide sufficient guidance.

This seems to be the case in corporate governance research. There are different categories of stakeholders. Freeman (1984) distinguishes between the following strategies on the basis of the number of stakeholder categories: the specific stakeholder strategy; the stockholder strategy; the utilitarian strategy; the Rawlsian strategy; and the social harmony strategy.[47] The specific stakeholder strategy[48] and the stockholder strategy[49] are probably the most popular in business practice. However, the utilitarian strategy seems to predominate in corporate governance and corporate law research.[50] The utilitarian strategy does not give sufficient guidance, because it fails to identify the overriding objective of the firm, the relevant stakeholders, the stakeholders' relevant interests, and their relative weight.

One can illustrate this problem with the characteristics of the modern stakeholder approach mentioned by a British scholar:[51]

---

[45] La Porta R, Lopez-de-Silanes F, Shleifer A, Vishny RW, Investor protection and corporate governance, J Fin Econ 58 (2000) p 4.

[46] See Williamson OE, The Economic Institutions of Capitalism. Free Press, New York (1985) pp 298–300.

[47] *Ibid*, p 102.

[48] *Ibid*, p 102: "Specific Stakeholder Strategy. Maximize benefits to one or a small set of stakeholders."

[49] *Ibid*, p 102: "Stockholder Strategy. Maximize benefits to stockholders. Maximize benefits to 'financial stakeholders'".

[50] *Ibid*, pp 102–105: "Utilitarian Strategy: Maximize benefits to all stakeholders (greatest good for greatest number). Maximize average welfare level of all stakeholders. Maximize benefits to society."

[51] Keay A, Moving Towards Stakeholderism? Constituency Statutes, Enlightened Shareholder Value, and More: Much Ado About Little? EBLR 2011 pp 6–7.

- It is fundamental to stakeholding that organisations are to be managed for the benefit of ... all stakeholders
- All those who contribute critical resources to the firm should benefit
- The company works towards creation of value for all stakeholders
- The duty of managers is to create optimal value for all social actors who might be regarded as parties who can affect, or are affected by, a company's decisions
- It is necessary for the managers ... when making decisions to have the aim of making the company a place where stakeholder interests can be maximised in due course
- The purpose of the company is that it is a vehicle to serve in such a way as to co-ordinate the interests of stakeholders
- It is necessary for the managers to balance the interests of all stakeholders in coming to any decision
- Organisations are to be managed ... accountable to all stakeholders

The example shows that it remains unclear what interests are regarded as stakeholder interests. As a result, it is unclear what exactly should be coordinated, balanced, and maximised, to whom exactly organisations should be accountable, and how one should deal with conflicting interests. Moreover, managers cannot be expected to have enough information about external stakeholder interests for coordination and balancing purposes, and one may ask why a stakeholder would delegate the coordination and balancing of interests to managers rather than try to obtain the best possible bargain. In addition, maximisation is not a feasible goal for corporate decision-making,[52] and there is a measurement problem.[53]

Shareholder primacy. The stakeholder approach fails to provide sufficient guidance, but the same can be said of the shareholder primacy approach.

First, real shareholders can have different subjective interests. All real shareholders of the same company do not share the same subjective interests. Real shareholders of different companies can have different subjective interests.

Second, decisions on corporate strategy and decisions made in the course of operations management and financial management would not make any sense without taking into account the interests of stakeholders. They will thus require the balancing of many aspects.

Third, as the subjective interests of real shareholders can vary, there can be a conflict between the interests of different real shareholders, or between the interests of some shareholders and what is regarded as rational and reasonable in the context of corporate strategy, operations management, and financial management. For example, the phenomenon that financial investors prefer short-term profits while managers can take a long-term view was known already in the latter half of the 19th century when American railroad companies were financed by outside equity

[52] See already Alchian AA, Uncertainty, Evolution, and Economic Theory, J Pol Econ 58 (1950) p 213.

[53] Tirole J, Corporate Governance, Econometrica 69 (2001) pp 25–26.

investors.[54] Moreover, the aggressive use of the target's assets in the funding of corporate takeovers was common practice already in the 1980s.[55] It can increase the firm's debts and risk-level and reduce its long-term survival prospects.

Fourth, the interests of some shareholders can be illegal or contrary to fundamental societal values, or a shareholder may be looking for non-pecuniary private benefits that are unreasonable[56] rather than the reasonable pecuniary benefits of a shareholder in its capacity as shareholder.

6.3.4 *The Problem of Separate Legal Personality*

From a legal perspective, the chosen approach should be compatible with the separate legal personality of corporations. Separate legal personality means that the company is not identified with its shareholders or any third party. It is a fundamental rule of company law that the main duties of employees, sub-board managers, and board members are owed to the company as the legal person and enforceable by the company itself.[57] No other party is regarded as the appropriate direct beneficiary of their main duties; many other parties can nevertheless benefit indirectly.

---

[54] Bratton WW, The New Economic Theory of the Firm: Critical Perspectives from History, Stanford L Rev 41 (1989) p 1486 (on American railroad companies that were financed by outside equity investors).

[55] *Ibid*, pp 1520–1521.

[56] An example of non-pecuniary private benefits that are *unreasonable* (and bad) is when a foreign country buys a block of shares in a company in order to force the company to further the country's foreign policy interests. An example of non-pecuniary private benefits that are *reasonable* (and good) is when a wealthy investor supports a loss-making book publisher or football club for the pleasure of it.

[57] See, for example, Section 1 of Chapter 29 of the Swedish Company Act; Section 8 of Chapter 1 and Section 1 of Chapter 22 of the Finnish Company Act; § 93(1) of the German Aktiengesetz; Salomon v A Salomon & Co Limited [1897] AC 22 (House of Lords) (separate corporate personality, a company is not identified with its shareholders); Re Smith & Fawcett Ltd [1942] Ch 304, [1942] 1 All ER 1032 (directors must exercise their powers "bona fide in the interests of the company" and "not for any collateral purpose"). The business judgment rule applied in the US and many other countries means that a court "will not substitute its own notions of what is or is not sound business judgment" [Aronson v. Lewis, 473 A.2d 805, 812 (Delaware Supreme Court 1984)] if "the directors of a corporation acted on an informed basis, in good faith and in the honest belief that the action taken was in the best interests of the company" [Sinclair Oil Corp. v. Levien, 280 A.2d 717, 720 (Delaware Supreme Court 1971)].

6.3.5 Previous Attempts to Solve the Problems

There have been various attempts to solve these problems in the past. They include: using fictive rather than real circumstances; defining "the company" in new ways to suit the chosen approach; the Entity Maximisation and Sustainability Model; and diluting the stakeholder approach.

Fictions. The shareholder primacy model tries to deal with the problem of conflicting interests by fictions.

To begin with, all shareholders can be assumed to have just one goal in any company if the shareholders are *fictive* rather than real and the goal is a *fictive* one rather than real. In some cases, these fictive shareholders are assumed to be long-term investors that take a long-term view. In other cases (takeovers), they are assumed to be short-term investors with a short-term view. (In fact, the most vocal shareholders in the context of large takeovers are investment funds with very short-term interests.). The representatives of the shareholder primacy model do not regard this kind of variation as a problem although it makes one wonder whether the fictive shareholders have a long-term or short-term perspective.

What remains then is the need to align the shareholder primacy model with the separate legal personality of corporations. The customary way to achieve this result is to assume that the fictive interests of those fictive shareholders are really the interests of the company as well or that there are no collective corporate interests.[58]

These two shareholder primacy related approaches lead to obvious problems: they are based on several fictions; they do not reflect the interests of real shareholders and the different circumstances of real companies; they require the identification of the company with its shareholders contrary to the principle of separate legal personality; and the identification is proposed to work just one way (benefits) but not the other (responsibilities, liability).

Entity Maximisation and Sustainability Model. The Entity Maximisation and Sustainability Model (EMS) proposed by Keay (2008) is another attempt to address the problems. As the model's name implies, it has two core elements: "First, there is a commitment to maximise the entity. This involves, inter alia, enhancing the company's wealth . . . The second part is to sustain the company as a going concern, that is, to ensure its survival and more. An important aspect of the model is that there is focus on the company as an entity or enterprise, that is the company is an institution in its own right."[59] Influenced by English law, this model does not distinguish between the legal entity and the firm.

It is hard to argue against sustainability (it is accepted as a fundamental goal below). However, there are three problems with EMS.

---

[58] See also Bratton WW, *op cit*, p 1499: "Since no cognizable corporate collectivity appears amidst the nexus of contracts, no tension arises between collective and individual interests."

[59] Keay A, Ascertaining The Corporate Objective: An Entity Maximisation and Sustainability Model, MLR 71(5) (2008) p 679, citing Suojanen W, Accounting Theory and the Large Corporation, Acc Rev 29 (1954) pp 391, 393.

The first is the choice of the legal entity as the principal. The legal entity can change although the identity of the firm remains the same.[60] For example, a Finnish parent company listed in Helsinki (say, Nokia) can functionally be replaced by an American parent company listed in New York without the group losing its identity. (Nokia would still be a firm that makes and sells mobile phones.) Moreover, a model focusing on the maximisation and sustainability of a legal entity becomes unworkable in quite normal structural transactions such as mergers, re-incorporations, takeovers, or other transactions in which at least one legal entity ceases to exist or is reduced in size, and it does not explain the widespread popularity of corporate groups (subsidiaries) and business networks (outsourcing, the make or buy decision).

The second is its behavioural assumption: the maximising orientation.[61] How much is the maximum? Neither entity maximisation nor profit maximisation are feasible goals for corporate decision-making.[62] This is reflected in corporate laws which generally do not require profit maximisation.[63]

The third problem relates to the choice of two goals: maximisation and sustainability. Which goal should prevail? Keay (2008) suggests that EMS really has one overall goal and that maximisation and sustainability are complementary.[64] It should therefore be possible to identify a higher level goal (such a goal will be proposed below).

Dilution of the stakeholder approach. The stakeholder approach exists even in a diluted form. If the stakeholder approach means that the board and managers are asked to take into account the interests of stakeholders and any other circumstances to the extent that it is in the interests of the company to do so, there is no conflict between the stakeholder approach and company law. This is the position of company law as well.

There are similar approaches in management science. In strategic management, one of the solutions is to: regard the survival of the firm as the firm's most important objective; and choose a more specific enterprise strategy that focuses on the interests of a certain group of stakeholders as a way to improve the survival chances of the firm (Freeman 1984).[65] The concept of "shared value" (Porter and Kramer 2011) is an example of a similar diluted stakeholder approach.

---

[60] See Mäntysaari P, The Law of Corporate Finance. Volume I. Springer, Berlin Heidelberg (2010) p 86.

[61] Williamson OE, The Economic Institutions of Capitalism. Free Press, New York (1985) p 44: "Three levels of rationality are usefully distinguished. The strong for contemplates maximizing. Bounded rationality is the semistrong form. The weak form is organic rationality."

[62] See already Alchian AA, Uncertainty, Evolution, and Economic Theory, J Pol Econ 58 (1950) p 213.

[63] See, for example, Bruner CM, The Enduring Ambivalence of Corporate Law, Alabama L Rev 59 (2008) pp 1400, 1402–1403, 1407, 1420, and 1425.

[64] See nevertheless Keay A, Ascertaining the Corporate Objective: An Entity Maximisation and Sustainability Model, MLR 71(5) (2008) p 687.

[65] Freeman RE, Strategic Management. A Stakeholder Approach. Cambridge U P, Cambridge (originally published in 1984) p 107.

6.3.6 The Interests of the Firm as a Way to Solve the Problems

6.3.6.1 General Remarks

Focusing on the interests of the firm rather than the interests of shareholders or stakeholders would be an alternative way to deal with conflicting interests and separate legal personality. For various reasons, this is the most important way from a legal perspective. We can start with the bigger picture.

6.3.6.2 Why Laws Further the Interests of the Firm

The position of traditional company law has developed over a long period of time. Since company law is normative, company representatives must apply it or risk legal sanctions. It has, therefore, been tested in practice, and it has formed the business practices of firms in the West. Corporate strategy, operations management, financial management, and corporate risk management would not have developed as they have without being compatible with the legal regulation of companies.

Now, after the industrial revolution, capitalistic firms were recognised as the most important producers of goods and the most important market participants in the West. [66] In economics, this gave reason to define the firm and the factors that explain their existence (Chap. 2). For example, the firm could be defined by authority,[67] as an organisational construction or governance structure[68] whose members can be motivated in various ways,[69] or as a "team" whose members act from self-interest but realise that their destinies depend to some extent on the survival of the team in its competition with other teams.[70]

If firms exist and are capable of rational actions as firms, one can assume that they generally try to survive.[71] They "struggle for existence" by adapting to the

[66] Weber M, Wirtschaft und Gesellschaft. Grundriss der verstehenden Soziologie (1922), Erster Teil, Kapitel II, § 31: "Nur der Okzident kennt rationale kapitalistische Betriebe ... Also: die kapitalistische Form der formal rein voluntaristischen Organisation der Arbeit als typische und herrschende Form der Bedarfsdeckung breiter Massen ..." See Marx K, Das Kapital (1872).

[67] Coase RH, The Nature of the Firm, Economica, New Series 4(16) (1937) pp 388–389.

[68] Williamson OE, The Economic Institutions of Capitalism. Free Press, New York (1985).

[69] Simon HA, Organizations and Markets, J Econ Persp 5(2) (1972) p 30. For an application in company law, see Eisenberg MA, The Structure of the Corporation. Beard Books, Washington, D.C. (1976) pp 30–31.

[70] Alchian AA, Demsetz H, Production, Information Costs, and Economic Organization, Am Econ Rev 62 (1972) pp 777–795; Jensen MC, Meckling WH, Theory of the Firm: Managerial Behavior, Agency Costs and Ownership Structure, J Fin Econ 3 (1976) pp 305–360.

[71] Alchian AA, Uncertainty, Evolution, and Economic Theory, J Pol Econ 58 (1950) pp 211–221. The survival of organisations is also studied in organisational theory. See its classics Barnard CI, The Functions of the Executive. Harv U P, Cambridge, Mass. (1938) pp 60–61; Thompson JD, Organizations in Action: Social Science Bases of Administration. McGraw-Hill, New York (1967) p 13 (the central problem of complex organisations is one of coping with uncertainty).

competitive environment and other circumstances.[72] One can therefore say that strategic choices, operations management ("engineering"), financial management ("financial engineering"), and corporate risk management are ways to adapt to external and internal circumstances for the purpose of improving the firm's survival chances in a competitive environment.

States recognise the existence, importance, and diversity of firms and the market economy. For example, states have facilitated the survival and growth of firms by adopting rules on business forms. Firms can choose from a pool of legally recognised business forms. Some cannot be separated from the persons behind the business venture (sole traders, partnerships). Others have separate legal personality and are artificial persons not owned by anyone (foundations, co-operatives, corporations).

The existence of such artificial persons makes it necessary to adopt three kinds of rules: rules made necessary by separate legal personality, rules made necessary by the firm having an organisation (or because the firm is an organisational structure), and rules made necessary by the fact that the legal organisation and the real organisation can be different.[73]

Such issues must be addressed in some way or another. However, it is not sufficient to try to address them in a "mathematically rational" way. There are two preliminary questions which can only be answered according to what is regarded as reasonable. First, in whose interests should the questions be answered? There must be a "principal". Second, it must be defined what the interests of the principal are.

It is suggested here that traditional company law is based on the choice of the firm as the principal. The most fundamental interest of the firm is its own survival.[74]

This is reflected in the most fundamental rules of traditional company law such as separate legal personality, asset partitioning, separation of functions, and rules that set out to whom duties are owed. In the legal regulation of companies, it is customary to provide that the duties of employees, sub-board managers, and board members are owed to the legal person as the carrier of the firm.

---

[72] For the struggle for existence, see Darwin C, The Origin of Species (1859).

[73] See Mäntysaari P, The Law of Corporate Finance. Volume I. Springer, Berlin Heidelberg (2010), Chapter 8.

[74] Compare Dooley MP, Two Models of Corporate Governance, Bus Law 47 (1991–1992) p 463 distinguishing between the "Authority Model" and the "Responsibility Model". At p 463, Dooley mentions the survival of the firm as an objective: "It should be readily apparent that neither Model exists in pristine form in the real world. Standing alone, neither Model could provide a sensible guide to the governance of firm-organized economic activity because each seeks to achieve a distinct and separate value that is essential to the survival of any firm. Accordingly, any feasible governance system must and does contain elements of both Models, and it is only one's assessment of which value seems to predominate in a given system that justifies categorizing the system as primarily concerned with Authority or Responsibility." At p 466, Dooley nevertheless argues that "decisions are to be made to the benefit the interests of the residual claimants".

6.3.6.3 German Law as an Example

German law provides the clearest example of this approach. The company is regarded as the carrier of the firm (Unternehmensträger). The duties of the board members of an AG are owed to *the company*.[75] All board members have a duty to act in the interests of *the firm* (Unternehmensinteresse). The most basic interests of the firm can be summarised as its own survival.[76] The main rule is that sanctions for the breach of such duties are enforced by the company.[77]

This view has been part of German law since 1965. When the Aktiengesetz of 1937 was replaced by the Aktiengesetz of 1965, the previous requirement to direct the company in accordance with the common benefit to the people and the empire was abolished.[78] The requirement to act in the interests of the firm remained,[79] complemented by a general duty under the German constitution to use property rights even in the public interest.[80]

In Germany, this manner of solving the problems is understandable not only in the light of the importance of firms but also in the light of the realist theory of von Gierke (according to which a company is treated as a person) and the doctrine of the firm in itself or Unternehmen an sich (which suggested that the firm exists and is not the same thing as any particular individual).[81] One can also find other reasons.[82]

---

[75] § 76(1) AktG: "Der Vorstand hat unter eigener Verantwortung die Gesellschaft zu leiten." § 93 (2) AktG: "Vorstandsmitglieder, die ihre Pflichten verletzen, sind der Gesellschaft zum Ersatz des daraus entstehenden Schadens als Gesamtschuldner verpflichtet . . ."

[76] Kuhner C, Unternehmensinteresse vs. Shareholder Value als Leitmaxime kapitalmarktorienterter Aktiengesellschaften, ZGR 2/2004 pp 249–250, citing Raiser T, Unternehmensrecht als Gegenstand juristischer Grundlagenforschung, Festschrift Potthoff. Nomos, Baden-Baden (1989) pp 31–45.

[77] See § 147 AktG and § 112 AktG.

[78] See, for example, Flume W, Allgemeiner Teil des Bürgerlichen Rechts, Erster Band. Zweiter Teil, Springer, Berlin Heidelberg (1983) § 2 IV.

[79] § 93(1) AktG. See, for example, Teubner G, Corporate Fiduciary Duties and Their Beneficiaries. In: Hopt K, Teubner G, Corporate Governance and Directors' Liabilities. de Gruyter, Berlin (1994) pp 149–177; Kuhner C, Unternehmensinteresse vs. Shareholder Value als Leitmaxime kapitalmarktorienterter Aktiengesellschaften, ZGR 2/2004 pp 245–248; Mäntysaari P, Comparative Corporate Governance. Springer, Berlin Heidelberg (2005) p 340.

[80] Art 14(2) GG: "Eigentum verpflichtet. Sein Gebrauch soll zugleich dem Wohle der Allgemeinheit dienen."

[81] See Riechers A, *op cit*, pp 53–55.

[82] Kuhner C, Unternehmensinteresse vs. Shareholder Value als Leitmaxime kapitalmarktorienterter Aktiengesellschaften, ZGR 2/2004 p 247: Hegenialism or idealistic tendencies in German legal culture, the early introduction of worker co-determination in the Weimar republic, the secondary role of shareholders' capital as a source of funding, the national socialist ideology, and corporative tendencies.

6.3.6.4 Other Jurisdictions

Because of the importance and diversity of firms, laws are designed to further the interests of firms even in other countries.

Because of the *importance* of firms, the problem of potentially conflicting interests has traditionally been solved in similar ways. The main duties of a company's board members are owed to the company as the carrier of the firm, and they are enforceable by the company. For example, the position of English common law is that a company is not identified with its shareholders (separate corporate personality)[83] and that directors must exercise their powers "bona fide in the interests of the company" and "not for any collateral purpose".[84]

Because of the *diversity* of firms and the market economy, the main rule is that the board must be given plenty of discretion. Board members' general duty of care owed to the company as the carrier of the firm[85] is qualified by the "business judgment rule" or similar rules. In the US, the business judgment rule means that a court "will not substitute its own notions of what is or is not sound business judgment"[86] if "the directors of a corporation acted on an informed basis, in good faith and in the honest belief that the action taken was in the best interests of the company".[87] There is a similar rule in Germany.[88]

Company laws do not lay down a general duty to maximise welfare, entity size, profits, or anything else, because it would not be possible to enforce such a duty in

[83] Salomon v A Salomon & Co Limited [1897] AC 22 (House of Lords).

[84] Re Smith & Fawcett Ltd [1942] Ch 304, [1942] 1 All ER 1032. There are similar rules in Nordic company laws. See, for example, § 1 of Chapter 29 of the Swedish Company Act: "En stiftare, styrelseledamot eller verkställande direktör som när han eller hon fullgör sitt uppdrag uppsåtligen eller av oaktsamhet skadar bolaget skall ersätta skadan ..." For Finnish law, see § 8 of Chapter 1 of the Finnish Company Act: "Bolagets ledning skall omsorgsfullt främja bolagets intressen." § 1 of Chapter 22: "En styrelseledamot, en förvaltningsrådsledamot och verkställande direktören skall ersätta skada som de i sitt uppdrag, i strid med den omsorgsplikt som föreskrivs i 1 kap. 8 §, uppsåtligen eller av oaktsamhet har orsakat bolaget ..."

[85] See, for example, § 1 of Chapter 29 of the Swedish Company Act: "En stiftare, styrelseledamot eller verkställande direktör som när han eller hon fullgör sitt uppdrag uppsåtligen eller av oaktsamhet skadar bolaget skall ersätta skadan ..." For Finnish law, see § 8 of Chapter 1 of the Finnish Company Act: "Bolagets ledning skall omsorgsfullt främja bolagets intressen." § 1 of Chapter 22: "En styrelseledamot, en förvaltningsrådsledamot och verkställande direktören skall ersätta skada som de i sitt uppdrag, i strid med den omsorgsplikt som föreskrivs i 1 kap. 8 §, uppsåtligen eller av oaktsamhet har orsakat bolaget ..."

[86] Aronson v. Lewis, 473 A.2d 805, 812 (Delaware Supreme Court 1984).

[87] Sinclair Oil Corp. v. Levien, 280 A.2d 717, 720 (Delaware Supreme Court 1971).

[88] § 93(1) AktG: "Die Vorstandsmitglieder haben bei ihrer Geschäftsführung die Sorgfalt eines ordentlichen und gewissenhaften Geschäftsleiters anzuwenden. Eine Pflichtverletzung liegt nicht vor, wenn das Vorstandsmitglied bei einer unternehmerischen Entscheidung vernünftigerweise annehmen durfte, auf der Grundlage angemessener Information zum Wohle der Gesellschaft zu handeln ..."

any meaningful way. However, they do recognise the central role of profitability for the survival of the firm.[89]

6.3.7 Summary

The shareholder primacy model fails to provide sufficient guidance in the event of conflicting interests. It tries to solve the problem by fictions. In addition, it is difficult to combine it with separate legal personality. The stakeholder approach fails to provide sufficient guidance unless it is diluted and means that it is permitted to take into account any interests to the extent that it is in the interests of the firm to do so. The Entity Maximisation and Sustainability model focuses too much on the legal entity (the form, a mere shell). In real life, the legal entity is always used for a purpose, and it has a function.

The newer approaches do not seem to beat traditional company law. In the legal regulation of companies, it is customary to provide that the duties of employees, sub-board managers, and board members are owed to the legal person which is the carrier of the firm. The duty to act in the interests of the company means a duty to act in the interests of the firm.

6.4 Shareholders

We can move on to the next big question, the question why there are shareholders. There is no doubt about the answer in mainstream corporate governance research. Shareholders are regarded as the most important principal and shareholder primacy as the "standard model".

But all business forms do not have shareholders with freely transferable shares. Business forms that do not have them range from partnerships and co-operatives to mutual insurance companies and foundations. Moreover, most firms are rather small family firms without freely transferable shares.

There must, therefore, be something that explains: the choice of a business form that does have shareholders; the degree of transferability of shares; and the share ownership structure. The answer can depend on the function of shareholders.

[89] Spindler G, Unternehmensinteresse als Leitlinie des Vorstandshandelns – Berücksichtigung von Arbeitnehmerinteressen und Shareholder Value. Gutachten im Auftrag der Hans-Böckler-Stiftung. Hans-Böckler-Stiftung, Düsseldorf (2008): "Einigkeit besteht darüber, dass auf jeden Fall der Bestand des Unternehmens zu sichern und für eine dauerhafte Rentabilität zu sorgen ist, was zum Teil auch als 'angemessene' Gewinnerzielung konkretisiert wird." See also section 4.1.1 of the German Corporate Governance Code.

Mainstream research is unable to properly explain the function of shareholders and why they exist in the first place. Most corporate governance research takes the existence of shareholders for granted.[90]

This is caused by two things. First, mainstream corporate governance research is mostly limited to the very small minority of firms that are large listed companies. By definition, they have shareholders with freely transferable shares. Second, the function of shareholders is irrelevant when shareholders are chosen as the principal. It is not necessary to explain the existence and function of the principal. It is necessary to explain the function of the agent.

When mainstream research does try to explain the existence and function of shareholders, it tends to use weak arguments.

First, mainstream research assumes that shareholders are "owners" of the firm.[91] Fama nevertheless (1980) finds that ownership of the firm is an irrelevant concept when the firm is regarded as a nexus of contracts.[92] From a legal perspective, separate corporate personality ensures that shareholders of a company are not owners of the firm[93] any more than bondholders can be regarded as its owners. Neither bondholders nor shareholders own the company's assets or the company itself. All they own are securities that confer certain rights to their holders. Separate legal personality explains even limited liability. If shareholders or bondholders were regarded as owners of the firm rather than holders of securities issued by the company, it would be more difficult to explain their limited liability for the company's obligations. With ownership come not just rights but even obligations.

Second, mainstream research assumes that shareholders are providers of capital. However, this does not make them unique. From a financial perspective, retained earnings are the most important source of funding, and most of the capital raised from investors is in the form of debt. From a legal perspective, buyers of existing shares do not provide any funding.[94] Moreover, capital can flow in the opposite direction. Before the recent financial crisis, the amount of capital distributed by listed companies to shareholders in the form of dividends and share buybacks tended to exceed the amount of capital that they raised from shareholders.[95]

---

[90] For example, Williamson is no exception. See Williamson OE, The Economic Institutions of Capitalism. Free Press, New York (1985) pp 274, 298 and 304–305. Neither is Bainbridge. Bainbridge S, Director Primacy: The Means and Ends of Corporate Governance, Northw U L Rev 97 (2003) p 550: "... director primacy claims that shareholders are the appropriate beneficiaries of director fiduciary duties."

[91] See already Berle AA, Means GC, *op cit*, Book Four, Chapter I.

[92] Fama EF, Agency Problems and the Theory of the Firm, J Pol Econ 88(2) (1980) p 290.

[93] See, for example, Salomon v A Salomon & Co Ltd [1897] AC 22.

[94] This was pointed out already by Berle A, Property, Production and Revolution. A Preface to the Revised Edition. In: Berle AA, Means GC, *op cit*: "The purchaser of stock does not contribute savings to an enterprise, thus enabling it to increase its plant or operations."

[95] See, for example, Ireland P, Company Law and the Myth of Shareholder Ownership, MLR 62(1) (1999) pp 54–55.

The relative weight of shareholders as actual providers of funding can depend on the business cycle of the firm (start-ups may need equity capital, and some firms may need to issue new shares in order to raise capital). However, this does not change the fact that shareholders are not the only providers of capital and that many shareholders are not providers of capital.

Third, mainstream research assumes that shareholders are "risk bearers" as residual claimants. However, the employees, creditors and business partners of failed companies can tell you that shareholders are not the only risk bearers. Shareholders are not necessarily the biggest risk bearers. The higher the leverage, the more risk is allocated to creditors, and corporate failure can generally have a bigger impact on employees than on wealthy shareholders who have diversified their holdings. One can also add that acting as a residual claimant when a company is liquidated does not really explain the role of shareholders during the life of the company. During the life of the company, shareholders do not have an automatic claim to the residual. What they do have is a claim to distributions to the extent that the company has lawfully decided to distribute funds to shareholders. This decision is typically controlled by the board.

What is left are moral or social arguments.[96] However, it would be stretching the point too far to argue that company laws were adopted in all western countries just to create a rentier class whose wealth should be maximised by everybody else. Company laws are older than the shareholder primacy model. The mainstream view of the role of shareholders is just an ideological choice.

6.5 The Board

The last of the four big questions discussed here relates to the board. According to the mainstream models, large public corporations should have a board acting as a monitoring board, that is, a board that oversees managers instead of attempting to run the business directly. This has been a mandatory statutory requirement in Germany since the Commercial Code of 1897.[97] In the US, it was recommended by Eisenberg (1976) as well as by Fama and Jensen (1983).[98]

[96] Such as those used by Berle. Berle AA, Property, Production and Revolution. A Preface to the Revised Edition. In: Berle AA, Means GC, *op cit*: "Why have stockholders? . . . Wealth unquestionably does add to an individual's capacity and range in pursuit of happiness and self-development . . . Privilege to have income and a fragment of wealth without a corresponding duty to work for it cannot be justified except on the ground that the community is better off – and not unless most members of the community share it." Generally, see also Ireland P, *op cit*, pp 32–57.

[97] § 246 HGB 1897.

[98] Eisenberg M, The Structure of the Corporation. Beard Books, Washington, D.C. (1976) p 170; Fama EF, Jensen MC, Separation of Ownership and Control, J Law Econ 26 (1983) pp 301–325.

If a large company has a unitary (one-tier) board, it is now customary to recommend or require the use of two-tier structures with committees and "independent" non-executive members acting as monitoring bodies. This can be a recommendation (many corporate governance codes recommend it) or a mandatory legal requirement (like the requirements based on the Sarbanes-Oxley Act).

However, most firms in the world are privately-owned family businesses rather than large listed firms. Not all limited-liability companies have a board (for example, the board is not mandatory for the German GmbH and the European SPE[99]), and if they do, their structures and functions may vary (there are one-tier models, two-tier models, and other board models).

A theory of corporate governance should be able to explain for what purpose it is necessary for the board to monitor management and have other functions. There are different views about what that purpose is. Moreover, a theory of corporate governance should explain why there are boards in the first place.

Shareholder primacy. The most popular starting point is the shareholder primacy model. It dominates the theoretical literature. For example, Williamson (1985) argues that "the board of directors should be regarded primarily as a governance structure safeguard between the firm and owners of equity capital and secondarily as a way by which to safeguard the contractual relation between the firm and its management".[100] Primarily, the board can be "a governance structure that holders of equity recognize as a safeguard against expropriation and egregious mismanagement".[101]

The stakeholder approach. The stakeholder approach customarily does not attempt to explain the existence of the board. One can say that the starting point of the stakeholder approach is the shareholder primacy model. The stakeholder approach (such as Ireland 1999) tries to modify it.[102] According to the "communitarian" or "progressive" school of corporate scholars, corporate law ought thus to require directors to serve not only the shareholders' interests, but also those of employees, consumers, creditors, and other corporate stakeholders.

Team production. The team production theory of Blair and Stout (1999) is a variation of the stakeholder approach theme.[103] What explains the existence of the board is that it acts as a "mediating hierarchy". According to Blair and Stout, stakeholders are "team members" who give up important rights to the legal entity. Corporate assets belong to the corporation itself. Within the corporation, control over the assets is exercised by "an internal hierarchy whose job is to coordinate the activities of the team members, allocate the resulting production, and mediate

---

[99] §§ 6 and 52 GmbHG; Article 28 of the draft SPE Regulation.

[100] Williamson OE, The Economic Institutions of Capitalism. Free Press, New York (1985) p 298.

[101] *Ibid*, p 305. For an application of this theory, see Bainbridge S, Director Primacy: The Means and Ends of Corporate Governance, Northw U L Rev 97 (2003) p 550.

[102] Ireland P, Company Law and the Myth of Shareholder Ownership, MLR 62(1) (1999) p 53.

[103] Blair MM, Stout LA, A Team Production Theory of Corporate Law, Virginia L Rev 85 (1999) pp 247–328.

disputes among team members over that allocation. At the peak of this hierarchy sits a board of directors whose authority over the use of corporate assets is virtually absolute and whose independence from individual team members … is protected by law." Blair and Stout further argue that directors should not be under direct control of either shareholders or other stakeholders.

Board-centric corporate governance. Team production is an example of board-centric corporate governance. Many mainstream corporate governance scholars have advanced theories that emphasise the board's superior decision-making capacities.[104]

On the other hand, their analysis tends to be limited to large US companies with a dispersed share ownership structure (and exclude companies that have an entrepreneur-manager-shareholder or another kind of controlling shareholder) and the board has superior information about relatively few issues in such companies (people responsible for the day-to-day management of the firm tend to have more information than a body that convenes a few times a year).

According to one extreme approach, the board should, therefore, act as a monitoring board that appoints and removes the chief executive but should not do much else.[105] The opposite approach could be to regard the board as the nexus of all contracts, "a sui generis body that hires all of the factors of production necessary for the corporation to conduct its business and affairs".[106]

Individual directors. It is also customary to study board composition and the function of different categories of board members. For example, non-executive board members fulfil both control and service functions according to current theory (Shleifer and Vishny 1997; Becht et al. 2003; Tirole 2006; Adams et al. 2010). The function of different categories of board members should nevertheless reflect the function of the board as a whole.

6.6 Summary

The customary research approaches fail to answer the most fundamental corporate governance questions or answer them only partly. Of the shareholder primacy approach and the stakeholder approach, the former is particularly problematic from a legal perspective, because it fails to recognise separate corporate personality. The shareholder primacy approach fails to give sufficient guidance in real

104 For an overview, see Bruner CM, The Enduring Ambivalence of Corporate Law, Alabama L Rev 59 (2008) pp 1396–1405.

105 For example, Eisenberg argues that the main function of the board of a publicly-held corporation is the selection and removal of the chief executive. Eisenberg MA, The Structure of the Corporation. Beard Books, Washington, D.C. (1976) pp 162–170.

106 Bainbridge S, The New Corporate Governance in Theory and Practice. OUP, Oxford (2008) p 24.

corporate practice, because it is both too rigid and based on too many fictions. The problem with the Entity Maximisation and Sustainability Model is that it focuses on the legal entity and the form rather than the firm and the function. Tested in business practice over a long period of time, traditional company law gives firms enough flexibility to adapt to changes in the market and other circumstances. Whereas traditional company law is not a theory of corporate governance itself, a theory of corporate governance could help to explain its contents. This is what we will try to study in the following two chapters.

Chapter 7
Theory of Corporate Governance: Proposed Legal Theory

7.1 Introduction

Because of the failings of the mainstream approaches, there is room for a new legal corporate governance theory. The proposed theory is an application of Management-based Commercial Law (MBCL) and defines the law of corporate governance as a functional area of law and a branch of MBCL.[1] Unlike most corporate governance theories, the proposed theory is not limited to listed limited-liability companies.[2] It can be applied to all forms of commercial cooperation that are sufficiently ring-fenced and self-contained.

Context. One can identify certain issues that must be addressed in the context of corporate governance.

Some issues can be identified in a "mathematically-rational" way (Zweckrationalität), that is, by the force of logic alone. In the context of corporate governance, it is necessary to address issues caused by three things. The first is the existence of a *legal entity*, that is, a legal institution facilitating a ring-fenced and self-contained organisation. The firm will need a business form in order to operate. Typically, the business form is a legal entity and an artificial person. The second is the existence of an *organisation*. These two aspects are reflected already in early legal theories of corporations (Sect. 5.2). In addition, there may be a difference

[1] See Fleischer H, Gesellschafts- und Kapitalmarktrecht als wissenschaftliche Disziplin – Das Proprium der Rechtswissenschaft'. In: Engel C, Schön W (eds), *op cit*, p 50 (where corporate governance is identified as a functional branch of law); Mäntysaari P, Comparative Corporate Governance. Springer, Berlin Heidelberg (2005) pp 16 and 30 (where it is discussed from a functional perspective in the context of comparative law); Mäntysaari P, The Law of Corporate Finance. Volume I. Springer, Berlin Heidelberg (2010) pp 1 and 165 (where it is defined functionally).

[2] For example, Bainbridge's director primacy model is limited to large US corporations with a dispersed share ownership structure. Bainbridge S, The New Corporate Governance in Theory and Practice. OUP, Oxford (2008) pp 12–13.

P. Mäntysaari, *Organising the Firm*,
DOI 10.1007/978-3-642-22197-2_7, © Springer-Verlag Berlin Heidelberg 2012

between the firm's legal form and its *real organisation*. These issues raise various questions which will have to be answered in some way or another.[3]

However, one cannot provide answers to such questions without deciding in whose interests they should be answered and what the interests are. One must therefore *choose the principal* and *determine the interests* of the principal. These choices cannot be made in a "mathematically-rational" way. They require the use of another form of rationality, that is, rationality as reasonableness (Wertrationalität). This means that they are more political.

Definition. One can, therefore, define the law of corporate governance as a functional area of law that focuses on the study of the use of legal tools and practices for the management of issues caused by the existence of legal entities and organisations. One can distinguish between three levels of questions: What must be addressed? In whose interests should it be done? What are the interests?[4]

7.2 First Level Questions

There are certain questions that must be addressed in the context of corporate governance. First, there are questions caused by two fundamental matters. The firm will need a business form in order to operate. Typically, the business form is a *legal entity* and an artificial person. The firm will also need an *organisation*. These two fundamental matters raise various questions which will have to be answered in some way or another[5] (for example, according to the principles of self-enforcing governance models discussed in Chap. 8, according to the principles of governance models that foster innovation discussed in Chap. 9, and/or the principles of organisational design discussed in Sect. 8.1).

Legal entity. There are particular questions that must be answered somehow in all artificial persons: small privately-owned limited-liability companies, NGOs, co-operatives, and other artificial persons.

---

[3] Mäntysaari P, Comparative Corporate Governance. Springer, Berlin Heidelberg (2005) pp 16 and 30; Mäntysaari P, The Law of Corporate Finance. Volume I. Springer, Berlin Heidelberg (2010) pp 165–174.

[4] For previous models, see Bainbridge S, Director Primacy: The Means and Ends of Corporate Governance, Northw U L Rev 97 (2003) pp 549–550: "Essentially, all of [the previous] models are ways of thinking about the means and ends of corporate governance. They strive to answer two basic sets of questions: (1) as to the means of corporate governance, who holds ultimate decisionmaking power? and (2) as to the ends of corporate governance, whose interests should prevail? When the ultimate decisionmaker is presented with a zero-sum game, in which it must prefer the interests of one constituency class over those of all others, which constituency wins?"

[5] See Mäntysaari P, Comparative Corporate Governance. Springer, Berlin Heidelberg (2005) pp 16, 30; Mäntysaari P, The Law of Corporate Finance. Volume I. Springer, Berlin Heidelberg (2010) p 165–174.

- To whom do assets linked to the entity belong? Some form of "asset partitioning" is necessary. It is necessary to designate a separate pool of assets that are associated with the entity, and that are distinct from the personal assets of the entity's shareholders, if any, and managers. The second component of asset partitioning is the assignment of rights in this distinct pool of assets (Hansmann and Kraakman 2000; Fleischer 2004).[6]
- Who is to be regarded as acting as or on behalf of the entity? An artificial person cannot act on its own in the physical sense.
- How should the persons acting as or on behalf of the entity act? It may be necessary to make these persons act in a certain way.
- How should the various stakeholders act? It may also be necessary to make stakeholders act in a certain way. Even their behaviour must be modified. There must be rules telling stakeholders what to do.
- How are these persons and stakeholders motivated? The self-interest of all these parties may not always lead them to act in the desired way. The entity stakeholders and people acting as or on behalf of the entity must be given incentives.

Organisation. Various corporate governance tools and practices are necessary because an artificial person has an organisation:[7]

- How is power allocated?[8]
- How is risk allocated?
- How is information produced, distributed, and disclosed?

Legal organisation v real organisation. The legal organisation of the firm is not necessarily the same as its real or relational organisation.[9] This raises additional questions:

- How are the questions addressed in corporate groups and networks? For example, a large firm customarily uses a fleet of legal entities rather than just one legal

[6] See Hansmann H, Kraakman R, The Essential Role of Organizational Law, Yale L J 110 (2000) pp 392–393; Fleischer H, Gesetz und Vertrag als alternative Problemlösungsmodelle im Gesellschaftsrecht, ZHR 168 (2004) p 679.

[7] Mäntysaari P, Comparative Corporate Governance. Springer, Berlin Heidelberg (2005) p 30; Mäntysaari P, The Law of Corporate Finance. Volume I. Springer, Berlin Heidelberg (2010) p 167.

[8] Bainbrige distinguishes between "shareholder primacy" (here a first level question) and "shareholder value maximization" (here a second and third level question). Bainbridge S, Director Primacy: The Means and Ends of Corporate Governance, Northw U L Rev 97 (2003) p 574: "Although often used interchangeably, the terms 'shareholder primacy' and 'shareholder wealth maximization' express distinct concepts. As we have seen, shareholder primacy encompasses a decisionmaking model vesting ultimate control in the shareholders. In contrast, the narrower concept of shareholder wealth maximization charges directors with managing the corporation so as to maximize shareholder wealth, but without prescribing any particular model of corporate decisionmaking."

[9] See, for example Aoki M, Toward a Comparative Institutional Analysis. The MIT Press, Cambridge, Mass. (2001) pp 116–117 and 222.

entity. A large firm can use a combination of different types of legal entities and contracts. A private equity firm can choose one of many available business forms (for example, a partnership, a limited partnership, a privately-held limited-liability company, or a listed limited-liability company) for its own management, pool its own and investors' assets in funds that are limited partnerships, use special purpose vehicles owned by the fund when making business acquisitions, and limit its own liability by using particular limited-liability companies as vehicles for its own investments in the fund as well as for the management services it provides to the fund and the companies acquired by the fund.
- How are the legal organisation and the real organisation different?

7.3 The Second Level Question

The first level questions can be identified rationally (Zweckrationalität). However, they cannot be answered without choices that are regarded as reasonable (Wertrationalität). It is necessary to determine *whose interests* one should further when answering the first level questions (Mäntysaari 2010a).[10] This means that it is necessary to choose the *principal*. There are different views about who should reasonably be chosen as the principal.

According to the shareholder primacy model and the mainstream view, shareholders are the most important principal. According to the stakeholder approach (communitarian models, die Lehre vom Unternehmen an sich, team production), shareholders are not the only principal; even other stakeholders can be principals.

Both models are nevertheless problematic. There are artificial persons that do not have shareholders in any meaningful sense. If the artificial person is a limited-liability company that does have shareholders, its real shareholders may have different and conflicting interests. Some real shareholders may have interests that are not only in conflict with the interests of other shareholders but also with the interests of the firm. One could circumvent this problem by choosing fictive shareholders as the principal. For example, one could assume that all shareholders of the company are long-term investors whose interests are perfectly aligned. However, fictive shareholders do not exist; in real life, it is necessary to deal with the real interests of real shareholders. Choosing other stakeholders as additional principals would make it impossible to determine whose interests should prevail and why.

It seems reasonable to choose the firm itself as principal. This view can be aligned with traditional company law (Sect. 6.3) and leaves just one main master. Accordingly, there should be a duty to act in the interests of the company as the

[10] Mäntysaari P, The Law of Corporate Finance. Volume I. Springer, Berlin Heidelberg (2010) p 169.

carrier of the firm that is, a duty to act in the interests of the firm owed to the company. This would mean a duty to protect the firm against all stakeholders.[11]

If the firm is the principal, all stakeholders – managers, board members, creditors, shareholders, contract parties, the state – can be regarded as its agents.

7.4 The Third Level Question

The third level question is *how to define the interests* of the principal. Of course, the interests depend on who is chosen as the principal.

According to the mainstream view, the interests of the principal (shareholders) can be defined as wealth maximisation. The stakeholder approach makes it more difficult to define the interests, as there are various kinds of principals.[12]

If the hypothetical firm can be assumed to have interests, its most basic interest is its own *long-term survival* in a competitive environment (Sects. 4.2 and 4.4).

The interests of the firm are sometimes recognised implicitly even by representatives of competing models. This can be illustrated with two examples.

Hansmann and Kraakman are representatives of the *shareholder primacy* model.[13] On one hand, they suggest that "there is no longer any serious competitor to the view that corporate law should principally strive to increase long-term shareholder value". They call this model the standard model. On the other, they also argue that firms compete on increasingly international product and financial markets and that "[f]irms organized and operated according to the standard model can be expected to have important competitive advantages over firms adhering more closely to other models" – depending on their needs and the circumstances.[14] This leads to the question, why do firms seek those competitive advantages? Do firms exist, and do they have objectives of their own? Do all firms regardless of the governance model have one or more similar objectives? Obviously, the long-term competitive advantages that firms may gain do not matter unless it is assumed that firms exist and have objectives, and the choice between, say, shareholder orientation and stakeholder orientation by firms cannot be explained unless firms try to achieve a higher level objective.

Bainbridge is a representative of shareholder wealth maximisation and *director primacy*.[15] According to Bainbridge, a higher cost of capital increases the

---

[11] The need for such a duty was identified already in the Weimar republic by Rathenau and Bernhard. See Riechers A, *op cit*, p 10.

[12] See, for example, Tirole J, Corporate Governance, Econometrica 69 (2001) pp 4 and 25–26.

[13] Hansmann H, Kraakman R, The end of history for corporate law. In: Gordon JN, Roe MJ, Convergence and Persistence in Corporate Governance. Cambridge U P, Cambridge (2004) p 33.

[14] *Ibid*, p 47.

[15] Bainbridge S, The New Corporate Governance in Theory and Practice. OUP, Oxford (2008) pp 65–67.

probability of firm failure or takeover. Due to the negative effects of firm failure, directors will seek to minimise the cost of capital. Shareholders will demand a higher rate of return, if directors expose shareholders to greater risk. Greater risk translates directly into a higher corporate cost of capital. For this reason, shareholder wealth maximisation should apply according to Bainbridge. On the other hand, this makes one wonder whether this is the highest objective. Is the highest objective not reducing the probability of firm failure (and increasing the firm's long-term survival chances)? Moreover, do shareholders matter when they are not a source of funding or not the most important source of funding? Most of the external funding is provided by banks and bondholders, and shareholder wealth maximisation can increase the firm's overall funding costs (Sect. 7.9).

7.5 The Fourth Level

One can also add a fourth level. One should provide answers to the first level questions in the interests of the principal, that is, in the light of what is regarded as reasonable answers to the second and third level questions. For example, rational decisions on the allocation of power between shareholders and corporate bodies will depend on the choice of the principal, because the choice of the interests to be served should influence the allocation of power in the company.[16]

7.6 The Entity

We can now discuss the four fundamental questions that a general theory of corporate governance should be able to answer: (1) Why is the *legal entity* with its characteristic governance model chosen in the first place? (2) Whose *interests* should the people acting as or on behalf of the legal entity further? (3) Why does a legal entity have a *board*? (4) Why does a legal entity have *shareholders*?

According to the theory of MBCL, the firm is not the same thing as the legal entity. Legal entities are tools used by firms for the purpose of managing: cash flow and the exchange of goods and services; risk, principal-agency relationships; and information. Depending on the circumstances, the firm may benefit from different business forms and different corporate structures. The firm adapts to circumstances by changing its business form and corporate structure.

One can illustrate this with railroad companies and private equity. The building of railroads is capital intensive. The railroad firms of the nineteenth century raised

[16] This was identified already by Tolonen JP, *op cit*, pp 93–96 and 101.

locked-in funding by *incorporating* as limited-liability companies and issuing *shares* to the public. This lead to a dispersed share ownership structure.

A private equity firm manages other people's money in the context of leveraged buyouts. Like the building of railroads, leveraged buyouts are capital intensive. However, a private equity firm needs neither to be incorporated as a limited-liability company nor to issue shares to investors in order to raise locked-in funding. Instead, investors are asked to invest directly in the *core transactions* (leveraged buyouts) and to share profits with the private equity firm. The assets are locked in *contractually* for many years. Investors pay a fixed fee and a slice of profits to the private equity firm for its services. Much of the risk is allocated to banks that provide most of the required capital, and target companies that will end up repaying the takeover debts. This means that a private equity firm can invest in very large transactions without diluting its own share ownership structure and with very low risk exposure. – In practice, investors' investments are pooled in a limited partnership (private equity fund). The fund is managed by the private equity firm, or rather, a limited-liability company that the private equity firm uses as a tool in order to limit its own risk exposure. A limited-liability company is used as a takeover vehicle in order to manage risk and facilitate refinancings.

7.7 The Interests

The choice of interests is a fundamental question according to the proposed legal theory of corporate governance. It is necessary to choose the principal and define the principal's interests. According to the proposed theory, this is a question of what is regarded as reasonable, and a political question. For reasons discussed above, the proposed theory chooses the interests of the firm as an organisational structure (governance construction). The most fundamental interests of the firm consist of its own long-term survival.

7.8 The Board

Neither separate legal personality nor the fact that the firm has an organisation can explain the use of boards. There can be limited-liability companies without a "board" in any meaningful sense.[17] The board is therefore not a necessary

[17] The German GmbH, § 6(1) GmbHG: "Die Gesellschaft muß einen oder mehrere Geschäftsführer haben. "The English company, section 154(1) of the Companies Act 2006: "A private company must have at least one director." Section 154 (2): "A public company must have at least two directors." The SPE, Recital 13 of the Proposal for a Council Regulation on the Statute for a European private company: "Since small businesses need legal structures that can be adapted to their needs and size and are able to evolve as activity develops, shareholders of the SPE should be

ingredient of the corporation. Moreover, the existence of a board is not a central characteristic of the governance model of private equity.

What is necessary is that there is at least one person that acts as or on behalf of the legal entity (a first level question)[18] and that there is at least one person that protects the interests of the principal (a second level question). Because of separate legal personality, the state that facilitates the use of the corporate form must ensure that somebody is responsible for compliance with laws (a third level question). The firm also needs somebody to decide on fundamental issues in the interests of the firm (a first, second, and third level question). These issues may relate to strategy, major investments, and the allocation of value and risk between the firm and stakeholders and between stakeholders inter se.

Such functions could be in the same hands or in different hands, and they could be in the hands of many people or just one person.

In order to save direct administrative costs, all such functions could be in the hands of the same person. The interesting question is then why there are boards that consist of more than one person, have many functions, and have more than minimum functions.

The fact that boards exist and have more than minimum functions can be explained by the existence of costs, risk, agency relationships (as well as agency costs), and information-related issues. (a) Generally, there are benefits brought by *specialisation* (Fama and Jensen 1983[19]; an alternative explanation is provided by Blair and Stout 1999 who argue that there must be a "mediating hierarchy"[20]).

---

free to determine in their articles of association the internal organisation which is best suited to their needs. An SPE may opt for one or more individual managing directors, a unitary or a dual board structure."

[18] See, for example, Article 2(1) of Directive 68/151/EEC (First Company Law Directive): "Member States shall take the measures required to ensure compulsory disclosure by companies of at least the following documents and particulars: . . . (d) The appointment, termination of office and particulars of the persons who either as a body constituted pursuant to law or as members of any such body: (i) are authorised to represent the company in dealings with third parties and in legal proceedings; (ii) take part in the administration, supervision or control of the company."

[19] Fama EF, Jensen MC, Separation of Ownership and Control, J Law Econ 26 (1983) pp 301–325: ". . . separation of the management and control of decisions contributes to the survival of any organization where the important decision managers do not bear a substantial share of the wealth effects of their decisions – that is, any organization where there are serious agency problems in the decision process."

[20] Blair MM, Stout LA, A Team Production Theory of Corporate Law, Virginia L Rev 85 (1999) pp 247–328: ". . . an internal hierarchy whose job is to coordinate the activities of the team members, allocate the resulting production, and mediate disputes among team members over that allocation". "In other words, boards exist not to protect shareholders per se, but to protect the enterprise-specific investments of all the members of the corporate 'team,' including shareholders, managers, rank and file employees, and possibly other groups, such as creditors." See also Bainbridge S, Director Primacy: The Means and Ends of Corporate Governance, Northw U L Rev 97 (2003) pp 551–552 for the difference between "team production" and "director primacy".

Specialisation can reduce costs, improve the quality of corporate decision-making, and reduce risk. (b) The *separation* of decision-making powers (decision management and decision control) belongs to the generic tools used in the management of agency relationships.[21] The use of boards can be an efficient way to manage agency relationships and reduce agency costs and agency-related risks. (c) In particular, there should be a suitable *top decision-maker* for various categories of corporate decisions. The use of boards is a way to manage agency relationships between (1) the firm as the principal and (2) executives at lower levels of hierarchy or shareholders as agents. Because of agency problems, company laws generally do not provide for "shareholder primacy" in corporate decision-making.[22] There are decisions that should not be left to the discretion of agents whose interests are not aligned with those of the principal. (d) The same can be said of *monitoring* and transparency. There should be a top monitor acting in the interests of the firm.

The fact that boards have more than one member can be explained by three things. First, it can be explained by risk management.[23] If the board consists of just one member, many risks are increased. If the board consists of more members, risks can be reduced. Second, it is also an example of the management of agency relationships with the firm as the principal and board members as agents. The existence of many members can facilitate mutual monitoring that reduces the need to rely on external monitors. Mutual monitoring can also be part of a governance structure that helps to answer the "who monitors the monitors" problem (for self-enforcing corporate governance models, see Chap. 8). The third reason relates to information. Boards that have more than one member have a better knowledge base and can take better decisions.

Firms use boards in different ways. Many differences can be explained by legal requirements, as different types of legal entities must comply with different sets of laws. There are also differences between firms that have chosen the same business form.[24] For example, the company's share ownership and management can be in the same hands or separated; the company can have one controlling shareholder or a dispersed share ownership structure; control and management can be in the same hands or separated; and societal and corporate culture combined with path dependency can favour a certain board model.

---

[21] Mäntysaari P, The Law of Corporate Finance. Volume I. Springer, Berlin Heidelberg (2010), Chapter 6.

[22] For the limited powers of shareholders, see, for example, Mäntysaari P, Comparative Corporate Governance. Springer, Berlin Heidelberg (2005). See also Bainbridge S, Director Primacy: The Means and Ends of Corporate Governance, Northw U L Rev 97 (2003) p 559: "the board is the nexus".

[23] Mäntysaari P, The Law of Corporate Finance. Volume I. Springer, Berlin Heidelberg (2010) p 130.

[24] *Ibid*, section 9.4.3.

7.9 Shareholders

The choice of the firm as the principal makes it possible to define the function of shareholders as the firm's agents, the reason for their existence, the services they are paid for, and the firm's share ownership structure.

Generally, investors can be providers of funding and ancillary services. Whereas investors in private equity funds are predominately providers of funding, the private equity management firm is mainly a provider of services. Banks provide both funding and ancillary services, and their ancillary services are particularly important in relational banking. Shareholders are not always providers of funding, but they are always providers of at least some ancillary services.

Shareholders are providers of funding in their capacity as shareholders when they subscribe for new shares issued by the company or buy existing shares from the company. However, most shareholders of large listed companies have not subscribed for new shares, and the distributions that large listed companies make to shareholders often exceed the funding raised from shareholders.

Shareholders can provide various kinds of ancillary services:

- Shareholders can be providers of *equity* capital (in addition to other forms of funding). The availability of equity capital can increase the long-term survival prospects of the firm.
- The existence of equity capital can increase the availability of debt capital and reduce its cost.
- Shareholders are a mechanism to monitor the profitability of the company. As residual claimants, self-interested shareholders can be expected to demand better profitability.
- Shareholders are a pricing mechanism for shares. Shares issued by the company have a value for investors, because shareholders are residual claimants and shares are transferable. A high share price makes it easier for the company to use its shares as a means of payment and reduce its funding costs.
- The existence of shareholders can help to separate control and management and to avoid dead-lock situations.
- Depending on the case, shareholders or a certain shareholder can provide even other ancillary services such as signalling services, management services, takeover defences, access to markets, access to technology, or rescue in corporate crisis. Their services can be actual or contingent.[25]

The function of shareholders explains why shareholders exist, what shareholders are paid for, why shareholders have company law rights, why there may be

[25] For "contingent governance", see Aoki M, Toward a Comparative Institutional Analysis. The MIT Press, Cambridge, Mass. (2001) p 300.

company law provisions according to which the purpose of the company is to make a profit, and why the share ownership structure matters.[26]

Shareholders are paid for the provision of funding and the provision of ancillary services. The *relative weight* of shareholders and each task nevertheless depends on the company. For example, in order to prevent hostile takeover bids, a medium-sized listed company with a dispersed share ownership structure must ensure that both its share price and its leverage are high. This can require large distributions to shareholders and mean that the overall cost of shareholders' services is high. A privately-owned company with a controlling shareholder may end up paying less for its shareholders' services, provided that the controlling shareholder's interests are long-term and aligned with those of the firm. On the other hand, a firm that is dependent on the inputs of the company's controlling shareholder may have reason to pay that shareholder more compared with other shareholders, and a firm completely dependent on the personal input of a charismatic manager may need to make the manager a large shareholder.[27]

Shareholders' company law rights are primarily designed to facilitate the provision of shareholders' *ancillary services*, because shareholders are always providers of ancillary services but not necessarily providers of funding.[28] For example, company law rights can be designed to increase the valuation of shares by reducing shareholders' perceived risk; the rights can act as constraints on management or make transactions subject to shareholders' consent. Another example is that voting rights can be vested in shareholders where there is no other reasonable way to separate control and management or to avoid dead-lock situations.

Company law rules that set out that the purpose of the company is to make a profit (or to make a profit for shareholders in particular) can thus be explained in three ways. First, legal entities are legal tools used by firms (Sect. 4.6). Second, such statutory constraints on the management of the firm are designed to improve the firm's survival chances directly, as long-term survival requires profitability. Third, they are designed to improve long-term survival chances even indirectly, as such statutory constraints can: change the behaviour of the board and managers; reduce the perceived risk of shareholders; increase the availability of equity capital; and reduce its cost.

---

[26] Compare Bainbridge S, Director Primacy: The Means and Ends of Corporate Governance, Northw U L Rev 97 (2003) p 563: "In contrast, director primacy accepts shareholder wealth maximization as the proper corporate decisionmaking norm, but rejects the notion that shareholders are entitled to either direct or indirect decisionmaking control." The director primacy model cannot explain the existence and function of shareholders.

[27] Rajan and Zingales discuss how Saatchi and Saatchi, a British advertising agency, failed due to the fact that the value of its charismatic chairman was not recognised. See Rajan RG, Zingales L, The Governance of the New Enterprise (2000).

[28] The standard law and economics explanation is different. See, for example, Easterbrook FH, Fischel DR, The Economic Structure of Corporate Law. Harvard U P, Cambridge, Mass. (1991) pp 66–72.

It should be irrelevant whether such rules state that the purpose of the company is to "make a profit" or to "make a profit for shareholders", because shareholders benefit in both cases as residual claimants, and such rules cannot set out how much profit a company should make, how it should make a profit, when it should make a profit, or how much profit it should distribute to shareholders. The essential thing is that the company's board and management have a legal duty to try to make a profit for the company, not that the various kinds of equity investors (providers of debt-based equity or share-based equity)[29] or residual claimants will be better off in the event that the company does make a profit. The reference to shareholders in connection with making a profit has nevertheless been used as an argument for shareholder primacy and/or shareholder wealth maximisation in legal dogmatics.[30]

Share ownership structure is likely to influence the availability and cost of equity capital, and the provision of shareholders' ancillary services. The quality of shareholders as providers of ancillary services varies greatly, for which reason share ownership structure matters even where shareholders are not required as providers of fresh capital. For example, in a large listed company with dispersed ownership, all shareholders may be short-term investors. The board should then try to protect the firm against shareholders and reduce their relative weight – it would be absurd to give such shareholders more power or align the interests managers with their interests[31]; however, the entry of a friendly long-term block-holder might help.

Limited liability can be explained by separate legal personality (in addition to historical reasons). The main rule is that a person is not responsible for the obligations of another person, and neither lenders nor shareholders are responsible for the obligations of a corporation. Separate legal personality is designed to help both the firm and all its stakeholders to manage risk in an efficient way. Another main rule is that unlimited liability exists in the context of entities that are not regarded as separate legal persons. This can be the case with partnerships and unlimited partnerships depending on the jurisdiction.[32] There are also intermediate

---

[29] Mäntysaari P, The Law of Corporate Finance. Volume III. Springer, Berlin Heidelberg (2010), section 5.2 (on share-based equity and equity that is not share-based) and Chapter 6 (on mezzanine funding).

[30] See Dodge v. Ford Motor Co., 170 N.W. 668 (Mich. 1919); Bainbridge S, Director Primacy: The Means and Ends of Corporate Governance, Northw U L Rev 97 (2003) pp 574–576; Bainbridge S, The New Corporate Governance in Theory and Practice. OUP, Oxford (2008) p 59.

[31] This is certainly *not* the mainstream view in the financial markets. See, for example, Shareholders v stakeholders. A new idolatry. The Economist, April 2010: ". . . the problem is not the emphasis on shareholder value, but the use of short-term increases in a firm's share price as a proxy for it. Ironically, shareholders themselves have helped spread this confusion. Along with activist hedge funds, many institutional investors have idolised short-term profits and share-price increases rather than engaging recalcitrant managers in discussions about corporate governance or executive pay. Giving shareholders more power to influence management (especially in America) and encouraging them to use it should prompt them and the managers they employ to take a longer view."

[32] See Mäntysaari P, The Law of Corporate Finance. Volume III. Springer, Berlin Heidelberg (2010), sections 5.6.3 and 5.6.4.

business forms. Unlimited liability can thus be applied in the context of separate legal entities that nevertheless resemble partnerships.

Because of separate legal personality, a corporation is not owned by its shareholders. There is no difference between shareholders and creditors in this respect. Both own legal instruments issued by the legal entity with particular limited rights and duties attached to the respective instruments. One could say that the separate legal personality of corporations works in the same way as the legal personality of men. Neither free men nor separate legal persons are owned by anyone.

7.10 Summary

This chapter was based on the theory of MBCL. MBCL assumes that firms exist and try to survive in the long term. In order to improve their long-term survival chances in a competitive environment, firms try to reach their generic legal objectives by generic legal tools and practices at the strategic level, operational level, and transaction level. MBCL is a functional area of law. One can define particular branches of MBCL by identifying the particular functional issues that must be addressed by the firm in a certain commercial context. This is also a way to define a functional theory of corporate governance.

In the context of corporate governance, the most general issues that must be addressed are caused by the existence of legal entities (separate legal persons or other ring-fenced and self-contained legal institutions for the management of organisations) and the fact that the firm has an organisation (or is an organisational structure). One can define the particular questions caused by these two issues. This is a rational excercise. However, the answers will not be reasonable without answering two preliminary questions. One should choose the principal and define the interests of the principal.

In this chapter, it was suggested that the choice of the firm as the principal and its own long-term survival in a competitive environment as its objective can explain existing laws and the real behaviour of firms better compared with the mainstream models. For example, the shareholder primacy model is unable to explain the existence and function of shareholders.

However, this chapter primarily focused on *what* should be addressed. It did not explain *how* exactly these issues should be addressed. The choice of a particular organisational model as a way to achieve the generic objectives of the firm can depend on several other aspects such as *self-enforcement* and the need to ensure the firm's ability to *innovate*. We will discuss these issues in Chaps. 8 and 9.

Chapter 8
Self-enforcing Governance Models

8.1 Introduction: Corporate Governance and Organisational Design

The legal corporate governance theory proposed in Chap. 7 explains what issues must be managed in some way or another, and for what purpose they should be managed. However, it does not explain how exactly they should be managed. How should one organise the firm?

Organisational design. There are many models for organisational design. The answer can depend on the choice between generality or detail, and on the issues that are regarded as relevant.

For example, Aoki and Jackson (2008) study organisational architecture at a very high level of generality. They identify four models on the basis of equilibrium modes of linkage between the basic stakeholders' assets (managers' human assets, workers' human assets, and investor-supplied physical or financial assets). The four models are: (1) property-rights-based control of organisational hierarchies (the traditional US/UK model); (2) co-determination and workers' participation in work-site control (German); (3) relational contingent governance of the team-like organisational architecture (Japanese); and (4) the venture capitalist governance of tournament among entrepreneurial start-up firms (Silicon Valley).[1] According to Aoki and Jackson, the performance of any governance model or mode of organisational architecture may be relative. History matters (path dependency), and a model may not be absolutely superior to other models independently of the nature of markets, technology, social values, political economy features, and other circumstances.[2]

[1] Aoki M, Jackson G, Understanding an emergent diversity of corporate governance and organizational architecture: an essentiality-based analysis, Ind Corp Change 17 (2008) pp 2–3 and 11.

[2] *Ibid*, pp 10–11.

DOI 10.1007/978-3-642-22197-2_8,

Focusing more on corporate units, it is customary to distinguish between the "unitary corporation" (U-form corporation) and the "multidivisional corporation" (M-form corporation, Sect. 9.4.6). U-form corporations are organised into functional departments such as sales or manufacturing. M-form corporations have operating units organised as divisions (Chandler 1962, 1977, 1991, Williamson 1975).[3]

Alternatively, one could use organisational design principles that enable firms to choose more detailed governance models. There are some widely-used organisational design frameworks.

One of them is Galbraith's Star Model which identifies five design policies and five basic structures.[4] (a) In the Star Model, design policies fall into five categories. *Strategy* determines direction and establishes the criteria for choosing among alternative organisational forms. *Structure* determines the location of decision-making power in the organisation. *Processes* determine the functioning of the organisation and address the flow of information. *Rewards* and reward systems align the goals of employees with organisational goals. *People* policies or human resources policies are designed to influence the employees' mind-sets and skills.[5] (b) Five basic structures can be derived from such strategies: (1) the *functional* structure (organised around activities or functions, also known as the U-form); (2) the *product* structure (also known as the M-form); (3) the *market* structure (organised around customers or markets); (4) the *geographical* structure; and (5) the *process* structure (organised around a complete flow of work).

There are also other design models. According to Booz-Allen & Hamilton's Natural Business Unit (NBU) model, the customer perspective should serve as the starting point. Firms should be built around capabilities required for satisfying customer needs. Once such specific business needs are defined, the firm should create a structure that serves them. When applied in its purest form, the NBU model means that each NBU is structured and managed as if it were an independent entity with outsourced services.[6]

---

[3] See Chandler AD, The Visible Hand: The Managerial Revolution in American Business. Belknap Press, Cambridge, Mass. (1977) pp 5–12; Williamson OE, Markets and Hierarchies: Analysis and Antitrust Implications. The Free Press, New York (1975) pp 135–138; Williamson OE, The Economic Institutions of Capitalism. The Free Press, New York (1985) pp 289 and 320; Bainbridge S, Director Primacy: The Means and Ends of Corporate Governance, Northw U L Rev 97 (2003) pp 547–606 at 566–567.

[4] Galbraith JR, Organization Design. Addison-Wesley, Reading, Mass. (1977); Galbraith J, Designing Organizations: An Executive Briefing on Strategy, Structure, and Process. Jossey-Bass Inc., San Francisco, Calif. (1995).

[5] Compare Mäntysaari P, Comparative Corporate Governance. Springer, Berlin Heidelberg (2005) pp 16, 30; Mäntysaari P, The Law of Corporate Finance. Volume I. Springer, Berlin Heidelberg (2010) p 165–174.

[6] Jones J, Keller S, Neilson G, Spiegel E, Organizing for Agility: Creating Natural Business Units. Booz-Allen & Hamilton, USA (1999).

Goold and Campbell (2002) present nine tests that can be used to either evaluate an existing organisation design or create a new one. (a) Four "fit" tests are used for screening (the market advantage test, the parenting advantage test, the people test, and the feasibility test). (b) Five "good design" tests can help the firm to refine its organisational design (the specialist cultures test, the difficult links test, the redundant hierarchy test, the accountability test, and the flexibility test).[7]

Self-enforcement. A different approach is chosen in this book. This chapter focuses on self-enforcement as one of the key issues that influence the governance structure of firms.[8] The next chapter suggests that governance models are not sustainable unless they also foster innovation. Both chapters try to explain why firms are organised the way they are organised. For example, management authority tends to be vested in a management body and monitoring authority in a monitoring body, because the separation of management and monitoring is one of the core components of the self-enforcing governance model. Moreover, corporate law tries to facilitate the use of self-enforcing governance models, because it would be very expensive and contrary to the interests of firms to use the court or the government as a monitoring or control device on a large scale.

A governance model is here defined as self-enforcing when it requires little external monitoring inputs in addition to (1) the inputs of customers and contract parties, and (2) the enforcement of general laws.[9]

There are two main elements in self-enforcing corporate governance models, the delegation of power and the concentration of power. Both give rise to characteristic problems in addition to general agency problems. When power is delegated, there is a coordination problem. When power is concentrated, problems can relate to bureaucracy and constraints on innovation. For this reason, these two seemingly contradictory elements must be combined.

Self-enforcing governance models are used by various kinds of organisations ranging from large industrial firms to law firms, and from co-operatives to NGOs and terrorist organisations. We will study self-enforcing governance models in the light of illustrative examples and previous theories. The previous theories that will

[7] Goold M, Campbell A, Do You Have a Well-Designed Organization? HBR 80(2) (2002) pp 117–124.

[8] For self-enforcement and the equilibrium state, see Aoki M, Toward a Comparative Institutional Analysis. The MIT Press, Cambridge, Mass. (2001) pp 6–9 and 15 (discussing Hurwitz 1993, 1996). See also Aoki (2001) p 281: "... a corporate governance mechanism is a set of self-enforceable rules (formal or informal) that regulates the contingent action choices of the stakeholders ... in the corporate organization domain".

[9] Compare Greif A, Commitment, coercion, and markets: The nature and dynamics of institutions supporting exchange. In: Menard C, Shirley MM (eds), Handbook of New Institutional Economics. Springer, Dordrecht (2005) pp 756–757: "Self-governance entails having bodies of collective decision-making, mechanisms, such as judicial processes and police forces, to overcome the free-rider problem and motivate and induce members to participate in sanctions."

help to understand self-enforcing models include Ostrom (1990) and Black and Kraakman (1996).[10]

Four basic types of self-enforcing models can be distinguished on the basis of the examples and theories: the model based on the delegation of power; the model based on the concentration of power; the Ostrom model; and the model that fosters innovation. Self-enforcing corporate governance models should contain elements of all four models.

8.2 The Problem

Why should the firm choose a self-enforcing model? Let us assume that the firm is the principal. In this case, external monitors can be regarded as the firm's agents. The firm will thus incur agency costs.[11] No agency costs for external monitoring will be incurred to the extent that no external monitors are required (no agency). This can mean savings. For example, if shareholders as a class are not an important provider of monitoring services, other ancillary services, or funding, the firm will not need to distribute as much funds to shareholders or to use funds to maintain a high share price.

Alternatively, one can assume that investors as a class are the principal. Board members and managers can then be regarded as their agents. If the governance model is self-enforcing, investors do not have to monitor the firm to the same extent. This means savings for them. For example, shareholders of a large listed company with a dispersed share ownership structure customarily do not want to invest time and money in monitoring. Savings can increase the price that investors are prepared to pay for securities issued by the firm and reduce the firm's funding costs.

The firm can thus benefit from a self-enforcing corporate governance model. In the long run, it can increase the firm's survival chances. This is reflected in corporate law. Separate legal personality, the existence of shareholders with transferable shares, the limited liability of shareholders, and the existence of corporate organs responsible for monitoring and management achieve two things. First, they reduce shareholders' risks and their need to monitor the firm. Second, they make the people that belong the organisation of the firm responsible for monitoring and management and give them incentives to do so. Many of the fundamental characteristics of corporations are thus designed to facilitate self-enforcement.

Now, the self-enforcing model relies on internal agents rather than external ones. This is what makes it *self*-enforcing. But reliance on internal agents gives rise to characteristic problem areas:

---

[10] Ostrom E, Governing the Commons: The Evolution of Institutions for Collective Action. Cambridge U P, Cambridge (1990); Black B, Kraakman R, A Self-Enforcing Model of Corporate Law, Harv L Rev 109 (1996) pp 1911–1982.

[11] Jensen MC, Meckling WH, Theory of the Firm: Managerial Behavior, Agency Costs and Ownership Structure, J Fin Econ 3 (1976) pp 308–309.

1. Management of internal agency relationships. This is the key problem area, since most of the target-setting and monitoring is, by definition, done internally, that is, by members of the organisation.
2. Target-setting. Even target-setting must be done internally. This creates problems, because the organisation's members may have incentives to further their own personal interests rather than the interests of the organisation (the firm) when setting the targets.
3. Monitoring. By definition, there should be minimal reliance on external monitors. But this increases the problem of who monitors the monitors.
4. Coordination. The model is not sustainable, unless it enables sufficient coordination of activities. But there can be too little coordination, as members of the organisation may prefer more discretion. There can also be too much bureaucracy, as the lack of external monitors means that internal bodies will need to be created to solve the problem of who monitors the monitors.
5. The role of mandatory laws. Laws can be used to influence behaviour. Many corporate governance models require the existence of laws in general (for example, company laws that facilitate the existence of companies), and mandatory laws in particular (for example, much of the German Aktiengesetz, the UK Listing Rules, and the US Sarbanes-Oxley Act). However, the enforcement of external legal norms can be time-consuming and expensive, and, as one cannot be sure of the outcome, combined with exposure to legal risk. The rule of law is not always enforced to the benefit of the firm, and it is not enforced in most countries of the world.

The self-enforcing model should therefore deal with such issues. The model should: work with minimal resort to legal authority, including the courts; work with minimal resort to other external monitoring inputs; reduce internal agency problems; enable the effective coordination of activities; and be sustainable. We can now study how these issues might be dealt with.

8.3 Delegation of Power

The first model could be to give members of the organisation plenty of discretion by delegating power to them. However, when participants in the self-enforcing model have plenty of discretion, there is a coordination problem. This model can be illustrated with the al-Qaeda case.

The al-Qaeda case. The loose network known as al-Qaeda is notorious but secretive. We can assume that the following aspects are characteristic of al-Qaeda and its governance model:

1. It exists outside the law (in the sense that it is illegal and states try to kill or capture its members) but not completely outside the general legal system (it tries

to benefit from laws, such as company laws, banking laws, human rights laws, and so forth).[12]
2. It consists of a number of local cells that largely act independently (the capture or killing of members will not endanger the whole network).
3. Information flows are restricted (for security reasons, see number 2).
4. Members of the organisation share a common culture.
5. There is a training camp for future terrorists.
6. Future terrorists are recruited by reliable local representatives from a pool of locally known fanatics (information management is important, because wrong recruitment choices may endanger the whole network, see number 1).
7. There is a reliable moneyman controlling centralised funding (Osama Bin Laden was a wealthy businessman that controlled funding, among other things).
8. The network needs donations.

The most obvious problems here are: coordination (numbers 1–3); and insufficient protection by laws (number 1). In other words, how can you coordinate anything if information flows are restricted (if states get to know the whereabouts of al-Qaeda's members, the members might be killed) and the cells must act independently?

The main ways to deal with this problem are: reliance on a strong *culture*; careful *recruitment*; centralised *training*; and centralised *funding*. (a) Members of al-Qaeda tend to be highly committed to the network's goals. The network would not exist unless all its members shared the common culture and were committed to its cause. (b) It is vital not to employ wrong people in the first place. Careful recruitment is supported by the screening of members locally and at the training site. (c) It is customary for members of the organisation to learn the trade in a standardised way. This can also contribute to the network's common culture. (d) Centralised funding is a powerful instrument as it is difficult for local cells to raise funding openly.

Like all self-enforcing models, even this model is complemented by monitoring by *customers* and the market. In this case, donors can be regarded as customers. Al-Qaeda is not an exception from the rule that all organisations need funding. In addition, al-Qaeda would not survive without business partners that provide valuable services.

8.4 Centralisation of Power

The opposite of delegation of power is centralisation of power. In this case, coordination is not the problem. There are two kinds of characteristic problems.

[12] For example, a basic level of law and order may be necessary for pirates to ply their trade. De Groot OJ, Rablen MD, Shortland A, Gov-aargh-nance – "even criminals need law and order", CEDI Discussion Paper Series 11–01, Centre for Economic Development and Institutions, Brunel University (February 2011).

First, it can be difficult to monitor the monitors and manage internal agency relationships. The reason is that all monitoring must be taken care of internally. By definition, you try not to rely on external monitors in the self-enforcing model.

The customary ways to manage these problems include, in particular: *separation* of functions (initiation of decisions, ratification of decisions, execution of decisions); *mutual monitoring* (boards, the participation of many people in the decision process and monitoring); *mixed monitoring* (different classes of monitors participate in the monitoring process); and a *common goal*.

Second, centralisation of power can increase bureaucracy and reduce innovation. Both can make it more difficult for the firm to adapt and survive in the long term. The ways to address this problem will be discussed in Chap. 9.

This model can be illustrated with the governance model of large listed German companies (AG) and the Black and Kraakman model. We can start with the latter.

The Black and Kraakman model. The Black and Kraakman (1996) model[13] was intended for emerging capitalist economies that still lacked strong institutional, market, cultural, and legal constraints on the governance of companies. The purpose of this model is to allow large "outside shareholders" to protect themselves from insider opportunism with minimal resort to legal authority, including the courts.

The central features of the Black and Kraakman self-enforcing model of corporate law are:

- Enforcement, as much as possible, through actions by direct participants in the corporate enterprise
- Greater protection of outside shareholders than is common in developed economies
- Reliance on procedural protections
- Use of bright-line rules rather than standards
- Strong legal remedies on paper, to compensate for the low probability that the sanctions will be applied in fact

As the Black and Kraakman model is a model for the protection of "outside shareholders", self-enforcement takes place "primarily through a combination of voting rules and transactional rights". Transactional rights include pre-emptive rights, appraisal rights, and sell-out rights. The central voting elements include, for example, shareholder approval for broad classes of major transactions and self-interested transactions, and approval of self-interested transactions by a majority of outside directors.

The Black and Kraakman model thus focuses on the management of the relationships between minority or outside shareholders and corporate insiders. Black and Kraakman chose outside shareholders as the principal. The most

[13] Black B, Kraakman R, A Self-Enforcing Model of Corporate Law, Harv L Rev 109 (1996) pp 1911–1982.

important way to manage this relationship is by regulating the scope of agency:[14] the right to decide on important issues is vested in shareholders or outside shareholders rather than corporate insiders.

The Black and Kraakman model seems to contain some elements of continental European and EU company law without going as far as the governance model of large German companies (see below).[15] Unlike the German corporate governance model, the Black and Kraakman model:

- Requires the active participation of shareholders
- Does not clearly separate decision management and decision control (initiation of decisions, ratification of decisions, execution of decisions)
- Relies less on mutual monitoring and mixed monitoring
- Does not rely on a favourable societal and corporate culture and
- Tries to replace the absence of a favourable corporate culture with legal rules

As a result, this model is less self-enforcing than the German corporate governance model designed to work even without minority shareholders' active monitoring inputs. Overreliance on legal rules is also bound to cause problems in a society that does not enforce the rule of law.

The German model. Like all corporate governance models, the German model is embedded in an institutional environment that consists of several complementary institutions. Before studying the German model, it is therefore useful to keep in mind the differences between the German and UK markets. Germany and the UK have:

- Traditionally different approaches to regulation (mandatory regulation through laws in Germany, industry self-regulation in the UK)
- Different industries (manufacturing is more important in Germany, financial services are more important in the UK)
- Different corporate governance cultures (the interests of the firm prevail in Germany, shareholder primacy prevails in the UK)
- Different share ownership structures (it is customary to have a controlling shareholder in Germany, share ownership is more dispersed in the UK)
- Different roles for banks (it used to be customary for firms to have a close long-term relationship with a "house bank" in Germany, banks do not have such a relationship with their customers in the UK)
- Different approaches to self-enforcement (it is characteristic of German corporate governance, it is less important in the UK)

The following aspects are characteristic of the governance model of a German AG:

---

[14] See Mäntysaari P, The Law of Corporate Finance. Volume I. Springer, Berlin Heidelberg (2010) p 105.

[15] See also Bebchuk LA, The Case for Increasing Shareholder Power, Harv L Rev 118 (2005) pp 833–914.

1. The governance model of the AG is facilitated by the largely mandatory provisions of the Aktiengesetz (AktG).
2. There is statutory separation of powers and mixed monitoring.
3. The AG has a supervisory board that is responsible for monitoring but must not manage.
4. The AG has a management board that must manage the firm.
5. All members of the management board are executives.
6. The supervisory board and the management board have no common members.
7. Members of the management board and supervisory board have a duty to act in the interests of the firm (Unternehmensintresse).
8. Up to half of members of the supervisory board are employee representatives (co-determination).
9. The AG often has a controlling shareholder.
10. The AG often has a "house bank" (Hausbank).
11. Even small shareholders have relatively extensive legal rights.

The German model is thus a combination of several mutually consistent institutional arrangements.[16]

It is an example of *mixed monitoring* (or "shared control"[17]). The core of the mixed monitoring system is the two-tier board. Mixed monitoring is increased by the existence of other monitors. The most important of them is the controlling shareholder. A controlling shareholder has both legal and de facto powers. Employees have influence through members of the supervisory board. Moreover, the house bank can have de facto powers as a provider of funding, as an adviser, or in some cases through its representative in the supervisory board.

This model is also an example of *mutual monitoring* since both the management board and the supervisory board are collegiate organs consisting of many members.

In order to work, the mixed monitoring system requires *clear rules* on the allocation of power, the separation of functions, and the corporate objective. The most important rules are set out in the AktG. The AktG lays down detailed and mandatory rules on the separation of functions. The AktG was originally designed for large companies with a dispersed share ownership structure,[18] and the purpose of its many mandatory provisions is to reduce shareholders' need to monitor the

[16] See Mäntysaari P, Comparative Corporate Governance. Springer, Berlin Heidelberg (2005) pp 239–242; Aoki M, *op cit*, p 17; Aoki M, Jackson G, *op cit*, p 7: "... corporatism, co-determination and the Hausbank system in the traditional German model may be considered as constituting an institutionally complementary cluster, while another cluster may include stock market control, hierarchically ordered [human assets], and the liberal state".

[17] Tirole J, Corporate Governance, Econometrica 69 (2001) pp 28–29.

[18] See Cheffins BR, Mergers and Corporate Ownership Structure: The United States and Germany at the Turn of the 20th Century, Am J Comp L 51 (2003) pp 473–503.

monitors and the management.[19] For example, all members of corporate bodies must further *the interests of the firm* (Sect. 6.3).[20]

The German model is embedded in German societal and business culture. The model relies on compliance and forces corporate bodies to cooperate and seek consensus. (a) This can perhaps make decision-making slower and reduce the organisation's agility and ability to adapt to changes in circumstances. Moreover, the large number of participants with potentially conflicting interests may increase agency costs. (b) On the other hand, increasing the number of participants in the decision-making process can mean that decisions are based on better information and that the participants are more committed. Agency costs can be reduced by a strong culture. The participation of employees and banks can reduce excessive risk-taking. In the light of the strength of the German manufacturing industry, this governance model seems to bring benefits at least in business sectors that require long-term investment and long-term commitment to innovation and quality.[21]

The German model seems to comply with many of the principles of the self-enforcing model (see above) although it is largely based on mandatory law and the existence of a compliance culture. One may ask whether it would be possible to design a self-enforcing model that does not rely on external rules to the same extent. We will study this question in the next section.

8.5 Delegation and Centralisation

Both the al-Qaeda case and the German corporate governance model indicate that you cannot design a self-enforcing model without combining the delegation and centralisation of power. A combination is necessary in order to mitigate inherent problems. The question is how delegation and centralisation should be combined.

Obviously, the answer can depend on the circumstances and the firm. We can study two earlier attempts to solve this problem. The first is the Ostrom model. The second is a model used by a Finnish group of co-operatives. We will discuss this question even in Sect. 8.6 and Chap. 9.

The Ostrom model. Elinor Ostrom's self-enforcing model is based on a combination of centralisation and delegation. Ostrom (1990) studies the "tragedy of the commons" or common property rights (CPR). Ostrom points out that "analyses in modern resource economics conclude that where a number of users have access to a common-pool resource, the total of resource units withdrawn from the resources

---

[19] See Mäntysaari P, Comparative Corporate Governance. Springer, Berlin Heidelberg (2005) p 389; Aoki M, *op cit*, p 290: "When control rights are shared with the worker, more external financing will be made in the form of long-term debt contracts."

[20] § 93(1) AktG; § 116 AktG; § 242 BGB; BGHZ 65, 15 (ITT).

[21] For a hostile view on co-determination, see, nevertheless, Bainbridge S, The New Corporate Governance in Theory and Practice. OUP, Oxford (2008) pp 45–49.

will be greater than the optimal economic level of withdrawal".[22] Simply put, the problem is that "everybody's property is nobody's property". There used to be two traditional solutions to the problem. One could either add a central authority such as the state to regulate and manage the resource, or make the resource "somebody's property" through private property rights. Ostrom proposes a third solution.

Ostrom's solution is to use a self-enforcing model that consists of five design principles and rules that:

- Define a set of "appropriators" who are authorised to use a CPR (design principle 1)
- Relate to the specific attributes of the CPR and the community of appropriators using the CPR (design principle 2)
- Are designed, at least in part, by local appropriators (design principle 3)
- Are monitored by individuals accountable to local appropriators (design principle 4) and
- Are sanctioned using graduated punishments (design principle 5)[23]

For example, one could try to apply Ostrom's theory to professional firms such as law firms:[24]

- Choice of resources. One could study the use of the common resources of a law firm.
- Appropriators. Partners could be chosen as appropriators (design principle 1).
- Attributes. The rules on the use of the resources should make sense for law firms in general and the firm's partners in particular (design principle 2).
- Design. In this case, the rules should be designed by the partners (design principle 3).
- Monitoring. The rules and compliance should be monitored by people and bodies elected by the partners, for example by committees and a partner that acts as a CEO (design principle 4).
- Sanctions. The sanctions for non-compliance could range from a friendly discussion to the application of rules on exit (design principle 5).

But there are limits to Ostrom's theory. First, it is designed for certain types of CPR. Ostrom studies renewable rather than non-renewable resources. Second, she studies situations in which users must rely on the CPR for their living and have no other choice. As a result, users of the CPR can substantially cause each other harm. However, the firm's employees and managers do have a choice and it is customary for them to move from one firm to another. Because of the freedom to exit the firm, members of the "team" are less likely to be able to cause each other harm and less dependent on the CPR. Third, although Ostrom explains that certain things should

[22] Ostrom E, Governing the Commons. Cambridge U P, Cambridge (1990) p 3.

[23] *Ibid*, pp 185–186.

[24] *Ibid*, p 25: "Examples of self-organized enterprises abound. Most law firms are obvious examples . . . Most cooperatives are also examples."

be coordinated by the users, she does not explain how coordination (rule-making, monitoring, execution of decisions, and enforcement of sanctions) should be organised. Fourth, as a large increase in the number of users makes it more difficult to coordinate things, it may be unclear to what extent Ostrom's model would scale up. For example, Ostrom's model can perhaps be applied to a middle-sized law firm, but can it be applied to a large industrial firm (or to global resources such as the atmosphere)?

One can therefore say that Ostrom's model focuses more on delegation than on centralisation or coordination. If one wants to design a self-enforcing model for a large firm, one should therefore complement Ostrom's model with the coordination approach or the German model (Sect. 8.4). On the other hand, Ostrom mentions cooperatives as an example of "self-organized enterprises". We can study whether this can be done in a cooperative.

A group of Finnish cooperatives. The S Group is a group of Finnish retail cooperatives.[25] It consists of local cooperatives and a cooperative of the local cooperatives at the top. The group is very successful and has obtained a large market share in Finland.

Finnish cooperatives are governed by the Cooperative Act (1488/2001).[26] In addition, there is a voluntary international code for cooperatives (the Rochdale Principles).

The following are the core elements of the governance model of the S-Group:

- There are local cooperatives ensuring proximity to the local retail markets
- There is a cooperative of cooperatives for economies of scale and coordination
- There are no shareholders
- Each cooperative has members, either retail customers (in the local cooperatives) or cooperatives (in the cooperative of cooperatives)
- In each cooperative, each member must by law have exactly one vote
- Membership in a local cooperative is not possible without a capital investment but members are entitled to bonuses, discounts, and other benefits
- Each cooperative has a similar governance structure with a cooperative meeting, a supervisory board, an executive board, and a CEO who is chairman of the executive board

There are similarities and differences between this model and the Ostrom model. Like in the Ostrom model, the rules are made by the participants (members). But whereas the Ostrom model leaves open how coordination should be organised, the S Group model combines the Ostrom model with a governance structure that ensures coordination. Like in the model used by German AGs, there is a clear separation of functions (a cooperative meeting, a supervisory board, an executive board); mutual

[25] *Ibid.*

[26] For the SCE, see Regulation 1435/2003, implemented in Finland through the SCE Act (906/2006).

monitoring; mixed monitoring; and a strong culture. One can now try to formulate a theory of self-enforcing corporate governance models.

8.6 How Can You Make the Model More Self-enforcing?

Several legal techniques (or institutions) can be combined to make the model more self-enforcing. They should be mutually consistent to create an environment that changes behaviour in the intended way.

First, if you cannot or will not rely on laws, you need to rely on patterns of *human behaviour* rather than laws, and on *organisational measures* (Simon 1991, Ostrom 1990). Reliance on patterns of human behaviour and on organisational measures means the use of: generic legal tools for the management of agency relationships[27]; principles of organisational risk management[28]; as well as stewardship and intra-firm competition.[29]

Second, the following practices are particularly important:

- A strong culture[30] (supported by other legal and non-legal tools and practices)
- Careful recruitment (high personal integrity of participants)
- Better transparency of the required behaviour (in particular, more bright-line rules and better documentation of the required behaviour, documented procedures for access to money)
- Better transparency of the actual behaviour since "sunlight is the best disinfectant" (increasing the number of organisation members that participate in decision management and decision control, the use of boards, joint acts, joint representation, documentation and transparency of payments)
- Mixed monitoring and mutual monitoring
- Clearer separation of functions (principle of four eyes, two-tier boards)
- Control of funding and money in safe hands (ownership of a controlling block or de facto control, money not in the hands of those who use it, money in a safe country and in a safe bank that has high integrity)
- Enforcement of sanctions for non-compliance

---

[27] See Mäntysaari P, The Law of Corporate Finance. Volume I. Springer, Berlin Heidelberg (2010), Chapter 6; Kraakman R, Davies P, Hansmann H, Hertig G, Hopt KJ, Kanda H, Rock EB, *op cit*, Chapters 1–2.

[28] Mäntysaari P, The Law of Corporate Finance. Volume I. Springer, Berlin Heidelberg (2010), section 7.4.

[29] Davis JH, Schoorman FD, Donaldson L, Toward a Stewardship Theory of Management, Acad Man Rev 22 (1997) pp 20–47; Mäntysaari P, The Law of Corporate Finance. Volume I. Springer, Berlin Heidelberg (2010) pp 106–107 and 223–224.

[30] Mäntysaari P, The Law of Corporate Finance. Volume I. Springer, Berlin Heidelberg (2010), section 6.2.

Third, power is both delegated and concentrated. Power is concentrated even in models that exhibit a high level of delegation, because it is necessary in order to: manage corporate culture; manage recruitment (and the choice of "agents"); co-ordinate rule-making; coordinate training; and coordinate the enforcement of sanctions (see also Ostrom 1990). Furthermore, the long-term survival of the firm tends to require a board and the vesting of certain powers in the board (Sect. 7.8).[31]

Fourth, when the self-enforcing model requires a high level of concentration of power at the top, the following aspects become important: clear separation of functions (in particular, a two-tier board); mutual monitoring; and mixed monitoring.

Fifth, when the self-enforcing model requires the participation of multiple parties, agency costs can be reduced if the model is embedded in a favourable legal framework. The model can benefit from the existence of mandatory provisions of law.[32]

Sixth, stewardship is important. Stewardship means the use of methods that increase social incentives to act in the interests of the organisation. Social incentives can be enhanced, for example, by: collegiate decision-making supported by monitoring procedures; and competition, combined with rewarding managers that have high integrity (Simon 1991). Whereas stewardship can increase the level of self-enforcement, a high level of self-enforcement is likely to increase stewardship, and both can contribute to a stronger culture. Self-enforcement will thus create social capital that makes self-enforcement stronger.[33]

Seventh, even other factors must be taken into account when choosing the balance between delegation and concentration. The firm's ability to innovate is studied as such a factor in the next chapter.

---

[31] See also Mäntysaari P, The Law of Corporate Finance. Volume I. Springer, Berlin Heidelberg (2010) p 174.

[32] See even Mäntysaari P, Comparative Corporate Governance. Springer, Berlin Heidelberg (2005), Chapter 6; Mazé A, Ménard C, Private ordering, collective action, and the self-enforcing range of contracts, Eur J Law Econ 29 (2010) p 138: "supervision by public institutions may extend the self-enforcing range of contract".

[33] For social capital as civic capital, see Guiso L, Sapienza P, Zingales L, Civic Capital as the Missing Link. EUI Working Paper ECO2010/08. European University Institute, Department of Economics (2010).

Chapter 9
Corporate Governance and Innovation

9.1 General Remarks

It is not enough to have a governance structure that is self-enforcing. The firm's long-term survival is not possible without continuous adaptation. The sustainability of the firm is increased, if the firm is able to innovate.

Innovation means more than mere maximising, optimising, or reacting to changes in circumstances. Innovation is a form of useful organisational learning and change. This requires two things. First, the firm should create and maintain organisational capabilities (Chandler 1990),[1] and improve and adapt its skill base (Lazonik 2010).[2] Organisational capabilities and skills can enable the firm to "set the agenda" before its competitors do (Arrow 1974).[3] Second, the firm should use an organisation structure that is "built to change". The necessary capabilities change as the business environment changes.[4]

---

[1] Chandler AD, Scale and Scope: The Dynamics of Industrial Enterprise. Harvard U P, Cambridge, Mass. (1990) p 594.

[2] Lazonik W, The Chandlerian corporation and the theory of innovative enterprise, Ind Corp Change 19 (2010) p 333: "Precisely because innovative enterprise depends on social conditions, the development and utilization of skill bases that occur in one institutional environment may not, at a point in time at least, prevail in another institutional environment. Moreover, even within the same industry and same nation, dynamic capabilities that yielded innovative outcomes in one historical era may become static capabilities that inhibit innovative responses in a subsequent historical era."

[3] Arrow KJ, The Limits of Organization. Fels Lectures on Public Policy Analysis. Norton, New York (1974) p 47.

[4] Worley CG, Lawler EE, Designing Organizations That Are Built to Change, MIT Sloan Man Rev 48(1) (2006) pp 19–23; Jones J, Keller S, Neilson G, Spiegel E, Organizing for Agility: Creating Natural Business Units. Booz-Allen & Hamilton, USA (1999).

P. Mäntysaari, *Organising the Firm*,

DOI 10.1007/978-3-642-22197-2_9,

Innovation can relate to all business processes. It is not limited to product development or to what takes place in the R&D department.[5] For example, the ability of the firm's top management to change the organisational architecture of the firm is particularly important for the firm's sustainability.

Ensuring the firm's ability to innovate requires the right combination of strategy, organisation, and finance (Lazonik 2010).[6] From the perspective of commercial law, it requires the use of a large number of legal tools and practices at all three levels of corporate decision-making (strategic, operational, and transaction level, see Sect. 4.7).

There are threats to the firm's ability to innovate. Some of them are characteristic of the self-enforcing corporate governance model. When choosing the balance between delegation and centralisation (Sects. 8.3 and 8.4), ensuring the firm's ability to innovate should therefore be one of the key objectives.

The purpose of this chapter is to study the firm's governance structure as a way to foster innovation. The firm must use various legal tools and practices in order to achieve and maintain its ability to innovate. The firm is again studied as an organisational construction (governance structure).

9.2 The Problem of Measurement

When is the firm innovative? There are alternative ways to measure the firm's ability to innovate. The choice can depend on the research area. Innovation can be studied in different disciplines. In addition, the perspective may vary.

Traditional corporate governance research. In traditional corporate governance research, it is customary to choose between the shareholder primacy approach, the managerial approach, and the stakeholder approach.

For example, one could focus on the effect of various innovation-related aspects on the financial performance of the firm (shareholder primacy approach). One could also try to formulate a theory of an innovative firm that explains "how, by generating output that is higher quality and/lower cost, a particular enterprise can differentiate itself from its competitors and emerge as dominant in its industry" (managerial approach).[7] The opposite approach could be sustainability innovation

[5] Compare Pavitt K, Innovating routines in the business firm: what corporate tasks should they be accomplishing? Ind Corp Change 11 (2002) p 119 (distinguishing between three overlapping processes: producing scientific and technological knowledge; transforming knowledge into working artifacts; and matching working artifacts with users' requirements).

[6] Lazonik W, The Chandlerian corporation and the theory of innovative enterprise, Ind Corp Change 19 (2010) p 326.

[7] *Ibid.*

research that focuses on ideas that improve environmental and/or social performance and how firms can foster such sustainability (stakeholder approach).[8]

Economics. In economics, mainstream corporate governance research focuses on relatively few innovation-related aspects for two reasons. The first is that the neoclassical theory of the firm studies the firm as a "black box" (see below).[9] This is likely to have reduced the overall volume of innovation-related corporate governance research. The second is that the shareholder primacy model does not include a theory of the firm's ability to innovate (Lazonick 2007).[10]

The main innovation-related streams focus on funding constraints and the effect of the share ownership structure.[11] There is plenty of research on funding constraints.[12] There is relatively little research on the effect of governance structures on the firm's ability to innovate.[13]

Organisational research. Organisational research can take a broader view, because it is not constrained by the neoclassical theory of the firm and the shareholder primacy model.

The theory of an innovative enterprise can have as its starting point the three generic activities in which the firm engages: strategy, organisation, and finance. One can then identify three social conditions of the innovative enterprise: strategic control, organisational integration, and financial commitment (Lazonik 2010).[14]

Proxies. It is necessary to choose proxies for the firm's ability to innovate. One alternative could be to use profitability, growth, the number of patents, or mere

---

[8] See Siebenhüner B, Arnold M, Organizational learning to manage sustainable development, Bus Strat Env 16 (2007) pp 339–353; Arnold MG, Hockerts K, The Greening Dutchman: Philips' Process of Green Flagging to Drive Sustainable Innovations, Bus Strat Env (2010).

[9] Lazonik W, The Chandlerian corporation and the theory of innovative enterprise, Ind Corp Change 19 (2010) pp 321–323.

[10] Lazonick W, The US stock market and the governance of innovative enterprise, Ind Corp Change 16 (2007) pp 984 and 997.

[11] See Hall BH, Rosenberg N (eds), Handbook of the Economics of Innovation. North-Holland, Amsterdam (2010).

[12] For a review, see Bond S, Van Reenen J, Microeconometric models of investment and employment. In: Heckman JJ, Leamer E (eds), Handbook of econometrics. North Holland, London (2007) pp 4417–4498.

[13] See also Belloc F, Corporate governance and innovation: an organizational perspective, MPRA Paper No. 21495 (10 January 2010): ... "to ask what makes a firm innovative means that we must ask what are conditions *internal* to the firm conducive to innovation and to ask how systems of corporate governance affect firms' investment strategies. Surprisingly, unlike traditional studies on the economics of innovation, such a field of research has not benefited so far from a systematic discussion and review of its major contributions." Lazonick W, Prencipe A, Dynamic Capabilities and Sustained Innovation: Strategic Control and financial Commitment at Rolls-Royce plc, Ind Corp Change 14(3) (2005) p 534: "Precisely because of the inherent uniqueness of each particular case, an accumulation of case studies ... is essential for the construction of a relevant and rigorous theory of innovative enterprise."

[14] Lazonik W, The Chandlerian corporation and the theory of innovative enterprise, Ind Corp Change 19 (2010) p 320 and pp 330–333.

survival as proxies for innovation (meaning that the firm must be innovative if it makes a profit, grows fast, or has a large number of patents). This approach would reflect "black box" theories of the firm that regard the firm as a production function.

But past profitability, growth, patent rights, or survival do not really explain what the firm should do now in order to remain innovative in the future. On the contrary, if the firm's managers use such factors as proxies, the result may be arrogance caused by past successes and failure to adapt to present and future changes in the market. There are many examples of large firms that have disappeared.

Firm size in particular. Large firm size would not be a suitable proxy for the firm's ability to innovate.

On one hand, large firm size may be the result of the successful exploitation of past innovations, and it may also bring benefits in the future. Generally, complex contracts with external parties can be avoided when things are done internally (Williamson 2002a, 2002b).[15] Large firm size brings organisational capabilities, economies of scale, and funding benefits (Chandler 1990).[16] The monopoly firm would be the extreme form of a large firm. Temporary monopolies can be necessary to provide the required incentive for firms to develop new products and processes (Schumpeter 1942).[17] After the Second World War, the monopoly firm was therefore regarded as the model that maximised innovation in a particular industry.[18]

On the other hand, the benefits of large firm size cannot be achieved without coordination. When the firm grows in size, continuing intra-firm specialisation results in new layers of hierarchy. The existence of many layers of hierarchy and bureaucracy can make it more difficult for the firm to manage information and adapt to changes in the market (Williamson 1984).[19]

Moreover, a large firm cannot be managed unless its governance structure is, to a large extent, self-enforcing. This requires coordination, but the tools and practices used for coordination (such as the separation of monitoring and management) will add new layers to hierarchy. The governance structure of the firm can thus be self-enforcing and relatively stable in the short term although it hampers innovation and is not sustainable in the long term.[20]

---

[15] Williamson OE (2002a), The Lens of Contract: Private Ordering. Am Econ Rev 92(2) (2002) pp 438–443; Williamson OE (2002b), The Theory of the Firm as Governance Structure: From Choice to Contract. J Econ Persp 16(3) (2002) pp 171–195.

[16] Chandler AD, Scale and Scope: The Dynamics of Industrial Enterprise. Harvard U P, Cambridge, Mass. (1990) p 594.

[17] Schumpeter JA, Capitalism, Socialism and Democracy. Harper and Brothers, New York (1942).

[18] See Lazonik W, The Chandlerian corporation and the theory of innovative enterprise, Ind Corp Change 19 (2010) p 337.

[19] Williamson OE, The Incentive Limits of Firms, Rev World Econ 120(4) (1984) pp 736–763.

[20] One can distinguish between the synchronic problem and the diachronic problem. Aoki M, Toward a Comparative Institutional Analysis. The MIT Press, Cambridge, Mass. (2001) pp 2–3.

The existence of innovation-related limits to the size of firms (Williamson 1984) reduces the maximum size of firms and increases their number.

New ways to measure innovation. One should, therefore, find other ways to measure innovation. We can study the question of resources as a preliminary question as it is certain that the firm's ability to innovate requires the availability of proper resources. The competitiveness of the firm's "innovation team" is chosen as a way to measure innovation.

9.3 The Innovation Team

Innovation work is not possible without human and other *resources*. Moreover, the resources must be *managed*. Firms manage the necessary resources and take decisions designed to foster innovation at all *three levels* of corporate decision-making (strategic, operational, and transaction level). Moreover, the ability of the firm to innovate depends not only on the internal organisation of resources within the firm but also on the *interaction* of the firm with outsiders (other firms and the market).

Internal and external resources. The resources can be internal and organised internally, or external and obtained from the market.[21] In the latter case, the firm can purchase them (business acquisitions, employment contracts), hire them (outsourcing, consultancy work), or share them through the pooling of resources with other firms (cooperation, joint ventures).

Innovation team. If the firm is regarded as an organisational structure, we can assume that innovation-related work is done by specialised innovation teams embedded in the general organisational framework of the firm. Innovation teams combine human resources and other resources. The firm can have one or more innovation teams, and there can be innovation teams shared by two or more firms. Different innovation teams may be responsible for different sectors depending on the business process (for example, sales, R&D, financial engineering, M&A) and the level of corporate decision-making (for example, customer account management, strategic management).

Competitiveness of the innovation team. Innovation teams compete against other innovation teams. The question of the ability of the firm's governance structure to foster innovation can thus be reduced to a question of the competitiveness of its innovation teams against other firms' innovation teams (or their competitiveness in the relevant "innovation market").

What makes the innovation team competitive? In the following, we will study certain things that might increase the competitiveness of the innovation team. They relate to the following:

[21] See Arora A, Fosfuri A, Gambardella A, Markets for Technology and their Implications for Corporate Strategy, Ind Corp Change 10 (2001) pp 419–451.

- Human and other resources. The firm cannot remain innovative in the long term without investing human resources, capital, and other resources in its innovation team or teams.
- Organisational framework. The general organisational framework of the firm should foster innovation.
- Culture. The firm needs a corporate culture that fosters innovation.
- Risk preferences. The firm should accept the high-risk nature of innovation work.
- Long-termism. The innovation team needs long-termism. It takes time and money to build a competitive innovation team.
- Effective decision-making process. In order to be competitive against other innovation teams, the innovation team needs a fast decision-making process and well-informed decision-makers.
- Discretion. The innovation team needs a sufficient amount of discretion and flexibility.
- Incentives. Moreover, it needs proper incentives.

These issues can be studied at different levels of corporate decision-making: the strategic level, the operational level, the level of innovation team members, and the transaction level. We will focus on the *strategic level.*

9.4 Strategic Level

9.4.1 General Remarks

At the strategic level, the factors that can foster innovation might relate to control, ownership structure, the availability of funding, the structure of the firm, and societal and corporate culture. We can start with culture.

9.4.2 Culture

Like any corporate goals, the ability to innovate should be supported by societal and corporate culture.[22] Corporate culture is not static.

First, the firm's corporate culture depends on the strategic choice of the societal or institutional environment. Firms are social structures embedded in larger institutional environments.[23] The choice of one institutional environment rather than the

[22] See, for example, Mäntysaari P, The Law of Corporate Finance. Volume I. Springer, Berlin Heidelberg (2010) p 101.

[23] Lazonik W, The Chandlerian corporation and the theory of innovative enterprise, Ind Corp Change 19 (2010) p 333.

other can influence access to information and incentives in the form of social expectations, career prospects, and financial rewards.

Societal and corporate culture can thus be influenced by the choice of industry, geographical location, and business partners. For example, a firm that develops and sells nanotechnological products (a knowledge-intensive and competitive industry) next door to MIT (access to high-quality information, high social expectations of innovation) in a network of innovative firms (access to information, convergence of innovation-friendly cultures) to NASA (high customer requirements) is likely to remain more innovative compared with a sawmill located in a remote part of Finland.

Second, the firm's culture depends on the firm's control structure and ownership structure (Sects. 9.4.3 and 9.4.4) as the firm's culture is the culture enforced by those in control.

9.4.3 Control Structure

The firm is more likely to be innovative when innovation-relevant issues are controlled by the right people, that is, people that have "the abilities and incentives to confront the technological, market and competitive uncertainties inherent in the innovation process" (Lazonick and Prencipe 2005).

Generally, they should ensure that the firm's "innovation teams" are competitive (Sect. 9.3). In particular, they should control the firm's institutional environment and culture, and the allocation of corporate resources (strategic control). They should also be able to ensure that financial and other resources remain locked in to sustain the innovation process (financial control).[24] Moreover, they should ensure that there is a balance between centralisation and delegation. The innovation team should be given enough discretion (organisational control).

One of the important factors influencing the control structure is the level of self-enforcement. If the firm's governance model does not work without external monitoring and control inputs (apart from control by customers and the enforcement of general laws), the firm's ability to innovate may suffer, because: external monitors can further different objectives and have different incentives; external monitors may be less informed when taking decisions; and their decision-making may be slower. Such problems can be mitigated if the governance model is self-enforcing.

[24] Lazonick W, Prencipe A, Dynamic Capabilities and Sustained Innovation: Strategic Control and financial Commitment at Rolls-Royce plc, Ind Corp Change 14(3) (2005) p 534; Lazonik W, The Chandlerian corporation and the theory of innovative enterprise, Ind Corp Change 19 (2010) p 331.

9.4.4 Ownership Structure

The firm's ownership structure can have a large impact on the firm's control structure, innovation culture and resource allocation. If the firm has shareholders, different existing or potential shareholders can have different qualities as sources of capital and/or providers of ancillary services such as control services or services designed to foster innovation (see Sect. 7.9).

Ownership concentration. For example, if the firm has a small number of entrepreneur-shareholders each committed to innovation (such as Hewlett/Packard, Gates/Allen, Page/Brien), the firm is more likely to have a strong innovation culture. The firm is less likely to have a strong innovation culture when it has a highly dispersed share ownership structure. In the latter case, vocal short-term shareholders (such as hedge funds) might try to block long-term investments in innovation projects, prevent the issuing of new shares to finance investments, and force the company to distribute excess funds to shareholders.

Ownership concentration is thus one of the factors that can bring benefits. Large shareholders are better at fostering innovation compared with small shareholders.

According to previous studies, there can be a positive correlation between ownership concentration and R&D expenditures,[25] and cuts in R&D following poor earnings performance are less likely, if the degree of institutional ownership is greater.[26] Moreover, a higher degree of institutional share ownership may encourage innovation. This has been explained by better monitoring and protection of managers in the event that an R&D project fails. There is also a more positive relationship between innovation and institutional ownership when product market competition is more intense or when there is protection from hostile takeovers.[27]

On the other hand, if the firm has a controlling shareholder, the quality of the controlling shareholder obviously matters. A "good" controlling shareholder can be a source of various kinds of necessary ancillary services. It might use its legal and de facto powers in innovation-friendly ways. It might provide know-how and other information, help in dealings with outsiders, management resources, and other services. A good controlling shareholder can even be a source of capital or a signalling mechanism that makes it easier for the firm to raise funding from other investors.

Even non-controlling shareholders can be sources of capital and/or suppliers of necessary ancillary services. For example, firms often cement technological

---

[25] Francis J, Smith A, Agency costs and innovation: Some empirical evidence, J Acc Econ 19 (1995) pp 383–409; Eng LL, Shackell M, The Implications of Long-Term Performance Plans and Institutional Ownership for Firms' Research and Development (R&D) Investments, J Acc Aud Fin 16 (2001) pp 117–139.

[26] Bushee B, The influence of institutional investors on myopic R&D investment behavior, Acc Rev 73 (1998) pp 305–333.

[27] Aghion P, Van Reenen J, Zingales L, Innovation and Institutional Ownership (February 3, 2009).

partnerships with share ownerships designed to align the parties' long-term interests.

Management discretion. The firm's ownership structure can also affect the level of management discretion.

Management discretion is highest in the "classical firm" with one sole shareholder-manager-entrepreneur, or in partnership-type firms.

In other firms, a high level of management discretion can be combined with access to capital and other resources in different ways. (a) A private equity fund or investor may be the sole shareholder but concentrate on ownership rather than management control. A venture capital investor may provide capital without interfering in the management of the firm. (b) In hyped industries, it may be possible to raise plenty of capital from the market with promises of future growth. (c) Moreover, as a very large firm with a huge market capitalisation is not really in the market for control, its management can enjoy a high level of discretion even where the firm has a highly dispersed share ownership structure.

Management discretion can also be increased if the firm chooses a business form that does not include shareholders. Such business forms include, for example, cooperatives (Sect. 8.5) and the business form of private equity. The business form of private equity gives fund managers plenty of discretion compared with the managers of traditional limited-liability companies.

9.4.5 The Availability of Funding

Innovation work requires funding. In particular, it requires "patient" capital (Lazonik 2010).[28] Patient capital is necessary, because capabilities that derive from collective learning cumulate over time and cannot be transferred as such. Capital may also be required for business acquisitions. Business acquisitions are customarily used for the purpose of purchasing capabilities embedded in the target's organisation.

Control and ownership. Once again, the firm's ownership structure and control structure matter. The firm is more likely to be innovative when its strategy is controlled by well-informed people committed to fostering innovation, and when they can ensure the availability of funding and financial commitment.[29] This may require strategic control over internal revenues.[30]

[28] Bushee B, *op cit*, p 331.

[29] Lazonick W, Prencipe A, Dynamic Capabilities and Sustained Innovation: Strategic Control and Financial Commitment at Rolls-Royce plc, Ind Corp Change 14(3) (2005) p 534.

[30] Lazonik W, The Chandlerian corporation and the theory of innovative enterprise, Ind Corp Change 19 (2010) pp 331–332.

The firm's ownership structure and control structure play an important role even due to the nature of innovation work. Because of the particular characteristics of innovation work, it can be difficult to raise funding.[31]

Problems. To begin with, innovation processes are time-consuming, and many innovation projects fail. This could mean that it is difficult to find investors that can accept the high-risk nature of the investment and provide funding for the whole duration of the project.

In principle, the nature of information could be another cause of problems. It has been assumed that it is difficult to raise funding for innovation work in a freely competitive marketplace, because the use of information does not preclude its use by others (Arrow 1959).[32] On the other hand, knowledge transfer is not costless. It requires investment in the firm's absorptive capacity (Cohen and Levinthal 1989).[33] This means that the firm's ability to innovate requires plenty of investment in prior knowledge and the innovation team's skills and that information cannot be used by others without a cost.

9.4.6 The Structure of the Business Organisation

9.4.6.1 General Remarks

In addition to control and ownership, the firm should choose the structure of its business organisation (organisational architecture). The firm's organisational architecture is customarily decided on by the board or whoever is in control.

The structure of the firm's business organisation influences the firm's ability to innovate in four main ways.

Size. The first relates to the overall size of the firm. Large firm size can increase bureaucracy and cause information and incentive problems (Williamson 1984).[34] Problems caused by the large size of the firm can be mitigated by dividing the firm into smaller units (independent divisions or subsidiaries).

Skill base. The second relates to the firm's skill base. The firm's skill base depends on the available resources, the division of labour within the firm,[35] and the

[31] There is plenty of research on funding constraints. For a review, see Bond S, Van Reenen J, Microeconometric models of investment and employment. In: Heckman JJ, Leamer E (eds), Handbook of econometrics. North Holland, London (2007) pp 4417–4498.

[32] Arrow KJ, Economic Welfare and the Allocation of Resources for Invention. The Rand Corporation, Economics Division (15 December 1959). For a survey of recent research, see also Hall BH, The Financing of Innovation (December 2005).

[33] Cohen WM, Levinthal DE, Innovation and learning: the two faces of R&D, Econ J 99 (1989) pp 569–596.

[34] Williamson OE, The Incentive Limits of Firms, Rev World Econ 120(4) (1984) pp 736–763.

[35] Lazonik W, The Chandlerian corporation and the theory of innovative enterprise, Ind Corp Change 19 (2010) pp 332–333.

matching of resources with the task at hand at any point in time. In other words, the firm's skill base can depend on the skills of "the man on the spot" (Hayek).[36]

Make or buy. The third is that the firm can change its skill base in various ways. The firm can change its organisational structure, acquire or divest capabilities through transactions with outsiders, or build up capabilities internally.

Agency. The fourth is that the organisational structure of the firm influences the behaviour of intra-firm agents.[37]

9.4.6.2 Organisational Structure

There are various ways to organise the firm (see Sect. 8.1) and widely-used organisational design frameworks such as the Star Model (Galbraith 1977, 1995) and the "fit" and "good design" tests (Goold and Campbell 2002). These particular models are nevertheless fairly static in the sense that they do not describe how they change over time or deal with change (although one of the "good design tests" is the flexibility test that asks whether the proposed design supports future innovations). Models that focus more on the organisation's agility include the NBU model (Booz-Allen and Hamilton 1999) and the model for "built-to-change" organisations (Worley and Lawler 2006).[38] On the other hand, both are less detailed compared with the other two frameworks.

If the widely-used organisational design frameworks do not provide sufficiently detailed information about organisational structures that foster innovation, it is useful to start with the most basic organisational structures and study how they differ in this respect.

U-form and M-form. One can, therefore, start with the basic distinction between the unitary corporation (U-form corporation) and the multidivisional corporation (M-form corporation). The choice between the U-form and the M-form will also raise questions about the centralisation or decentralisation of corporate functions (see also Sects. 8.3 and 8.4).

The U-form is the older model. U-form corporations are organised into functional departments such as sales or manufacturing.

In contrast, M-form corporations have operating units organised as divisions. There are limits to decentralisation. While the operating activities of M-form corporations tend to be decentralised down to the divisional level, supervisory and service operations are centralised at the corporate level.

---

[36] See Mäntysaari, The Law of Corporate Finance. Volume I. Springer, Berlin Heidelberg (2010), section 10.2.2.

[37] For the management of agency, see, for example, *ibid*, Chapter 6 and section 7.4.

[38] Jones J, Keller S, Neilson G, Spiegel E, Organizing for Agility: Creating Natural Business Units. Booz-Allen & Hamilton, USA (1999); Worley CG, Lawler EE, Designing Organizations That Are Built to Change, MIT Sloan Man Rev 48(1) (2006) pp 19–23.

The M-form is generally regarded as the appropriate governance structure for dealing with increasing corporate diversity (Chandler 1962, 1977, 1991, Williamson 1975).[39] It is customarily accepted that technology is one of the main drivers of corporate diversity and that technologies and organisational practices co-evolve (Thompson 1967, Chandler 1977).[40]

Variants of the M-form. There are variants of the M-form.[41] One of the basic choices is to organise the M-form corporation either as an integrated enterprise contained within a *single corporation* or as a *holding structure* with a parent and multiple subsidiary corporations.[42]

The variants can favour centralisation or delegation. For example, more *centralised* versions of the M-form include the strategic *planning* style M-form (in which headquarters is strongly involved in guiding the strategic development of the divisions) and the strategic *control* style M-form (in which headquarters focuses on controlling the implementation of divisional strategies).[43] Both tend to prevail in *less* diversified companies within *more* technology-intensive sectors.[44]

The choice between different variants of the M-form depends on corporate strategy. First, it can depend on the level of *diversification*.[45] One can distinguish between related diversification, vertical integration, and unrelated diversification. In related diversification, the related diversifier seeks to obtain synergistic economies. In vertical integration, the vertical integrator pursues vertical economies. Related diversifiers develop a broader range of businesses compared with vertical integrators. Vertical integrators develop a broader range of vertically linked value chain activities related to their dominant business areas.[46]

---

[39] See Chandler AD, The Visible Hand: The Managerial Revolution in American Business. Belknap Press, Cambridge, Mass. (1977) pp 5–12; Williamson OE, Markets and Hierarchies: Analysis and Antitrust Implications. The Free Press, New York (1975) pp 135–138; Williamson OE, The Economic Institutions of Capitalism. The Free Press, New York (1985) p 289; Bainbridge S, Director Primacy: The Means and Ends of Corporate Governance, Northw U L Rev 97 (2003) pp 547–606 at 566–567.

[40] Thompson JD, Organizations in Action: Social Science Bases of Administration. McGraw-Hill, New York (1967) p 13 suggests that "technologies and environments are major sources of uncertainty for organizations and that the differences in those dimensions will result in differences in organizations".

[41] See Christensen JF, Corporate strategy and the management of innovation and technology, Ind Corp Change 11 (2002) pp 264–265.

[42] See, for example, Muchlinski PT, Multinational Enterprises and the Law. Blackwell Publishing (1999), Chapter 3 (on the business and legal forms of multinational enterprise).

[43] Goold M, Campbell A, Strategies and Styles: The Role of the Centre in Managing Diversified Corporations (LBS Centre for Business Strategy). Blackwell, Oxford (1987), cited in Christensen JF, *op cit*, pp 264–265.

[44] Chandler AD, The Functions of the HQ Unit in the Multibusiness Firm, Strat Man J 12 (1991) pp 31–50, cited in Christensen JF, *op cit*, pp 264–265.

[45] See Christensen JF, *op cit*, p 266, Table 1.

[46] *Ibid*, pp 264–266.

Second, the choice between different variants of the M-form can also depend on the sector's *technology* intensivity:

- More centralised versions of the M-form tend to prevail in less diversified firms within more technology-intensive sectors.[47]
- The decentralised or financial control oriented M-form prevails in very diversified corporations in relatively low-technology sectors.[48]
- Related diversification and vertical integration require more centralised coordination compared with unrelated diversification.[49]
- Related diversifiers tend to use the M-form with more or less centralised functions to promote coordination across divisions.[50]
- Vertical integrators tend to rely on substantial top-level operational control to obtain vertical economies, and they tend to maintain a U-form structure. However, some vertical integrators move closer to the related diversifier position.[51]

Third, it can depend on the corporate and societal *culture* of the parent.[52]

Management of innovation. The choice between the U-form and different variants of the M-form will influence the management of innovation and vice versa.

The organisational mode of managing innovation depends on the overall organisational architecture of the firm and the need to centralise or decentralise innovation work.[53] Technology is one of the main drivers that cause corporate organisational practices to adapt.[54]

A *decentralised* mode of managing innovation can reflect (a) the M-form as the overall organisational structure of the firm and/or (b) an innovation strategy that "gives high priority to incremental innovation with a primary concern for downstream, inter-functional relations and engineering-based R&D".[55]

A *centralised* mode of managing innovation may reflect (a) the fact that the firm is a U-form vertical integrator or an M-form technology-related diversifier and/or

---

[47] Chandler AD, The Functions of the HQ Unit in the Multibusiness Firm, Strat Man J 12 (1991) pp 31–50, cited in Christensen, supra, pp 264–266.

[48] Goold M, Campbell A, Strategies and Styles: The Role of the Centre in Managing Diversified Corporations (LBS Centre for Business Strategy). Blackwell, Oxford (1987); and Chandler AD, The Functions of the HQ Unit in the Multibusiness Firm, Strat Man J 12 (1991) pp 31–50, cited in Christensen JF, *op cit*, pp 264–266.

[49] See Christensen JF, *op cit*, pp 264–266.

[50] *Ibid.*

[51] *Ibid.*

[52] Muchlinski PT, *op cit*, pp 60–61: "... US firms tend to be more centralized than non-US firms ..."

[53] *Ibid*, p 271, Table 3.

[54] Pavitt K, Innovating routines in the business firm: what corporate tasks should they be accomplishing? Ind Corp Change 11 (2002) pp 125–126.

[55] Christensen JF, *op cit*, p 270.

Table 9.1 Management of innovation: strategic focus and organisational focus (Christensen 2002)

Focus of innovation strategy	Innovation	Interface relations	Nature of R&D
Organisational focus for management of innovation: decentralised	Incremental innovation	Primary focus on downstream, inter-functional relations	Engineering-based application
Organisational focus for management of innovation: centralised	Radical innovation	Primary focus on upstream interdisciplinary relations	"Deep" or science-based R&D

(b) an innovation strategy "focusing on radical innovation with primary focus on upstream or inter-disciplinary relations and in-depth or science-based R&D" (Table 9.1).[56]

9.4.6.3 Make or Buy

As the ability to innovate is embedded in the firm's skill base and organisational routines, it is difficult for the firm to transfer the ability to innovate across organisational boundaries.[57] However, the firm can change its ability to innovate by managing its scope in various ways.

The firm can use a combination of five basic alternatives. It can: make, buy resources, pool, outsource, or buy. The firm can thus: (1) do innovation work internally by using its existing resources ("make"); (2) do innovation work internally after acquiring new resources; (3) pool resources with one or more other firms (networks, joint ventures); (4) purchase innovation work from outsource providers that are integrated into its organisation (outsourcing); or (5) purchase just innovation work from the market ("buy").

We can focus on the second alternative as a sustainable way to increase the firm's ability to innovate through transactions with third parties.[58]

The firm's ability to innovate can be improved: (1) by employing skilled people or members of innovation teams; (2) by acquiring innovations teams (without breaking them up); and (3) by acquiring complementary assets (Teece 1986) that

[56] *Ibid.*

[57] See Arora A, Fosfuri A, Gambardella A, Markets for Technology and their Implications for Corporate Strategy, Ind Corp Change 10 (2001) p 420.

[58] See *ibid*, p 427: "The resource-based theory of the firm suggests that to be a source of sustained above average performance resources must meet three criteria: they must be valuable, rare and imperfectly mobile (Barney, 1991; Peteraf, 1993; Markides and Williamson, 1996). In other words, a competitive advantage must be underpinned by resources for which well-functioning markets do not or cannot exist."

give the innovation team more options to use their skills and commercialise innovations.[59]

For example, the firm may acquire another firm: to improve its own skill base and ability to innovate; and to get access to complementary assets. (a) When the target firm and the acquirer are integrated, the combined firm may be able to benefit from a larger skill base, better complementary assets, and larger economies of scale. (b) Complementary assets can be particularly important, because the successful commercialisation of a product innovation may require access to specialised assets such as marketing services, competitive manufacturing, and after-sales support (Teece 1986). This can increase the price that industrial firms are prepared to pay for target firms.

9.4.6.4 Agency

The organisational architecture of the firm influences the behaviour of intra-firm agents and therefore also the firm's ability to innovate. There can be particular innovation-related agency issues. For example, they can relate to the scope of agency (discretion), information, and monitoring.

Discretion. First, the innovation team should have enough discretion. This requires the delegation of power to the team and changes the scope of agency.[60]

Increasing discretion at one level of corporate hierarchy can influence agency costs. It can *reduce* agency costs, if decisions can be taken by agents that have better information and better incentives to take decisions in the interests of the firm. On the other hand, an increase in the amount of discretion can also *increase* agency costs. It is, therefore, necessary to find a balance.

The M-form is regarded as the better alternative when corporate diversity is high, because the M-form enables: (a) better operational efficiency by giving managers more discretion; and (b) better separation of monitoring (central monitoring by top management) and management (operational management at the divisional level). The level of discretion can be higher, when the divisions are incorporated subsidiaries with separated assets and a separated governance structure, and lower, when the divisions are unincorporated.

On the other hand, the choice of a strategy that makes the M-form necessary (the choice of many business units and risk management through diversification) can

---

[59] See Teece DJ, Profiting from technological innovation: Implications for integration, collaboration, licensing and public policy, Research Policy 15 (1986) pp 285–305; Arora A, Fosfuri A, *op cit*, p 428.

[60] Mäntysaari P, The Law of Corporate Finance. Volume I. Springer, Berlin Heidelberg (2010), section 6.3.

influence investment decisions and make it easier for managers to invest in unprofitable businesses that need cash.[61]

Information. Second, the organisational structure influences many information-related issues such as: the innovation team's access to information; its ability to comply with expectations; the transparency of the innovation team; and monitoring.

To begin with, a small firm is more transparent and has less internal information-related problems compared with a very large firm.

In a large firm, changes in the organisational structure can change the innovation team's *access* to useful intra-firm information. Whereas a centralised organisational structure (U-form, the functional structure) may increase the size of the innovation team and the transfer of ideas, a decentralised organisational structure with decentralised innovation teams (M-form, product structure, market structure, NBU structure) may create barriers between innovation teams.

Monitoring. The innovation team has better access to information when the firm's other innovation teams are transparent. In addition, increasing the transparency of innovation teams can improve the monitoring of innovation work.

However, transparency is not enough. The monitoring of innovation work requires even particular skills. This can influence organisational architecture and the governance structure of the firm.

A *centralised* organisational structure (U-form) increases the proximity of monitors to the innovation team. This can increase *transparency* and make it easier to monitor the team. However, the *specialisation* of monitors and the quality of monitoring is *reduced*, if the firm is very diversified (in which case it would be customary to choose the M-form). The lack of sufficient monitoring skills can make it more difficult to separate monitoring and innovation management.

A *decentralised* organisational structure (M-form) can contribute to *increased specialisation* of monitors compared with the centralised organisational structure. But if monitoring is decentralised as well, the "embedded" monitors can be *biased* or have incentives not to monitor effectively. In practice, this can require an additional layer of *centralised monitoring*. But the quality of monitoring may suffer, if the distance between the monitors and the innovation team is increased and specialisation reduced. In this case, it is important to ensure that the firm is controlled by people who possess the necessary skills.

For example, the governance model of a German AG addresses these problems in three ways.[62] First, there is mandatory separation of management powers and monitoring powers at board level (a two-tier board). Second, the management board can have the necessary innovation-relevant skill base, because the management

---

[61] Bardolet D, Lovallo D, Rumelt R, The hand of corporate management in capital allocations: patterns of investment in multi- and single-business firms, Ind Corp Change 19 (2010) p 608: "... we find that more diversified firms invest relatively more in unprofitable business units, less in cash-needy businesses, and more in cash-needy unprofitable businesses".

[62] See Mäntysaari P, Comparative Corporate Governance. Springer, Berlin Heidelberg (2005), section 5.2.5.

board must consist of the company's top executives. Third, even the supervisory board can have the necessary skill base, because German law does not hamper the appointment of skilled and well-informed supervisory board members. Since the independence of the monitoring function is achieved by structural measures, the personal independence of each member of the supervisory body is less relevant. This makes it possible to appoint well-informed former managers as supervisory board members. The mandatory supervisory board membership of employee representatives can increase the skill base even more.

9.5 Operational Level

The firm can employ a large number of legal tools and practices at the operational level, and they can have an influence on the firm's ability to innovate. We can illustrate this with three examples: the organisation of the firm's top management and the board; incentives; as well as the size and number of innovation teams.

Top management and the board. The structure and composition of the firm's top management should foster innovation. This requires managers that have the necessary skills and represent an innovation-friendly culture.

Many entities have a board structure (Sect. 7.8). As a result of the separation of monitoring and management, self-enforcement (Sect. 8.6), or compliance with laws, the board may be the body responsible for controlling corporate strategy, much of the governance structure of the firm, the allocation of resources, risk management, and the firm's culture. The board can thus play a key role. This requires board members that possess the necessary qualities. A board dominated by monitoring specialists may lack the necessary skills and an innovation-friendly culture.

Incentives. Generally, the personal incentives of top managers, members of the innovation team, and board members should be aligned with the interests of the firm in innovation-friendly ways. This can require "the alignment of their personal interests with the interests of the business organization in attaining and sustaining its competitive advantage" (Lazonik 2010).[63]

The nature of innovation work should play a role. For example, as innovation work requires risk-taking, members of innovation teams should not be punished for failure. It may also be important to ensure that members of innovation teams have favourable career prospects.[64]

Size and number of innovation teams. Even the size and number of innovation teams can play a role. Generally, large entity size can improve the skill base but

[63] Lazonik W, The Chandlerian corporation and the theory of innovative enterprise, Ind Corp Change 19 (2010) p 331.

[64] See Aghion P, Van Reenen J, Zingales L, Innovation and Institutional Ownership (February 3, 2009).

increase bureaucracy and information problems. The entity should therefore not be too large. Moreover, each innovation team should have proper incentives. Internal competition is one of the ways to create incentives. On the other hand, there are processes that must be coordinated.

This leads to the question of the optimal number of innovation teams in the firm. First, there cannot be more than one innovation team for a *coordination process*. For example, there cannot be more than one top management team for the firm.

Second, it may bring benefits to designate one innovation team for each *innovation market*. If the work of an innovation team is dependent on the work of another innovation team, bad things may happen. There may be information, incentive, and coordination problems. The other team may not know what the innovation team is up to, may not focus on the right issues, may not provide the optimal answers, may not prioritise the same things, and so forth. For example, it would perhaps not be a good idea to use a matrix organisation for the development of mobile phones with different teams responsible for different components or mobile phone functions, as the matrix organisation might lead to coordination problems.

Third, an innovation team should have sufficient human and other *resources*. This can reduce the optimal number of innovation teams. However, the firm may benefit from internal *competition* between innovation teams, and a large firm may need to mitigate information problems caused by its size. A large firm may, therefore, double some innovation work by using use smaller cells or "teams within teams" embedded in a larger but transparent innovation team.

9.6 Summary

As the governance model of the firm can influence its ability to innovate and survive in the long term, the latter belongs to factors that can explain the choice of the former. In order to remain innovative, the firm should be controlled by people who share an innovation-friendly culture and have both the necessary skill base and enough discretion. If the firm has a management body and a monitoring body, both should have an innovation-relevant skill base. The board should not be dominated by monitoring specialists. Because of the nature of innovation work, the firm should encourage innovation-relevant risk-taking.

Chapter 10
Theory of Corporate Law: Proposed Theory

10.1 General Remarks

Earlier in this book previous theories of corporate law were divided into theories of corporate law and theories of corporations. Both have their characteristic failings. Theories of corporations tend to be narrow and based on a small group of existing norms. Theories of corporate law tend to be broader but not perfectly aligned with existing norms. In addition, theories of corporate law in the US focus on corporate governance and fail to address a large part of the regulation of companies.[1]

There is room for a new theory of corporate law. The new theory should help to define the scope of corporate law and explain the contents of existing norms. The theory should be broad enough and, as far as possible, aligned with existing norms.

10.2 Three Categories of Issues

According to MBCL, corporations are legal tools used by firms. Corporations are not the only legal tools used by firms. For example, even the smallest firms can use a very large number of contracts (Chap. 4). Corporations are thus used as an alternative mechanism, and different alternative mechanisms can be chosen during the life of the firm.[2]

[1] See, for example, Bruner CM, The Enduring Ambivalence of Corporate Law, Alabama L Rev 59 (2008) pp 1386 (three fundamental and related issues) and 1408 (problems with models that focus on pure corporate governance); Bainbridge S, The New Corporate Governance in Theory and Practice. OUP, Oxford (2008) pp 14–15.

[2] To say that a corporation is a contract, or that a corporation is a nexus of contracts, or that the board is the nexus, would not explain why corporations are used and why the legal structure of the firm can change over time.

P. Mäntysaari, *Organising the Firm*,
DOI 10.1007/978-3-642-22197-2_10, © Springer-Verlag Berlin Heidelberg 2012

The existence of corporations is facilitated by corporate law. Corporate law should address three kinds of issues: existential; governance-related; and financial. (1) During its life, the corporation needs an organisation and a governance structure in order to operate. Many provisions of corporate law are therefore governance-related. (2) Each transaction will raise not only governance-related questions but even questions that can be described as financial. (3) And finally, the life of the corporation has two ends. Corporations come into existence and expire. Both situations raise governance-related and financial questions.

As a result, corporate law must consist of a matrix of three regulatory systems consisting of: (1) legal norms on corporate governance; (2) legal norms on transactions and corporate finance; and (3) legal norms on the incorporation, restructuring, and expiry of companies. A theory of corporate law must consist of three sectoral theories: (1) a theory of the law of corporate governance; (2) a theory of the law of corporate finance; and (3) a theory that describes the incorporation, restructuring, and expiry of companies.[3] In addition to these systems, corporate law will always contain (4) norms that reflect the public policy preferences of the state.

Two of these areas – corporate governance and corporate finance – are functional areas of law rather than a collection of norms found in certain statutes or cases regarded as company law statutes or cases. These areas can be defined in a meaningful way provided that the firm is chosen as the hypothetical user of law and the principal. The third area is dominated by public policy. It is therefore a collection of norms typically found in certain company and insolvency law statutes and cases.

These issues will now be discussed one by one.

10.3 Corporate Governance

A legal theory of corporate governance was already proposed in Chap. 7. It defines the law of corporate governance as a functional area of law and as a branch of MBCL. The theory identifies the particular issues that are addressed by firms in the context of corporate governance.

A legal theory of corporate governance is also an integral part of a broader theory of corporate law. Corporate governance norms address issues raised by: the separate

[3] Compare Fleischer H, Zur Zukunft der gesellschafts- und kapitalmarktrechtlichen Forschung, ZGR 4/2007 p 506: "Innerhalb des Gesellschafts- und Kapitalmarktrechts sehe ich zwei Kermgebiete, die Corporate Governane als zukünftige Megathemen ablösen könnten: Corporate Finance und Corporate Insolvency." From a historical perspective, see Bratton WW, *op cit*, p 1485: from the 1850s to the 1880s, the American states enacted "general corporation laws" that included "provisions respecting corporate purposes, directors' powers, capital structure, dividends, amendments, and mergers". Bratton cites Hurst JW, The Legitimacy of the Business Corporation in the Law of the United States 1780–1970. The University Press of Virginia, the USA (1970) p 82.

legal personality of companies (asset partitioning, representation, guidance, motivation)[4]; the organisation of firms (allocation of power, risk, and information); and the fact that there can be differences between the firm's real organisation and its legal organisation (the regulation of groups, see Sect. 7.2). In addition, corporate governance norms define the interests to be served by designating the principal and defining its legally relevant interests (Sects. 7.3 and 7.4).

The self-enforcement of the governance structure (Chap. 8) is an important design principle in corporate law. Companies are designed as self-contained legal entities. They have corporate bodies responsible for their internal decision-making and dealings with third parties. Corporate law provides for the separation of functions. Shareholders have only limited powers, and the court or the administrative authority is only rarely responsible for decision-making.

Like self-enforcement, ensuring the firm's ability to innovate is an important design principle (Chap. 9). First, it is customarily accepted that corporate law should be flexible and not too prescriptive.[5] Second, corporate law vests important management powers in the board rather than shareholders in general meeting. Third, risk-taking is made easier by the business judgment rule and other constraints on shareholders rights to claim compensation in the event of failure.

10.4 Corporate Finance

A legal theory of corporate finance describes the law of corporate finance as a functional area of law. Like the legal theory of corporate governance, it can be defined as a branch of MBCL.

In the context of corporate finance, the firm tries to manage the four generic issues (cash flow and the exchange of goods and services; risk; principal-agency relationships; and information) in four characteristic contexts: investment decisions; funding decisions; exit decisions; and existential decisions.[6]

Corporate law facilitates such decisions by providing a legal framework. This explains why corporate law contains rules on: transactions in general (investments); the issuing of shares and the raising of capital (funding); distributions and share

---

[4] To whom do assets linked to the company belong? Who is to be regarded as acting as or on behalf of the company? How should the persons acting as or on behalf of the company act? How should the various stakeholders act? How are these persons and stakeholders motivated?

[5] See, for example, Regulation 2157/2001 (SE Regulation); The Department of Trade and Industry, Company Law Reform, White Paper, Cm 6456 (March 2005); Gesetz zur Modernisierung des GmbH-Rechts und zur Bekämpfung von Missbräuchen (MoMiG).

[6] Mäntysaari P, The Law of Corporate Finance. Volume I. Springer, Berlin Heidelberg (2010) pp 1–2.

buybacks (exit); corporate insolvency and takeovers (existential decisions); and similar matters.[7]

The exact contents of these rules depend on many governance-related issues. First, the legal framework for investment, funding, exit, and existential decisions cannot be designed without choosing the interests that the framework should protect (Sects. 6.3, 7.3, 7.4, and 7.7). Second, it will often mean the allocation of risk between the firm and its stakeholders and between stakeholders inter se (Sect. 7.2). There are many examples of this. The allocation of power to shareholders is designed to reduce their perceived risk and, indirectly, the firm's funding costs. Restrictions on distributions to shareholders and the equity-insolvency rule are designed to lock in assets and protect the firm against the company's shareholders, shareholders against other shareholders, and lenders against shareholders. Corporate insolvency rules are designed to allocate risk between creditors, shareholders, and the firm. Third, the management of agency relationships is particularly important in the context of matters relating to corporate finance (Sect. 7.2). Fourth, the duty to disclose information is particularly important as a corporate governance tool in these situations (Sect. 7.2).

10.5 Existential Issues

Existential issues relate to incorporation (the coming into existence of the company), restructuring, or expiry of the entity. For public policy, governance-related, and financial reasons, each of these situations may require a different regulatory approach.

Before incorporation. Before incorporation, a company does not exist as a legal person. The regulation of companies at this stage is influenced by various factors.

Public policy reasons will dictate much of the regulation of the founding of companies. The founding of companies can be made difficult or easy, it can require plenty of capital or no capital, it can require government permits or mere registration, the participation of a lawyer or a notary public may be necessary or not necessary, the founding of companies can take a couple of days or several months, and so forth. These differences can be explained by different approaches to business, the regulation of business, the protection of the public, other public policy concerns, or sleaze.

Even governance-related issues will require plenty of regulation at this stage. This is because normal rules on the representation of the company internally and in its dealings with third parties cannot apply unless adapted to this special situation. There is a difference in time between the stage when no steps have been taken and the moment when the person responsible takes the final step required for the

[7] Generally, see Mäntysaari P, The Law of Corporate Finance. Volume III. Springer, Berlin Heidelberg (2010).

attainment of legal personality through incorporation. Whereas normal rules on the representation of the company clearly cannot apply when the incorporation process is about to start, they may gradually become applicable the closer one gets to the point in time when the entity becomes the finished product and a legal person.

Some norms are necessary for financial reasons. First, there may be particular capital requirements because of public policy. Capital requirements may be general and part of a legal capital regime (for example, requirements implementing the Second Company Law Directive in the EU), or sector-specific (for example, requirements implementing the Capital Requirements Directive). Second, somebody should subscribe for shares and pay the amount payable for the shares, and somebody should ensure that the shares are paid in full.

After incorporation. After incorporation, the company is a legal person. Public policy, governance-related, and financial reasons will again influence the regulation of the restructuring of companies and corporate insolvency.

Public policy reasons play an important role in corporate insolvency. Corporate insolvency rules allocate risk between the firm and its stakeholders, and between stakeholders inter se. First, they give incentives not to let the company become insolvent in the first place. For example, there may be general standards, bright-line rules, and liability rules for the company's representatives. Second, there may be rules designed to protect the firm as a going concern. For example, there may be restrictions on payments to creditors and shareholders, and rules that enable creditors to convert their claims to shares at the cost of existing shareholders. Third, there can also be rules regulating the right of creditors to realise the assets of the company.

The choice of the regulatory framework will thus require a policy choice. In the US, Chap. 11 is an example of a corporate insolvency mechanism that protects the firm as a going concern. Traditional continental European bankruptcy laws are the opposite. They provide an example of a mechanism that favours existing creditors to the detriment of members of the firm's organisation (employees, network members) and the company's shareholders.

In corporate insolvency, public policy objectives will also influence many governance-related issues. The allocation of power is a major issue because of the conflicting interests of the various stakeholder classes and the firm in "pathological" situations. The allocation of power to a certain stakeholder class means that its interests have a better chance to prevail.

Governance-related issues predominate in corporate restructurings for three reasons. First, restructurings (such as mergers and demergers) may benefit one stakeholder category at the expense of other stakeholders. For example, they may have an adverse effect on the interests of existing shareholders and creditors. Second, they are important decisions – "rules of the game decisions"[8] – that should not be made lightly and not without the separation of initiation and ratification

[8] Bebchuk LA, The Case for Increasing Shareholder Power, Harv L Rev 118 (2005) pp 833–917.

powers. Third, the choice of principal is a key factor explaining the reason for restructuring. For example, a takeover might make industrial sense and bring long-term benefits to the firm under the circumstances, but if it reduces the amount of distributable funds in the short-term, many short-term shareholders of the buyer may vote against it. Corporate law sets out whose interests should matter.

Financial aspects are important in restructurings and corporate insolvency. Both can result in a change in the funding and share ownership structure of the company. Company laws can increase the survival chances of firms by facilitating restructurings and the refinancing of companies.

Expiry. After incorporation, it may become necessary to end the company's life. The regulation of companies will even in this case address different kinds of legal concerns.

There are obvious public policy issues. Some companies should not be permitted to exist as legal persons. And when any company expires, the interests of its existing contract parties must be protected.

Governance-related issues play an important role because of the impact that the company's expiry will have on its shareholders and other stakeholders. This raises again questions about the principal (Sects. 7.3 and 7.4). Shareholders are often regarded as residual claimants who have a claim to whatever is left after the company's debts have been paid. If shareholders may decide on the liquidation of the company (the carrier of the firm), one might ask whether the firm can be regarded as the principal at all. The answer is, first, that somebody must be able to decide on the liquidation of the company and that a decision of this kind requires a decision-making process that reflects its magnitude. It can be difficult to separate decision management (initiation) and decision control (ratification) in this case. One of the ways to achieve it is by vesting decision rights in shareholders or the court, or both. Second, the allocation of power to decide on the liquidation of the company can also be explained by financial aspects.

What happens at the end of the company's life will influence the risk exposure of investors, the availability and cost of funding, and the firm's long-term survival chances. If the power to decide on liquidation is reserved for shareholders, their perceived risk exposure is reduced. If it is reserved for somebody else, shareholders' perceived risk exposure is increased. Their perceived risk exposure will influence the availability and cost of equity capital and the long-term survival chances of the firm.

10.6 Public Policy Preferences of the State

Corporate law can contain various norms that reflect the state's particular public policy preferences. These norms do not have to be designed to foster "economic efficiency" or the "joint welfare of all stakeholders". The state can use corporate law as a means to achieve a wide range of social goals. Depending on the state, they could include: equality (prohibition of discrimination, gender-based board quotas, other quotas); discrimination (on the basis of gender, race, religion, ethnic origin, nationality, or political views); rent-seeking by the ruling class (business activities, share ownership, or board membership totally or partly reserved for members of a certain class); national security (restrictions on who may control companies in certain sectors); governance of risk in general; management of systemic risk (financial industry); or other goals.

References

Adams RB, Hermalin BE, Weisbach MS, The role of boards of directors in corporate governance: a conceptual framework and survey, Journal of Economic Literature 48(1) (2010) pp 58–107.

Aghion P, Van Reenen J, Zingales L, Innovation and Institutional Ownership (February 3, 2009).

Aglietta M, Rebérioux A, Corporate Governance Adrift. A Critique of Shareholder Value. Edward Elgar, Cheltenham (UK) Northampton (Mass) (2005).

Alchian AA, Uncertainty, Evolution, and Economic Theory, Journal of Political Economy 58 (1950) pp 211–221.

Alchian AA, Demsetz H, Production, information costs, and economic organization, American Economic Review 62(5) (1972) pp 777–795.

Almén T, Das skandinavische Kaufrecht: ein Kommentar zu den skandinavischen Kaufgesetzen unter eingehender Berücksichtigung ausländischen Rechts. Carl Winters Universitätsbuchhandlung, Heidelberg (1922).

Angell JK, Amess, Treatise on The Law of private corporations aggregate. 9th ed. Little, Brown, and Co., Boston (1871).

Aoki M, Toward a Comparative Institutional Analysis. Comparative Institutional Analysis 2. The MIT Press, Cambridge, Mass. (2001).

Aoki M, Jackson G, Understanding an emergent diversity of corporate governance and organizational architecture: an essentiality-based analysis, Industrial and Corporate Change 17 (2008) pp 1–27.

Armour J, Whincop, MJ. The Proprietary Foundations of Corporate Law, Oxford Journal of Legal Studies 27 (2007) pp 429–465.

Arnold MG, Hockerts K, The Greening Dutchman: Philips' Process of Green Flagging to Drive Sustainable Innovations, Business Strategy and the Environment (2010).

Arora A, Fosfuri A, Gambardella A, Markets for Technology and their Implications for Corporate Strategy, Industrial and Corporate Change 10 (2001) pp 419–451.

Arrow KJ, Economic Welfare and the Allocation of Resources for Invention. The Rand Corporation, Economics Division (15 December 1959).

Arrow KJ, Essays in the Theory of Risk Bearing. Markham Publishing Co., Chicago (1971).

Arrow KJ, The Limits of Organization. W. W. Norton & Company, New York (1974).

Bagley CE, Winning Legally. Harvard Business School Press, Boston, Mass. (2005).

Bainbridge S, Director Primacy: The Means and Ends of Corporate Governance, Northwestern University Law Review 97 (2003) pp 547–606.

Bainbridge S, Response to Increasing Shareholder Power: Director Primacy and Shareholder Disempowerment, Harvard Law Review 119 (2006) pp 1735–1749.

Bainbridge S, The New Corporate Governance in Theory and Practice. Oxford University Press, Oxford (2008).

P. Mäntysaari, *Organising the Firm*,
DOI 10.1007/978-3-642-22197-2, © Springer-Verlag Berlin Heidelberg 2012

Ballerstedt K, GmbH-Reform, Mitbestimmung, Unternehmensrecht, Zeitschrift für das gesamte Handelsrecht und Wirtschaftsrecht 135 (1971) pp 479–510.
Bardolet D, Lovallo D, Rumelt R, The hand of corporate management in capital allocations: patterns of investment in multi- and single-business firms, Industrial and Corporate Change 19 (2010) pp 591–612.
Barnard CI, The Functions of the Executive. Harvard University Press, Cambridge, Mass. (1938).
Barney JB, Firm Resources and Sustained Competitive Advantage, Journal of Management 17 (1991) pp 99–120.
Basedow J, The State's Private Law and the Economy–Commercial Law as an Amalgam of Public and Private Rule-Making, American Journal of Comparative Law 56 (2008) pp 703–722.
Baumann H, Strukturfragen des Handelsrechts, Archiv für die civilistische Praxis 184 (1984) pp 45–66.
Baumol WJ, Business Behavior, Value and Growth. Macmillan, New York (1959).
Baumol WJ, On the Theory of Expansion of the Firm, The American Economic Review 52 (1962) pp 1078–1087.
Bebchuk LA, The Case for Increasing Shareholder Power, Harvard Law Review 118 (2005) pp 833–917.
Bebchuk LA, Roe MJ, A Theory of Path Dependence in Corporate Ownership and Governance, Stanford Law Review 52 (1999) pp 127–170.
Bebchuk LA, Jackson RJ, Corporate Political Speech: Who Decides? Harvard Law Review 124 (2010) pp 83–117.
Becht M, Bolton P, Roell A, Corporate Governance and Control. In: Constantinides M, Harris M, Schulz RM (eds), Handbook of Economics and Finance. Nord Holland, Amsterdam (2003) pp 4–109.
Belloc F, Corporate governance and innovation: an organizational perspective, MPRA Paper No. 21495 (10 January 2010).
Berger KP, International Economic Arbitration. Studies in Transnational Economic Law 9. Kluwer Law and Taxation Publishers, Deventer (1993).
Berger KP, The Creeping Codification of the Lex Mercatoria. Kluwer Law International, The Hague (1999).
Bergström C, Samuelsson P, Aktiebolagets grundproblem. En rättsekonomisk analys. Nerenius & Santérus Förlag, Stockholm (1997).
Berle AA, Corporate Powers as Powers in Trust, Harvard Law Review 44 (1931) pp 1049–1074.
Berle AA, For Whom are Corporate Managers Trustees? Harvard Law Review 45 (1932) pp 1365–1372.
Berle AA, Property, Production and Revolution. A Preface to the Revised Edition. In: Berle AA, Means GC, The Modern Corporation and Private Property. Transaction Publishers, New Brunswick, New Jersey (1968).
Berle AA, Means GC, The Modern Corporation and Private Property. Transaction Publishers, New Brunswick, New Jersey (1932).
Binder JH, „Prozeduralisierung" und Corporate Governance. Innerbetriebliche Entscheidungsvorbereitung und Prozessüberwachung als Gegenstände gesellschaftsrechtlicher Regulierung – Entwicklungslinien und Perspektiven, Zeitschrift für Unternehmens- und Gesellschaftsrecht 5/2007 pp 745–788.
Black B, Kraakman R, A Self-Enforcing Model of Corporate Law, Harvard Law Review 109 (1996) pp 1911–1982.
Blair MM, Locking in Capital: What Corporate Law Achieved for Business Organizers in the Nineteenth Century, UCLA Law Review 51 (2003) pp 387–455.
Blair MM, Stout LA, A Team Production Theory of Corporate Law, Virginia Law Review 85 (1999) pp 247–328.
Bond S, Van Reenen J, Microeconometric models of investment and employment. In: Heckman JJ, Leamer E (eds), Handbook of econometrics. North Holland, London (2007) pp 4417–4498.
Booz-Allen & Hamilton, see Jones J et al (1999).

Bormann J, König DC, Der Weg zur Europäischen Privatgesellschaft, Recht der internationalen Wirtschaft 3/2010 pp 111–119.

Bratton WW, The New Economic Theory of the Firm: Critical Perspectives from History, Stanford Law Review 41 (1989) pp 1471–1527.

Brookings RS, Die Demokratisierung der amerikanischen Wirtschaft. Berlin (1925).

Brown LM, Manual of Preventive Law. Prentice-Hall, Inc., New York (1950).

Bruner CM, The Enduring Ambivalence of Corporate Law, Alabama Law Review 59 (2008) pp 1385–1449.

Bushee B, The influence of institutional investors on myopic R&D investment behavior, The Accounting Review 73 (1998) pp 305–333.

Calabresi G, Some Thoughts on Risk Distribution and the Law of Torts, Yale Law Journal 70 (1961) pp 499–553.

Canaris CW, Handelsrecht, 24. Auflage. C.H. Beck, München (2006).

Casciaro T, Determinants of governance structure in alliances: the role of strategic, task and partner uncertainties, Industrial and Corporate Change 12 (2003) pp 1223–1251.

Chandler AD, Strategy and structure: Chapters in the history of the industrial enterprise. MIT Press, Cambridge, Mass. (1962).

Chandler AD, The Visible Hand: The Managerial Revolution in American Business. Belknap Press, Cambridge, Mass. (1977).

Chandler AD, Scale and Scope: The Dynamics of Industrial Enterprise. Harvard University Press, Cambridge, Mass. (1990).

Chandler AD, The Functions of the HQ Unit in the Multibusiness Firm, Strategic Management Journal 12 (1991) pp 31–50.

Charreaux GJ, Corporate Governance Theories: From Micro Theories to National Systems Theories. Working Papers FARGO 1041202, December 2004. Available at: http://ideas.repec.org/p/dij/wpfarg/1041202.html.

Cheffins BR, Using Theory to Study Law: A Company Law Perspective, Cambridge Law Journal 58(1) (1999) pp 197–221.

Christensen JF, Corporate strategy and the management of innovation and technology, Industrial and Corporate Change 11 (2002) pp 263–288.

Clark RC, Corporate Law. Little, Brown & Co., Boston, Mass (1986).

Clark RC, Contracts, Elites, and Traditions in the Making of Corporate Law, Columbia Law Review 89 (1989) pp 1703–1747.

Coase RH, The Nature of the Firm, Economica, New Series 4(16) (1937) pp 386–405.

Coase RH, The Problem of Social Cost, Journal of Law and Economics 3 (1960) pp 1–44.

Cohen WM, Levinthal DE, Innovation and learning: the two faces of R&D, The Economic Journal 99 (1989) pp 569–596.

Cooter R, Ulen T, Law and Economics. 5th International Edition. Pearson/Addison-Wesley, Boston, Mass. (2007).

Cosack K, Lehrbuch des Handelsrechts. Sechste Auflage. Verlag von Ferdinand Enke, Stuttgart (1903).

Cyert RM, March JG, A Behavioral Theory of the Firm. Prentice-Hall, Inc., Englewood Cliffs, New Jersey (1963).

Daines R, Does Delaware Law Improve Firm Value? Journal of Financial Economics 62 (2001) pp 525–558.

Darwin C, The Origin of Species (1859).

Dau-Schmidt KG, Brun CL, Lost in Translation: The Economic Analysis of Law in the United States and Europe, Columbia Journal of Transnational Law 44 (2006) pp 602–621.

Davis JH, Schoorman FD, Donaldson L, Toward a Stewardship Theory of Management, The Academy of Management Review 22 (1997) pp 20–47.

DCFR. See von Bar C et al.

De Coninck J, The Functional Method of Comparative Law: Quo Vadis? Rabels Zeitschrift für ausländisches und internationales Privatrecht 74 (2010) pp 318–350.

Demsetz H, The Structure of Ownership and the Theory of the Firm. Journal of Law & Economics 26(2) (1983) pp 375–390.

Dewey J, The Historic Background of Corporate Legal Personality, Yale Law Journal 35 (1926) pp 655–673.

Djankov S, Glaeser E, La Porta R, Lopez-de-Silanes F, Shleifer A, The New Comparative Economics, Journal of Comparative Economics 31 (2003) pp 595–619.

Djankov S, La Porta R, Lopez-de-Silanes F, Shleifer A, The law and economics of self-dealing, Journal of Financial Economics 88 (2008) pp 430–465.

Dodd EM, For Whom are Corporate Managers Trustees? Harvard Law Review 45 (1932) pp 1145- 1163.

Dodd EM, Is Effective Enforcement of the Fiduciary Duties of Corporate Managers Practicable? University of Chicago Law Review 2 (1935) pp 194–207.

Dooley MP, Two Models of Corporate Governance, The Business Lawyer 47 (1991–1992) pp 461–528.

Druey JN, The practitioner and the professor – is there a theory of commercial law? In: Tison M, De Wulf H, Van der Elst C, Steennot R (eds), Perspectives in Company Law and Financial Regulation: Essays in Honour of Eddy Wymeersch. International Corporate Law and Financial Market Regulation. Cambridge University Press, Cambridge (2009).

Eidenmüller H, Effizienz als Rechtsprinzip. Die Einheit der Gesellschaftswissenschaften 90. Mohr Siebeck, Tübingen (2005).

Eisenberg M, The Structure of the Corporation. Originally published by Little, Brown & Co., Boston (1976). Reprinted in 2006 by Beard Books, Washington, DC.

Easterbrook FH, Fischel DR, The Economic Structure of Corporate Law. Harvard University Press, Cambridge, Mass (1991).

Eidenmüller H, Effizienz als Rechtsprinzip. 3. Auflage. Die Einheit der Gesellschaftswissenschaften. Band 90. Mohr Siebeck, Tübingen (2005).

Eidenmüller H, Forschungsperspektiven im Unternehmensrecht, Zeitschrift für Unternehmens- und Gesellschaftsrecht 4/2007 pp 484–499.

Eisenhardt KM, Agency Theory: An Assessment and Review. Academy of Management Review 14 (1989) pp 57–74.

Eng LL, Shackell M, The Implications of Long-Term Performance Plans and Institutional Ownership for Firms' Research and Development (R&D) Investments, Journal of Accounting, Auditing and Finance 16 (2001) pp 117–139.

Engel C, Schön W (eds), Das Proprium der Rechtswissenschaft. Recht – Wissenschaft – Theorie. Mohr Siebeck, Tübingen (2007).

Engel C, Schön W, Vorwort. In: Engel C, Schön W (eds), Das Proprium der Rechtswissenschaft. Recht – Wissenschaft – Theorie. Mohr Siebeck, Tübingen (2007) pp IX–XIV.

Epstein RA, Let "The Fundamental Things Apply": Necessary and Contingent Truths in Legal Scholarship, Harvard Law Review 115 (2002) pp 1288–1313.

Ernst W, Gelehrtes Recht – Die Jurisprudenz aus der Sicht des Zivilrechtslehrers. In: Engel C, Schön W (eds), Das Proprium der Rechtswissenschaft. Recht – Wissenschaft – Theorie. Mohr Siebeck, Tübingen (2007) pp 3–49.

Fai F, A structural decomposition analysis of technological opportunity, corporate survival, and leadership, Industrial and Corporate Change 16 (2007) pp 1069–1103.

Fama EF, Agency Problems and the Theory of the Firm. Journal of Political Economy 88(2) (1980) pp 288–307.

Fama EF, Jensen MC, Separation of Ownership and Control. Journal of Law and Economics 26 (1983) pp 301–325.

Farber DA, Economic Efficiency and The Ex Ante Perspective. In: Kraus JS, Walt SD (eds), The Jurisprudential Foundations of Corporate and Commercial Law. Cambridge Studies in Philosophy and Law. Cambridge University Press, Cambridge (2000) pp 55–86.

Ferran E, Principles of Corporate Finance Law. Oxford University Press, Oxford (2008).

Fleischer H, Grundfragen der ökonomischen Theorie im Gesellschafts- und Kapitalmarktrecht, Zeitschrift für Unternehmens- und Gesellschaftsrecht 1/2001 pp 1–32.
Fleischer H, Zur Zukunft der gesellschafts- und kapitalmarktrechtlichen Forschung, Zeitschrift für Unternehmens- und Gesellschaftsrecht 4/2007 pp 500–510.
Fleischer H, Gesetz und Vertrag als alternative Problemlösungsmodelle im Gesellschaftsrecht, Zeitschrift für das gesamte Handelsrecht und Wirtschaftsrecht 168 (2004) pp 673–707.
Fleischer H, Gesellschafts- und Kapitalmarktrecht als wissenschaftliche Disziplin – Das Proprium der Rechtswissenschaft. In: Engel C, Schön W (eds), Das Proprium der Rechtswissenschaft. Recht - Wissenschaft - Theorie 1. Mohr Siebeck, Tübingen (2007) pp 50–76.
Fleischer H, Supranational Corporate Forms in the European Union: Prolegomena to a Theory on Supranational Forms of Association, Common Market Law Review 47 (2010) pp 1671–1717.
Fleischer H, Supranationale Gesellschaftsformen in der Europäischen Union – Prolegomena zu einer Theorie supranationaler Verbandsformen, Zeitschrift für das gesamte Handelsrecht und Wirtschaftsrecht 174 (2010) pp 385–428.
Flohr M, Beyond the State? Rethinking Private Law. Symposium in Hamburg am 12. Und 13. Juli 2007, Rabels Zeitschrift für ausländisches und internationales Privatrecht 72 (2008) pp 391–396.
Flume W, Allgemeiner Teil des bürgerlichen Rechts. Band 1. Teil 2. Springer, Berlin Heidelberg (1983).
Foucault M, L'Archéologie du Savoir. Éditions Gallimard, France (1969).
Foss NJ, Lando H, Thomsen S, 5610 The Theory of the Firm. In: Bouckaert B, De Geest G (eds), Encyclopedia of Law and Economics. Volume III. The Regulation of Contracts. Edward Elgar, Cheltenham (2000) pp 631–658.
Foster NHD, Company Law Theory in Comparative Perspective: England and France. American Journal of Comparative Law 48 (2000) pp 573–621.
Foucault M, L'Archéologie du Savoir. Éditions Gallimard, France (1969).
Francis J, Smith A, Agency costs and innovation: Some empirical evidence, Journal of Accounting and Economics 19 (1995) pp 383–409.
Freeman RE, Strategic Management. A Stakeholder Approach. Cambridge University Press, Cambridge (print-on-demand edition, originally published in 1984).
Freeman RE, Harrison JS, Wicks AC, Parmar BL, de Colle S, Stakeholder Theory: The State of the Art. Cambridge University Press, Cambridge (2010).
Freud S, Massenpsychologie und Ich-Analyse. Internationaler Psychoanalytischer Verlag, Wien (1921).
Freund E, The Legal Nature of Corporations. University of Chicago Press, Chicago (1897).
Friedman M, The Social Responsibility of Business is to Increase its Profits, The New York Times Magazine, September 13, 1970.
Galan JI, Sanchez MJ, Influence of industry R&D intensity on corporate product diversification: interaction effect of free cash flow, Industrial and Corporate Change 15 (2006) pp 531–547.
Galbraith JR, Organization Design. Addison-Wesley, Reading, Mass. (1977).
Galbraith JR, Designing Organizations: An Executive Briefing on Strategy, Structure, and Process. Jossey-Bass Inc., San Francisco, Calif. (1995).
Geis GS, The Space Between Markets and Hierarchies. Virginia Law Review 95 (2009) pp 99–154.
Gillette CP (ed), The Creation and Interpretation of Commercial Law. The International Library of Essays in Law and Legal Theory. Ashgate, Dartmouth (2003).
Goetzmann WN, Rouwenhorst KG (eds), The Origins of Value. Oxford University Press, Oxford (2005).
Goldman B, Lex Mercatoria, Forum Internationale 3 (1983) pp 3–7.
Goldschmidt L, Handbuch des Handelsrechts. Erste Band. Erste Abtheilung. Universalgeschichte des Handelsrechts. Erste Lieferung. Ferdinand Enke, Stuttgart (1891).
Goode RM, The Wilfred Fullagar Memorial Lecture: The Codification of Commercial Law, Monash University Law Review 14 (1988) pp 135–157.

Goode RM, Commercial Law in the Next Millenium. The Hamlyn Lectures. Forty-ninth Series. Sweet & Maxwell, London (1998).
Goold M, Campbell A, Strategies and Styles: The Role of the Centre in Managing Diversified Corporations (LBS Centre for Business Strategy). Blackwell, Oxford (1987).
Goold M, Campbell A, Do You Have a Well-Designed Organization? Harvard Business Review 80(2) (2002) pp 117–124.
Greif A, Commitment, coercion, and markets: The nature and dynamics of institutions supporting exchange. In: Menard C, Shirley MM (eds), Handbook of New Institutional Economics. Springer, Dordrecht (2005) pp 727–786.
Großfeld B, Zur Geschichte der Anerkennungsproblematik bei Aktiengesellschaften, Rabels Zeitschrift für ausländisches und internationales Privatrecht 38 (1974) pp 344–371.
Grossman SJ, Hart OD, The Costs and Benefits of Ownership: A Theory of Vertical and Lateral Integration, Journal of Political Economy 94 (1986) pp 691–719.
Grotius H, De jure belli ac pacis libri tres (1625).
Guillaume F, The Law Governing Companies in Swiss Private International Law. In: Sarcevic P, Volken P, Bonomi A, Yearbook of Private International Law, Volume 6. Sellier, München / Staempfli Publishers, Berne / Swiss Institute of Comparative Law (2005) pp 251–289.
Guiso L, Sapienza P, Zingales L, Civic Capital as the Missing Link. EUI Working Paper ECO2010/08. European University Institute, Department of Economics (2010).
Hall BH, The Financing of Innovation (December 2005).
Hall BH, Rosenberg N (eds), Handbook of the Economics of Innovation. North-Holland, Amsterdam (2010).
Hansmann H, Kraakman R, The Essential Role of Organizational Law, Yale Law Journal 110 (2000) pp 392–393.
Hansmann H, Kraakman R, The end of history for corporate law. In: Gordon JN, Roe MJ (eds), Convergence and Persistence in Corporate Governance. Cambridge University Press, Cambridge (2004) pp 33–68. Originally published as Hansmann H, Kraakman R, The End of History for Corporate Law. Georgetown Law Journal 89(2) (2001) pp 439–468.
Hardin G, The Tragedy of the Commons, Science 162 (1968) pp 1243–1248.
Hatzimihail NE, The Many Lives—And Faces—of Lex Mercatoria: An Essay on the Genealogy of International Business Law, Law and Contemporary Problems 71 (2008) pp 169–190.
Hausmann F, Vom Aktienwesen und vom Aktienrecht. Mannheim (1928).
Herala N, Use of Qualitative Comparative Analysis (QCA) in Comparative Law. Comparison of the Legal Regulation of Sustainable Development in Physical Planning in Denmark and Finland. Acta Wasaensia 124, Universitas Wasaensis, Vaasa (2004).
Hofstetter K, Parent Responsibility for Subsidiary Corporations: Evaluating European Trends, International and Comparative Law Quarterly 39 (1990) pp 576–598.
Holahan PF, Markham SK, Factors Affecting Multifunctional Team Effectiveness. In: Rosenau MD Jr, Griffin A, Castellion G, Anschuetz N (eds), The PDMA Handbook of New Product Development. John Wiley & Sons, Inc., New York (1996) pp 119–135.
Holmes OW, The Path of the Law, Harvard Law Review 10 (1897) pp 457–490.
Holmström B, Moral Hazard in Teams. The Bell Journal of Economics 13(2) (1982) pp 324–340.
Holmström B, Roberts J, The Boundaries of the Firm Revisited, Journal of Economic Perspectives 12(4) (1998) pp73–94.
Holmström B, Tirole J, The Theory of the Firm. In: Schmalensee R, Willig RD (eds), The Handbook of Industrial Organization. Volume 1. North-Holland, Amsterdam (1989) pp 61–133.
Horwitz MJ, Santa Clara Revisited: The Development of Corporate Theory, West Virginia Law Review 173 (1986) pp 173–224.
Hug W, The History of Comparative Law, Harvard Law Review 45 (1932) pp 1027–1070.
Hunziker S, Das Prinzipal-Agent-Problem im schweizerischen Vertragsrecht. Informationsasymmetrien und Verhaltenssteuerung. Zürcher Studien zum Privatrecht 199. Schulthess, Zürich Basel Genf (2007).

Husa J, Farewell to Functionalism or Methodological Tolerance? Rabels Zeitschrift für ausländisches und internationales Privatrecht 67 (2003) pp 419–447.

Ireland P, Company Law and the Myth of Shareholder Ownership, Modern Law Review 62(1) (1999) pp 32–57.

Jansen N, Michaels R, Private Law and the State. Comparative Perceptions and Historical Observations, Rabels Zeitschrift für ausländisches und internationales Privatrecht 71 (2007) pp 345–397.

Jensen MC, Meckling WH, Theory of the Firm: Managerial Behavior, Agency Costs and Ownership Structure. Journal of Financial Economics 3(4) (1976) pp 305–360.

Jessup PC, Transnational Law. Yale University Press, New Haven (1956).

Jones J, Keller S, Neilson G, Spiegel E, Organizing for Agility: Creating Natural Business Units. Booz-Allen & Hamilton, USA (1999).

Kadner Graziano T, Die Europäisierung der juristischen Perspektive und der vergleichenden Methode – Fallstudien, Zeitschrift für Vergleichende Rechtswissenschaft 106 (2007) pp 248–271.

Kahan M, Kamar E, The Myth of State Competition in Corporate Law. Stanford Law Review 55 (2002) pp 679–749.

Kalss S, Maßgebliche Forschungsfelder in der nächsten Dekade im Bereich des Gesellschafts- und Kapitalmarktrechts, Zeitschrift für Unternehmens- und Gesellschaftsrecht 4/2007 pp 520–531.

Keay A, Ascertaining The Corporate Objective: An Entity Maximisation and Sustainability Model. Modern Law Review 71(5) (2008) pp 663–698.

Keay A, Moving Towards Stakeholderism? Constituency Statutes, Enlightened Shareholder Value, and More: Much Ado About Little? European Business Law Review 2011 pp 1–49.

Klages P, Die Wiederentdeckung schlafender Alternative in der Rechtslehre. Berliner Debatte Initial 18 (2007) pp 75–82.

Klausner MD, The Contractarian Theory of Corporate Law: A Generation Later. Journal of Corporation Law 31 (2006) pp 779–797.

Kornhauser LA, Constrained Optimization. Corporate law and the Maximization of Social Welfare. In: Kraus JS, Walt SD (eds), The Jurisprudential Foundations of Corporate and Commercial Law. Cambridge Studies in Philosophy and Law. Cambridge University Press, Cambridge (2000) pp 87–117.

Kraakman R, Davies P, Hansmann H, Hertig G, Hopt KJ, Kanda H, Rock EB, The Anatomy of Corporate Law: A Comparative and Functional Approach. Oxford University Press, Oxford (2004).

Kraus JS, Walt SD (eds), The Jurisprudential Foundations of Corporate and Commercial Law. Cambridge Studies in Philosophy and Law. Cambridge University Press, Cambridge (2000).

Kraus JS, Walt SD, Introduction. In: Kraus JS, Walt SD (eds), The Jurisprudential Foundations of Corporate and Commercial Law. Cambridge Studies in Philosophy and Law. Cambridge University Press, Cambridge (2000) pp 1–11.

Küting K, Gattung A, Konzerntheorien in der nationalen und internationalen Konzernrechnungslegung, Zeitschrift für Vergleichende Rechtswissenschaft 102 (2003) pp 505–527.

Kuhn TS, The Structure of Scientific Revolutions, Second Edition. University of Chicago Press, Chicago (1970).

Kuhner C, Unternehmensinteresse vs. Shareholder Value als Leitmaxime kapitalmarktorienterter Aktiengesellschaften, Zeitschrift für Unternehmens- und Gesellschaftsrecht 2/2004 pp 244–279.

Lando O, The Harmonization of European Contract Law through a Restatement of Principles. Centre for the Advanced Study of European and Comparative Law, University of Oxford (1997).

La Porta R, Lopez-de-Silanes F, Shleifer A, Vishny RW, Law and Finance, Journal of Political Economics 106 (1998) pp 1113–1155.

La Porta R, Lopez-de-Silanes F, Shleifer A, Vishny R, Investor protection and corporate governance, Journal of Financial Economics 58 (2000) pp 3–27.

Larenz K, Über die Unentbehrlichkeit der Jurisprudenz als Wissenschaft. Schriftenreihe der Juristischen Gesellschaft e. V. Berlin, Heft 26. Walter de Gruyter, Berlin (1966).
Larenz K, Allgemeiner Teil des deutschen Bürgerlichen Rechts. Ein Lehrbuch. 7. Auflage. Verlag C.H. Beck, München (1988).
Laux F, Die Lehre vom Unternehmen an sich. Walther Rathenau und die aktienrechtliche Diskussion in der Weimarer Republik. Schriften zur Rechtsgeschichte RG 74. Duncker & Humblot, Berlin (1998).
Lazonick W, The US stock market and the governance of innovative enterprise, Industrial and Corporate Change 16 (2007) pp 983–1035.
Lazonik W, The Chandlerian corporation and the theory of innovative enterprise, Industrial and Corporate Change 19 (2010) pp 317–349.
Lazonick W, Prencipe A, Dynamic Capabilities and Sustained Innovation: Strategic Control and financial Commitment at Rolls-Royce plc, Industrial and Corporate Change 14(3) (2005) pp 501–542.
Lieder J, Legal Origins und empirische Rechtsvergleichung. Zur Bedeutung des Rechts für die Entwicklung von Kapitalmärkten und Corporate-Governance-Strukturen, Zeitschrift für Vergleichende Rechtswissenschaft 109 (2010) pp 216–264.
Mäntysaari P, Comparative Corporate Governance. Shareholders as a Rule-maker. Springer, Berlin Heidelberg (2005).
Mäntysaari P (2010a), The Law of Corporate Finance: General Principles and EU Law. Volume I: Cash Flow, Risk, Agency, Information. Springer, Berlin Heidelberg (2010).
Mäntysaari P (2010b), The Law of Corporate Finance: General Principles and EU Law. Volume II: Contracts in General. Springer, Berlin Heidelberg (2010).
Mäntysaari P, En teoretisk referensram för handelsrätten, Tidsskrift for Rettsvitenskap 2/2011.
Malmendier U, Roman Shares. In: Goetzmann WN, Rouwenhorst KG (eds), The Origins of Value. The Financial Innovations That Created Modern Capital Markets. Oxford University Press, Oxford (2005) pp 31–42.
Mann BH, Republic of Debtors. Bankruptcy in the Age of American Independence. Harvard University Press, Cambridge London (2002).
Mann RJ, Explaining the Pattern of Secured Credit, Harvard Law Review 110 (1997) pp 625–680.
Manne HG, Mergers and the Market for Corporate Control, Journal of Political Economy 73 (1965) pp 110–120.
Martin R, The Age of Customer Capitalism. Harvard Business Review 1/2010.
Marx K, Das Kapital (1872).
Masson A, Shariff MJ, Through the Legal Looking Glass: Exploring the Concept of Corporate Legal Strategy, European Business Law Journal 2011 pp 51–77.
Mattei U, Comparative Law and Economics. University of Michigan Press, Ann Arbor (1997).
Mazé A, Ménard C, Private ordering, collective action, and the self-enforcing range of contracts, European Journal of Law and Economics 29 (2010) pp 131–153.
Means GC, The Corporate Revolution In America. The Crowell-Collier Press, New York (1962).
Merkl G, Reform der Corporate Governance in den USA, Schweizerische Zeitschrift für Wirtschaftsrecht/Revue Suisse de Droit des Affaires 1/2011 pp 28–46.
Merkt H, Wirtschaftsrechtsvergleichung im Zeitalter der Globalisierung: Tendenzen, Aufgaben, Perspektiven, Zeitschrift für Vergleichende Rechtswissenschaft 103 (2004) pp 263–267.
Merkt H, Die Zukunft der privatrechtlichen Forschung im Unternehmens- und Kapitalmarktrecht, Zeitschrift für Unternehmens- und Gesellschaftsrecht 4/2007 pp 532–541.
Mestmäcker EJ, A Legal Theory without Law. Walter Eucken Institut, Beiträge zur Ordnungstheorie und Ordnungspolitik 174. Mohr Siebeck, Tübingen (2007).
Michaels R, The True Lex Mercatoria: Law Beyond the State, Indiana Journal of Global Legal Studies 14:2 (2007) pp 447–468.
Mowery DC, Alfred Chandler and knowledge management within the firm, Industrial and Corporate Change 19 (2010) pp 483–507.
Muchlinski PT, Multinational Enterprises and the Law. Blackwell Publishing (1999).

Mustill MJ, The New Lex Mercatoria: The First Twenty-Five Years. In: Bos M, Brownlie I (eds), Liber Amicorum for the Rt. Hon. Lord Wilberforce, PC, CMG, OBE, QC. Clarendon Press, Oxford (1987) pp 149–183. Published also as Mustill MJ, Arbitration International 4 (1988) pp 86–119.

Neuner J, Handelsrecht — Handelsgesetz — Grundgesetz, Zeitschrift für das gesamte Handelsrecht und Wirtschaftsrecht 157 (1993) pp 243–290.

Nörr KW, Ein Gegenstand der Reflexion: Die Aktiengesellschaft in den Schriften Franz Kleins, Rudolf Hilferdings, Walther Rathenaus, Zeitschrift für das gesamte Handelsrecht und Wirtschaftsrecht 172 (2008) pp 133–143.

North DC, Institutions, Institutional Change and Economic Performance. Cambridge University Press, Cambridge (1990).

Nystén-Haarala S, Contract Law and Everyday Contracting. In: Wahlgren P (ed), A Proactive Approach. Stockholm Institute for Scandinavian Law, Scandinavian Studies in Law, Volume 49. Stockholm (2006) pp 263–283.

Ostrom E, Governing the Commons: The Evolution of Institutions for Collective Action. Cambridge University Press, Cambridge (1990).

Ostrom E, Crawford S, Classifying Rules. In: Ostrom E, Understanding Institutional Diversity. Princeton University Press, Princeton Oxford (2005), Chapter 7, pp 186–215.

Pavitt K, Innovating routines in the business firm: what corporate tasks should they be accomplishing? Industrial and Corporate Change 11 (2002) pp 117–133.

Peteraf MA, The Cornerstones of Competitive Advantage: A Resource-Based View. Strategic Management Journal 14 (1993) pp 179–191.

Porter ME, Kramer MR, Creating Shared Value, Harvard Business Review, January-February 2011.

Posner EA, Book Review: Kraus, Jody S., and Walt, Steven D., eds., The Jurisprudential Foundations of Corporate and Commercial Law, Ethics 112 (2002) pp 626–628.

Posner RA, The Decline of Law as an Autonomous Discipline: 1962–1987, Harvard Law Review 100 (1987) pp 761–780.

Posner RA, Frontiers of Legal Theory. Harvard University Press, Cambridge, Mass (2001).

Posner RA, Economic Analysis of Law. Seventh Edition. Wolters Kluwer Law & Business, Austin, Texas (2007).

Posner RA, Legal Scholarship Today, Harvard Law Review 114 (2002) pp 1314–1326.

Priest GL, Social Science Theory and Legal Education: The Law School as University, Journal of Legal Education 33 (1983) pp 437–441.

Priester HJ, Beginn der Rechtsperson – Vorräte und Mäntel, Zeitschrift für das gesamte Handelsrecht und Wirtschaftsrecht 168 (2004) pp 248–264.

Rabel E, Das Recht des Warenkaufs. Eine rechtsvergleichende Darstellung. Band I-II. de Gruyter, Berlin and Leipzig (1936) / Mohr, Tübingen (1957–1958).

Raisch P, Geschichtliche Voraussetzungen, dogmatische Grundlagen und Sinnwandlung des Handelsrechts. C.F. Müller, Karlsruhe (1965).

Raisch P, Die rechtsdogmatische Bedeutung der Abgrenzung von Handelsrecht und bürgerlichem Recht, Juristische Schulung 1967 pp 533–542.

Raiser T, The Theory of Enterprise Law in the Federal Republic of Germany. American Journal of Comparative Law 36(1) (1988) pp 111–129.

Raiser T, Unternehmensrecht als Gegenstand juristischer Grundlagenforschung. In: Eichhorn P (ed), Unternehmensverfassung in der privaten und öffentlichen Wirtschaft. Festschrift für Prof. Dr. Erich Potthoff zur Vollendung des 75. Lebensjahres. Nomos, Baden-Baden (1989) pp 31–45.

Rajan RG, Zingales L, The Governance of the New Enterprise. In: Vives X (ed), Corporate Governance, Theoretical & Empirical Perspectives. Cambridge University Press, Cambridge (2000) pp 201–227.

Rakoff TD, Introduction to Symposium: Law, Knowledge, and the Academy, Harvard Law Review 115 (2002) pp 1278–1287.

Ramberg J, International Commercial Transactions. ICC, Kluwer Law International, Norstedts Juridik Ab, Stockholm (1998).
Rathenau W (1917a), Vom Aktienwesen. Eine geschäftliche Betrachtung. D. Fischer, Berlin (1917).
Rathenau W (1917b), Von Kommenden Dingen. D. Fischer, Berlin (1917).
Rawls J, A Theory of Justice. Harvard University Press, Cambridge, Mass (1971).
Riechers A, Das "Unternehmen an sich". Die Entwicklung eines Begriffes in der Aktienrechtsdiskussion des 20. Jahrhunderts. Beiträge zur Rechtsgeschichte des 20. Jahrhunderts 17. Mohr Siebeck, Tübingen (1996).
Robé JP, The Legal Structure of the Firm, Accounting, Economics, and Law 1(1). Available at: http://www.bepress.com/ae1/vol1/iss1/5
Roe M, Strong Managers, Weak Owners: The Political Roots of American Corporate Finance. Princeton University Press, Princeton, New Jersey (1994).
Romer PM, Increasing Returns and Long Run Growth, Journal of Political Economy 94(5) (1986) pp 1002–1038.
Ross SA, The Economic Theory of Agency: The Principal's Problem. The American Economic Review 63(2) (1973) pp 134–139.
Roth WH, From Centros to Überseering: Free Movement of Companies, Private International Law, and Community Law, International and Comparative Law Quarterly 52 (2003) pp 177–208.
Ruckenstein M, suikkanen J, Tamminen S, Unohda innovointi. Keskity arvonluontiin. Sitra 291. Edita Prima Oy, Helsinki (2011).
Sakkab NY, Growing Through Innovation, Research Technology Management 50(6) (2007) pp 59–64.
Schmidt K, Vom Handelsrecht zum Unternehmens-Privatrecht? Juristische Schulung 1985 pp 249–257.
Schmidt K, Sitzverlegungsrichtlinie, Freizügigkeit und Gesellschaftsrechtspraxis. Grundlagen, für Unternehmens- und Gesellschaftsrecht 1999 pp 20–35.
Schmidt K, Gesellschaftsrecht, 4. Auflage. C. Heymann, Köln (2002).
Schmidt K, Zerfällt das Handelsgesetzbuch? Eine Gedankenskizz zur Zukunft des Vierten Buchs. In: Berger KP, Borges G, Herrmann H, Schlüter A, Wackerbarth U (eds), Zivil- und Wirtschaftsrecht im Europäischen und Globalen Kontext / Private and Commercial Law in a European and Global Context: Festschrift für Norbert Horn zum 70. Geburtstag. de Gruyter Recht, Berlin (2006) pp 557–570.
Schmitthoff CM, International Business Law: A New Law Merchant. In: Cheng CJ (ed), Clive M. Schmitthoff's Select Essays on International Trade Law. Martinus Nijhoff Publishers / Graham & Trotman, Dordrecht (1988) pp 20–37. Originally published as Schmitthoff CM, International Business Law: A New Law Merchant. In: St J MacDonald R (ed), 2 Current Law and Social Problems. University of Toronto Press, Toronto (1961).
Schmitthoff CM, The Unification of the Law of International Trade, Journal of Business Law 1968 pp 105–119.
Schumpeter JA, Capitalism, Socialism and Democracy. Harper and Brothers, New York (1942).
Scott HS, The Risk Fixers, Harvard Law Review 91 (1978) pp 737–792.
Shleifer A, Vishny RW, A Survey of Corporate Governance. Journal of Finance 52(2) (1997) pp 737–783.
Siebenhüner B, Arnold M, Organizational learning to manage sustainable development, Business Strategy and the Environment 16 (2007) pp 339–353.
Simon HA, A Behavioral Model of Rational Choice. In: Models of Man, Social and Rational: Mathematical Essays on Rational Human Behavior in a Social Setting. Wiley, New York (1957).
Simon HA, Theories of decision-making in economics and behavioral science. American Economic Review 49 (1959) pp 253–283.
Simon HA, Organizations and Markets. Journal of Economic Perspectives 5(2) (1991) pp 25–44.

Sjåfjell B, Towards a Sustainable European Company Law. A Normative Analysis of the Objectives of EU Law, with the Takeover Directive as a Test Case. European Company Law Series 3. Wolters Kluwer, Alphen Aan Den Rijn (2009).
Skeel DA Jr, Debt's Domain. A History of Bankruptcy Law in America. Princeton University Press, Princeton Oxford (2001).
Skeel DA Jr, Corporate Anatomy Lessons, Yale Law Journal 113 (2004) pp 1519–1577.
Smith A, The Wealth of Nations (1776).
Solow RM, Technical Change and the Aggregate Production Function, The Review of Economics and Statistics 39(3) (1957) pp 312–320.
de Sousa Santos B, Law: A Map of Misreading. Toward a Postmodern Conception of Law, Journal of Law and Society 14 (1987) pp 279–302.
Spindler G, Unternehmensinteresse als Leitlinie des Vorstandshandelns – Berücksichtigung von Arbeitnehmerinteressen und Shareholder Value. Gutachten im Auftrag der Hans-Böckler-Stiftung. Hans-Böckler-Stiftung, Düsseldorf (2008). Available at: http://www.boeckler.de/pdf/mbf_gutachten_spindler_2008.pdf.
Stiglitz JE, Information and the change in the paradigm of economics, American Economic Review 92 (2002) pp 460–501.
Teece DJ, Profiting from technological innovation: Implications for integration, collaboration, licensing and public policy, Research Policy 15 (1986) pp 285–305.
Teece DJ, Alfred Chandler and "capabilities" theories of strategy and management, Industrial and Corporate Change 19 (2010) pp 297–316.
Teichmann C, Die Societas Privata Europaea (SPE) als ausländische Tochtergesellschaft, Recht der internationalen Wirtschaft 3/2010 pp 120–127.
Teubner G, Substantive and Reflexive Elements in Modern Law, Law and Society Review 17 (1983) pp 239–285.
Teubner G, Enterprise Corporatism: New Industrial Policy and the "Essence" of the Legal Person. American Journal of Comparative Law 36 (1988) pp 130–155.
Teubner G, The Two Faces of Janus: Rethinking Legal Pluralism, Cardozo Law Review 13 (1992) pp 1443–1462.
Teubner G, Corporate Fiduciary Duties and Their Beneficiaries. In: Hopt K, Teubner G, Corporate Governance and Directors' Liabilities. De Gruyter, Berlin (1994) pp 149–177.
Teubner G, Global Bukowina: Legal Pluralism in the World-Society. In: Teubner G (ed), Global Law Without a State. Aldershot, Dartmouth (1997) pp 3–28.
Thompson JD, Organizations in Action: Social Science Bases of Administration. McGraw-Hill, New York (1967).
Tirole J, Corporate Governance, Econometrica 69 (2001) pp 1–35.
Tirole J, The Theory of Corporate Finance. Princeton University Press, Princeton Oxford (2006).
Tolonen JP, Der allgemeine Erklärungshintergrund der wirtschaftlichen Ordnung und seine Anwendung auf das Aktiengesellschaftsrecht. Rechtsvergleichende Untersuchung. Suomalainen Tiedeakatemia, Helsinki (1974).
Trakman LE, The Law Merchant: The Evolution of Commercial Law. Fred B. Rothman & Co., Littleton, Colorado (1983).
Van de Mieroop M, The Invention of Interest. Sumerian Loans. In: Goetzmann WN, Rouwenhorst KG (eds), The Origins of Value. Oxford University Press, Oxford (2005) pp 17–30.
Van Caenegem RC, Johnston DEL, An Historical Introduction to Private Law. Cambridge University Press, Cambridge (1992).
Veblen T, Absentee Ownership and Business Enterprise in Recent Times: The Case of America. B.W. Huebsch, New York (1923).
von Bar C, Clive E, Schulte-Nölke H, Beale H, Herre J, Huet J, Storme M, Swann S, Varul P, Veneziano A, Zoll F (eds), Principles, Definitions and Model Rules of European Private Law. Draft Common Frame of Reference (DCFR). Outline Edition. Prepared by the Study Group on a European Civil Code and the Research Group on EC Private Law (Acquis Group). Based in part on a revised version of the Principles of European Contract Law. Sellier, Munich (2009).

von der Pforten D, Was ist Recht? Eine philosophische Perspektive. In: Brugger W, Neumann U, Kirste S (eds), Rechtsphilosophie im 21. Jahrhundert. Suhrkamp Verlag, Frankfurt am Main (2008) pp 261–285.
von Hein J, Die Rezeption US-amerikanischen Gesellschaftsrechts in Deutschland. Beiträge zum ausländischen und internationalen Privatrecht 87. Mohr Siebeck, Tübingen (2008).
von Jhering R, Geist des römischen Rechts auf den verschiedenen Stufen seiner Entwicklung. Breitkopf & Härtel, Leipzig (1852–1865).
von Savigny FC, Das System des heutigen römischen Rechts (1840–1849).
Watson A, Legal Transplants: An Approach to Comparative Law. Scottish Academic Press, Edinburgh (1974).
Watson A, Aspects of Reception of Law, American Journal of Comparative Law 44 (1996) pp 335–351.
Watson A, Legal Transplants and European Private Law, 4.4 ELECTRONIC JOURNAL OF COMPARATIVE LAW, http://www.ejcl.org/ejcl/44/44–2.html (2000).
Weber M, Zur Geschichte der Handelsgesellschaften im Mittelalter. Nach südeuropäischen Quellen. Eure, Stuttgart (1889).
Weber M, Wirtschaft und Gesellschaft. Grundriss der verstehenden Soziologie (1922).
Wendehorst CC, The State as a Foundation of Private Law Reasoning, American Journal of Comparative Law 56 (2008) pp 567–604.
Wendell Holmes O Jr, The Path of the Law, Harvard Law Review 10 (1897) pp 457–478.
Wernerfelt B, The Resource-Based View of the Firm, Strategic Management Journal 5(2) (1984) pp 171–180.
Whaples R, Morris AP, Moorhouse JC, What Should Lawyers Know about Economics? Journal of Legal Education 48 (1998) pp 120–124.
Whitman J, Note, Commercial Law and the American Volk: A Note on Llewellyn's German Sources for the Uniform Commercial Code, Yale Law Journal 97 (1987) pp 156–175.
Wiedemann H, Auf der Suche nach den Strukturen der Aktiengesellschaft. The Anatomy of Corporate Law, Zeitschrift des Unternehmens- und Gesellschaftsrechts 2006 pp 240–258.
Williamson OE, The Economics of Discretionary Behavior: Managerial Objectives in a Theory of the Firm. Prentice-Hall, Englewood Cliffs, New Jersey (1964).
Williamson OE, Markets and Hierarchies: Analysis and Antitrust Implications. The Free Press, New York (1975).
Williamson OE, The Modern Corporation: Origins, Evolution, Attributes, Journal of Economic Literature 19 (1981) pp 1537–1568.
Williamson OE, The Incentive Limits of Firms: A Comparative Institutional Assessment of Bureaucracy, Review of World Economics 120(4) (1984) pp 736–763.
Williamson OE, The Economic Institutions of Capitalism. Free Press, New York (1985).
Williamson OE, Transaction Cost Economics: How it Works; Where It Is Headed, De Economist 146 (1998) pp 23–58.
Williamson OE (2002a), The Lens of Contract: Private Ordering, American Economic Review 92(2) (2002) pp 438–443.
Williamson OE (2002b), The Theory of the Firm as Governance Structure: From Choice to Contract, Journal of Economic Perspectives 16(3) (2002) pp 171–195.
Williamson OE, Transaction Cost Economics. In: Ménard C, Shirley MM (eds), Handbook of the New Institutional Economics. Springer, The Netherlands (2005) pp 51–65.
Wilson R, On the Theory of Syndicates, Econometrica 36 (1968) pp 119–132.
Worley CG, Lawler EE, Designing Organizations That Are Built to Change, MIT Sloan Management Review 48(1) (2006) pp 19–23.
Xanthaki H, Legal Transplants in Legislation: Defusing the Trap, International and Comparative Law Quarterly 57 (2008) pp 659–673.
Zimmer D, Internationales Gesellschaftsrecht. Das Kollisionsrecht der Gesellschaften und sein Verhältnis zum Internationalen Kapitalmarktrecht und zum Internationalen Unternehmensrecht.

Schriftenreihe Recht der Internationalen Wirtschaft. Band 50. Verlag Recht und Wirtschaft GmbH, Heidelberg (1996).

Zimmer D, Grenzüberschreitende Rechtspersönlichkeit, Zeitschrift für das gesamte Handelsrecht und Wirtschaftsrecht 168 (2004) pp 355–368.

Zöllner W, Wovon handelt das Handelsrecht? Zeitschrift für Unternehmens-und Gesellschaftsrecht 1/1983 pp 82–91.

Zweigert K, Kötz H, Einführung in die Rechtsvergleichung auf dem Gebiete des Privatrechts, 3. Auflage. Mohr Siebeck, Tübingen (1996).

MIX
Papier aus verantwortungsvollen Quellen
Paper from responsible sources
FSC® C105338

If you have any concerns about our products,
you can contact us on
ProductSafety@springernature.com

In case Publisher is established outside the EU,
the EU authorized representative is:
Springer Nature Customer Service Center GmbH
Europaplatz 3, 69115 Heidelberg, Germany

Printed by Libri Plureos GmbH
in Hamburg, Germany